Politics, postmodernity and critical legal studies

Critical legal studies has been one of the most exciting developments within contemporary jurisprudence. Although originally an American phenomenon, it has now made headway in Britain. This is the first work of contemporary jurisprudence systematically to apply critical philosophy to the common law. Specifically, the book develops a novel and interdisciplinary account of the politics and cultural significance of the substantive institutions of law. Contributions from leading British and American scholars raise the essential political and ethical challenges facing the law in postmodernity. The book explores the breakdown of traditional conceptions of legal reason. Drawing upon diverse disciplines – psychoanalysis, phenomenology, linguistics and ethical philosophy – the authors develop conceptions of the contingency of law and the plurality of legal experience.

Justice has recently been seen to miscarry. It is the task of critical legal studies to raise the question of justice in relation to the substantive disciplines of common law. This book returns to the theories of the text and to the texts of the law both as archives of repression and as resources for cultural change.

Costas Douzinas is Rudolph Palumbo Lecturer in Law at Birkbeck College, University of London; **Peter Goodrich** is Corporation of London Professor of Law at Birkbeck College, University of London; **Yifat Hachamovitch** has taught at several universities in the United States and is currently completing a book on psychoanalysis and law.

Politics, postmodernity and critical legal studies

The legality of the contingent

Edited by Costas Douzinas, Peter Goodrich and Yifat Hachamovitch

ROUTLEDGE

London and New York

First published 1994
by Routledge
11 New Fetter Lane, London EC4P 4EE

Simultaneously published in the USA and Canada
by Routledge
29 West 35th Street, New York, NY 10001

Typeset in Baskerville by
Pat and Anne Murphy, Highcliffe-on-Sea, Dorset
Printed and bound in Great Britain by
Mackays of Chatham PLC, Chatham, Kent

British Library Cataloguing in Publication Data
A catalogue record for this book is available from the British Library.

Library of Congress Cataloging in Publication Data
A catalogue copy for this book has been requested.

ISBN 0-415-08651-5 (hbk)
ISBN 0-415-08652-3 (pbk)

Contents

Chapter 1

Introduction

Politics, ethics and the legality of the contingent

Peter Goodrich, Costas Douzinas and Yifat Hachamovitch

> The discipline [of law] is disputatious because it rests on nothing more complete than a collection of fragments, reports, pieces themselves representing uncertain conjectures and incomplete divinations.
>
> Francois Hotman, *Anti-Tribonian ou discours d'un grand et renomme iurisconsulte sur l'estude des loix*

Contingency is the condition of legal judgment and the limit of its reason. While contingency may be subject to laws it must also always escape legality. The contingent is particular: it is accident or change, it is experience or *pathos* and its reason is finite, mutable and only ever probable. The legality of the contingent, of justice or 'lesbian rule' (Lambard 1591), with which this work is concerned, is a legality that is tied on the one hand to the local and the particular, to the specific geography, institutions, disciplines, categories and reasons of common law, and on the other to the unique person who comes before the law. The focus of this study upon the legality of the contingent is also in part an attempt to formulate a philosophy of critical legal studies that recognizes the history and current political situation of critique in law. This entails not least a recognition of the role or complicity of critical legal scholarship in the reproduction of the legal institution and the transmission of legal doctrine, including the doctrine of critique. It involves further the formulation of a response to the context of what may be termed broadly postmodern jurisprudence. The contemporary contingency of legality is aligned to the prolonged collapse of certain specific beliefs in a positivized and closed world of abstract legal rules. The demise of the various sciences of law and of their accompanying substrate of systemic concepts throws legal theory back into the life-world or the experience of the legal institution. It propels the critical scholar towards conceptions and practices of justice and injustice, judgement and decision, ethic and affection, subjectivity, speech and the other specific ephemera of the profession or teaching of law. To respond to the legality of the contingent is to formulate an account of the amorphous, incidental, fluid and indefinable realms of justice and judgement, carriage and miscarriage, politic and ethic of common law. This project is predicated upon a theoretical and political radicalism that returns to the specific histories and disciplines of common law and interrogates them in the strange-sounding name of justice.

HISTORIES

A sixteenth-century recusant, writing against Bishop Jewell and the reform of the Church of England, paraphrased a lengthy patriotic tradition of rationalist apologetics in the following warning: 'Beware that no man spoil you through philosophy and vain deceit. . . . For these heretics put all the force of their poisons in log-like, or dialectical disputation, which by the opinion of philosophers is defined not to have power to prove, but an earnest desire to destroy and disprove' (Harding 1565: 32b). The politics of reason, in short, has always been a dimension of governance, of ecclesiastical and civil law. The aspersion of destructiveness or of wanton 'disproving' has traditionally been levelled against all attempts to question the authority of established reason, its institutions and claims to custody of truth and law. When the civilian lawyer Sir Robert Wiseman deprecated the early common law as being a 'poor illiterate reason', he concluded of the unwritten tradition and its 'artificial' logic of particulars that 'there is not a more deceitful thing than reason; it being made use of frequently by false shows and colours to beautify the foulest and most deformed things . . . it is such a faculty, that those that are partakers of it in the meanest measure, do infinitely extol and admire what they apprehend to be reasonable, though to a right judgement it be nothing so' (Wiseman 1664: 2). The 'illiterate' reason of common law has been an object of criticism, of political denunciation and philosophical ridicule on many occasions and in very distinct historical circumstances. On each occasion criticism of the law accompanies a crisis in the tradition and in its claim both to necessity and to ethics or justice.

Critical legal studies is not a new phenomenon in jurisprudence, nor is postmodernity that unusual a category of historical context or crisis. The pervading postmodern sentiment that 'things are not going well', that justice has miscarried or law has separated itself from ethics, has accompanied innumerable distinct cultural movements and styles from asceticism to pursuit of the millennium, gnosticism to iconoclasm, romanticism to the baroque. Melancholia, mourning or dread are inevitably associated with periods of transition. A sense of nostalgia, of depression or of loss has always tended to accompany the birth or renewal of social forms and is expressed both in pessimism and in radicalism, in the return to tradition and the escape from the present associated with epochs and literatures as diverse as renaissance humanism, naturalism or surrealism. The fear of 'unreason', of irrationality, heresy or simple nihilism is the stagnated historical expression of an extant tradition, of a loss of confidence in orthodoxy, whether theological, jurisprudential or political. The attribution of darkness, melancholy, fragmentation, waste and irrationality are common themes in the early doctrinal tradition in common law, and the institution was constantly attacked for its arbitrary judgments, its sudden and inexplicable injustices, its harsh wastage of youth and promise as well as its fundamental philosophical irrationality and political inequity. Bentham, to take a later example, was equally scathing and bleak in his denunciation of common law in the age of statutes and of codes. The common lawyer preferred repetition to action, status to reason and the myopia of imitation to the politics of vision (Postema 1986). The American realists and their latter-day inheritors, to take one final example, find swift empathy amongst radicals in profaning the law review, satirizing legal language or simply further exposing the distance and subjection that passes as law in an age where all other cultural phenomena speak to a relentless uncertainty. The prognosis of failure, of dissolution or decay both within and without the legal institution, has returned quite as often as doctrine, prejudice, faith or some other species of modernity have promulgated the language of progress or the universality of science, dogma or truth. If the variously expressed, often contradictory and generally fragmentary sentiments of postmodernity are novel primarily by virtue of their contemporaneity, critical legal studies, which has come latterly in some quarters to be identified in part with postmodernity is equally both a return to a tradition of resistance or opposition to legal orthodoxy and a novel rewriting of the text or art of law.

The history of European critical legal studies, in the most basic common sense of movements critical of legal orthodoxy, can probably be traced, if not directly to the anomalist beliefs of certain early Roman jurists (Stein 1966: 53–67), at least to the critical reaction of renaissance legal humanists and neo-scholastics to the glossatorial tradition of continental law. François Hotman, to take but one striking example, argued proleptically in *Anti-Tribonian*, a work first published in 1567, that a legal system such as that of France, based upon mimicking the law of ancient Rome, was both morally and politically reprehensible. Roman law, he argued, existed to protect the interests of the Roman property-owning classes or bourgeoisie:

> And if it is necessary to speak of the civil law of the Romans, I would say unequivocally that it was neither made nor interpreted to the ends of equity or natural reason. It was never suitable for all nations, but was rather fashioned by a particular prerogative expressly invented for the purpose of maintaining bourgeois Romans (*bourgeois Romains*) in a higher degree and dignity than the other inhabitants of the country of Italy.
>
> (Hotman 1567: 74)

It was ethically inappropriate and socially illogical, he asserted further, to reason from the historical example of a classical law (*tenebras antiquitatis*) predicated upon extreme inequality to contemporary forms of regulation. Critical legal studies find here an early and exemplary statement which directly criticized law and particularly legal doctrinal writers, glossators and commentators, for failing to understand the social and political content of law, its reflection of inequalities and its potential for injustice. The subtitle of Hotman's work is, significantly enough, *Discourse upon the study of the Laws*. The underlying concern of this critical legal humanism was with the educational institution and the teaching or doctrine of national law. Hotman thus based his critique of law upon the specific character, practice and belief of contemporary legal institutions. His argument was that poor scholarship and even weaker intellectual standards had deprived the legal tradition of its meaning and had left students and practitioners of law alike with the empty symbolism of a misunderstood classical tradition: an art of law which had grown both oppressive, useless and unjust (Hotman 1567: 6). Hotman was concerned with the institution, with the study and teaching of law as a centrally located and culturally essential practice or 'properly speaking' art. He saw ignorance of the history and social context of law as the cause of its continued practical failure, its infelicities, its irrationalities, its errors and its injustices. The failure of legal reason, the historical ignorance of doctrine and the scholastic and abusive sophistry of contemporary jurisprudence were all indicative of the political failure of the republic itself.

The mission or project of humanist legal reform – of what is today called critical legal studies – was that of relating the reason of law to the politics of the legal institution. Hotman's concern was not simply with the borrowings and the doctrinal inadequacies of a legal system that lacked any authentic reason or identity, but also with its theoretical and pedagogic weakness, the failings of a law that had come to repeat the sclerotic or at least anachronistic decisions and rulings of a past and little-understood era in the name of nothing more convincing than tradition. The return to theory was intimately linked to the teaching and practice of law: so close was the link between poor scholarship and the failings of legal practice that Hotman ends by attributing the bulk of disputes to lack of intellectual discipline, to poor philology and worse historical interpretation, a barbarous reverence for ancient, inappropriate and mistranscribed texts. The discipline was 'an abyss' of ignorance, wrangling, abuse, sophistry and injustice for which the parties would suffer. The reformulation of the legal discipline endeavoured precisely to tie the substance and categories of contemporary law to conceptions of equality, judgment and justice. The subsequent history of western jurisprudence saw several resurgent critiques of law associated not simply with recognized moments of decline in the standards of legal education and judicial reasoning but also associated with broader social and political movements which argued, particularly from within anarchistic and socialistic frameworks, that law itself was an unnecessary and all-too-human evil.

The Renaissance and Reformation saw numerous comparable critiques both of the particularism – the elaborate pleadings – and of the reason of common law associated with a wide variety of legal scholars, rhetoricians and antiquarians or in the modern idiom historians. The specific tradition of critique within English law was only in part a feature of the peculiar historicism of common law, of the rediscovery and reception of indigenous and imported legal forms. It was also, and more topically, a feature of comparative legal antagonisms and of the ill-fated desire to separate the common law from its continental and specifically Roman reasons and sources. The Continent was associated in the legal mind with theory and reform, radicalism and alterity. The most potent critics of common law were thus not only the antiquarians, but also the English civilian lawyers who refused to accept the irrational particularism, the haphazard comparisons or kadi justice of a spuriously nationalistic common law (Wiseman 1664). In this context the critique of common law was directed at the insularity and the formalism of a loosely knit system of precedent which refused to recognize any reason of law beyond the judicial prerogative, namely the *arbitrium*, dictate or fiat of the judge (Fraunce 1588). Whether in the name of the universal reason of Roman law or in that of a law of nature, a calculus of utility or some other normative criterion, the criticism of common law, right up to and including the more iconoclastic speculations of the American legal realists, was ultimately directed at the irrational particularity or purely habitual criterion (the repetition) of legal reason and judgment. In political terms the tradition of critique of common law is much closer to ethical humanism and to radical historicism than it is to the nihilism with which it is most frequently charged.

In contradistinction to the claim that critical legal studies is simply a development of a political critique of law based in a vulgar reduction of the legal to the economic or social, this book argues for an ethically committed politics of law that faces directly the institutional complexity of law, and particularly the symbolic and substantive domains and implications of legal practice. It is not sufficient merely to reiterate the abstract complicity or dependence of law upon economic exploitation or political and social inequality. No matter how real or devastating the enforcement of law or the products of law's practice, an ethics of law or even a politics of legal judgment is an institutional issue in the sense that it is doctrine which determines the specific products, the designs, attitudes, complicities and judgments that govern institutional practice as sociality and political and ethical sensibility. The first stage in that expansion of critical legal studies into a doctrinal position involves a politics of legal education and of the substantive disciplines and practices which understand and explore law as a series of deeply historical phenomena (Murphy 1991). It demands a rethinking of the art and practice of law in the context of its history and the philosophy of its history. In specific terms, the doctrine of critical legal studies is a study both of the failures, of the injustices, the exclusions and the inequalities of the legal tradition and an examination of the future of law, of an ethics of legality in a context of acknowledged or confessed contingency. The contingency of common law only has a meaning, however, if it is related to the realm of principle as accident to essence, substance to form, particular to universal. In critical argument this relation of contingency to necessity implies that the practice of law take some account of the particular dictates of morality, ethics or justice. While most theories of law seek to achieve the best of all possible laws, to relate the realm of contingent judgment to the transcendental possibility of the good, common-law doctrine has increasingly assumed rather than proved or practised the relation of God, justice or truth to legal acts. This positivism of law has been expressed in a modernist jurisprudence which radically separates law from morality, norm from judgment and rule from interpretation. The history of such positivization and of its demise remains to be written, while the ethical consequences of the separation of law and morality are just beginning to be understood, their effects felt and their future questioned.

MARXISM AND THE DOCTRINE OF CRITIQUE

The contemporary cycle of intellectual movements in the study of law, of theoretical fashions, continental importations, schools and names is characterized by an accelerated rate of obsolescence. To the extent that contemporary critical legal studies may be loosely defined as an intellectual movement, as the emergence of a 'left intelligentsia' or politically radical institutional place within law, it has already changed its intellectual icons and traded-in its emblematic theoretical positions several times (Goodrich 1992b). Despite its youth, critical legal studies has generated so many histories of the movement itself that it is not only frequently and accurately characterized by its inwardness but is also depicted theoretically in terms of an uneasy self-referentiality (Schlegel 1992). That such self-referentiality is narcissistic was evident early on in the movement and is confirmed by the recognition that the principal subject-matter of critical legal studies in America was critical legal studies itself (Kennedy 1985: 1015). Whether defined in terms of fascination (fixation) or in terms of subjectification, the self-reference of critical legal studies has a further and more striking connotation. It is that critical legal studies has inevitably itself become a school and so is placed in the ironic position of propounding or teaching its critical doctrines as the orthodoxy of legal radicalism. Like the various schools and creeds of 'postmodernism', ranging from neo-conservatism to the politics of resistance (Foster 1985), critical legal scholarship comes by virtue of time and circumstance, if not by virtue of any more marked political success, to include and exclude, defend and denounce, accept and reject positions that have in their momentary turn come to define doctrine, canon and rule for critical scholars.

It is the argument of this book that critical legal studies, by virtue of becoming a school, by dint of its academic recognition and place, as well as its substantive applications in the teaching of law, takes on a new political responsibility. The school of critical legal studies may well be precarious in its status and varied in its generational and political positions yet it would be irresponsible in the extreme not to admit to the political commitments of institutional attachment. Institutionalization brings with it a series of practical, professional and pedagogic imperatives. Attachment to or capture by the institution also carries with it an organizational responsibility: the critical school, if such is an appropriate label, necessarily develops an internal organization, a hierarchy of members designated by institutional affiliation and position, age, publications, scholarly or academic reputation, editorships and other insignia of critical belief or academic prowess. It is thus not only doctrinal issues and the inevitable emergence of diversity or splits within critical legal thought that mark the rapid development of the movement from an external to an internal and institutional politics. Critical legal studies, as an institutional organization and particularly as a movement affiliated with the contemporary legal academy, has developed internally along a trajectory dictated by the dawning realization that the politics of legal critique are predominantly the politics of legal education and of its relation to professional practice. The politics of critical legal studies is no longer to be conceived in terms of a new clerical elite dedicated to proselytizing, to external conversion – to changing the outside world, to reforming others – but rather it is to be characterized as a politics of institutional reform (Fitzpatrick and Hunt 1987). This emergent sense of responsibility and its accompanying politicization of legal institutions can be traced briefly by reconstructing the trajectory of contemporary critical legal scholarship through the stages of its brief, though always controversial, development within the academy.

Three broad phases characterize the development of critical legal studies. Their trajectory has been in large measure that of a movement from external critiques of the effects of law to the internal reform of doctrine and the interstitial institutions of law. The development of critical legal studies has been marked by a shift from a sociology of legal governance to the textual politics of the legal academy, from empiricism to deconstruction, from realism to pluralism and finally from the espousal of creeds, positions and other political truths to a politics of contingency and a creed of (gregarious) uncertainty (Tushnet 1991). While it is necessarily invidious and somewhat arbitrary to catalogue specific phases and authors in this development and diversification of critical legal studies it is none the less necessary to confront directly the changing political focus and the at times antagonistic positions of critical legal scholars (Fitzpatrick 1991). In many instances it seems, perhaps surprisingly, that the divisions or antagonisms are as much the product of a difference of generation as they are of theoretical position. The homogeneity of generational groups is indeed an important feature not only of the internal hierarchy of the critical legal studies movement – and of its system of patronage – but is also a reflection of the increasing subjection of intellectual culture to the media-driven phenomena of fashion (Jacoby 1987).

The first phase of critical legal scholarship within a European and, to a lesser extent, American context was a direct reflection of Marxist sociological theory (Hunt 1986). This phase, which might be termed the pre-history of the movement, treated law and legal order more broadly as a superstructural phenomenon within an economically determined social order. Drawing upon Marx, but also upon English socialism and communitarian anarchism, law was represented in an unmediated fashion as the expression of class interest and of economic domination (Sugarman 1983). The legal order bound together, at a political and ideological level, a social order predicated upon massive inequalities of wealth and opportunity. The critique of law was accordingly a critique of the class content of law and of the ethical and political error of believing in the specific juridical precepts that constituted the rule of law (Bankowski and Mungham 1976). In synoptic terms, law was variously represented and studied as an apparatus both generated by and assisting in the reproduction of the conditions of class domination and exploitation (Klare 1978). The rule of law was a hollow facade behind which the sociologist could easily uncover the economic causes, the political mechanisms and the ideological effects of domination (Griffith 1977). The law itself was the legislative product of the dominant class, it was interpreted by an elite professional group and it was in practice applied selectively and almost exclusively to members of the working class (Mathieson 1980). The purpose of critical study of law in this context was to expose or demystify the determinations and real conditions of law's application. The meaning of the legal rule and of the normative order of law lay in its content. The critique of law – and the possibility of transcending legality – lay in reform of the content of law and most specifically in the political project of wresting the instruments of legal control out of the hands of the ruling class. Such critique, however, was always subordinate to the analysis and projection of economic determinations: law reflected and helped to reproduce a reality external to it and in consequence it was only the dissolution of the real conditions of class domination that would bring legal domination to an end (Fine *et al.* 1979).

The central project of the earliest phase of critical legal studies was a global critique of law which called for or preached the rejection and the future end of law. Most importantly, this critique was external to law, the critic was either professionally or existentially and politically an outsider to the law and an ideological opponent of all aspects of 'liberal legalism'. Critical legal scholars were likely to be sociologists or academic lawyers with few if any professional contacts or legal doctrinal commitments. Critical legal studies was part of the law and society movement, of the sociological analysis of law or latterly of socio-legal studies. If this diverse institutional grouping had an identity within the legal institution it was that of the marginal or of the periphery, of a young, at times utopian and at all times radical newcomer to the law. The critic was concerned to expose the politically oppressive character of law and as she could not identify ethically or intellectually with law she was forced, as an outsider and yet as one tainted in some sense by legality, to dream (often inauthentically) of the end of law (Schlag 1990).

The second phase of critique was associated most closely with the development and popularization of structuralism. Levi-Strauss, Althusser, Poulantzas and Pashukanis were variously the heroes of this political theology or more jurisprudential critique of law. The movement was from sociology to jurisprudence and an examination and critique of the legal form. Continuing with the explicitly Marxist current of critical legal studies, the work of Pashukanis, a post-revolutionary soviet legal theorist, enjoyed a brief and striking significance, and was in some respects an exemplary text (Pashukanis 1978). For Pashukanis, law was to be understood as the direct historical expression of the commodity form of production. The legal form was born with the commodity and it would survive only as long as the production of commodities. The legal subject – and by association, the legal form of human relation – was in its turn simply a reflection of the commodity and was to be understood as a primary condition of the possibility of the commodity: the circulation of commodities required the simultaneous creation and mobility of the consumer, the fictively free and equal legal subject who would come to the market and buy and sell. The legal form of human relation was based upon and typified by the contract, and for Pashukanis all legal relations were either directly or indirectly contractual: even citizenship was conceived in terms of a contractual relationship with the state and the sanctions of criminal acts were nothing other than remedies for the breach of this relation. Underlying this view of legality was a socio-economic account of the ideological atomization of social relations into the notionally free and equal form of exchange. The law of contract supposedly established and protected the legal subject yet this protection was the necessary or pre-determined political correlate of the economic form of commodity production and of its concomitant exploitation and domination.

Several features of the above analysis were to become significant aspects of the second phase of critical legal studies. The most striking characteristic of the commodity form theory was the focus upon the form of law as opposed to the earlier emphasis on content. Not only was law given a remarkable – and no doubt justified – economic and political significance but it was also represented as constitutive of social personality and of legal subjectivity. The relative autonomy of law not only granted law a role within the economic determination of social forms but also attributed the political restraint of subjectivity or the ideological capture of the subject to the legal form (Edelman 1979). Law was an exemplary dimension of what Althusser termed ideological state apparatuses whose ultimate function was to lock the individual into an imaginary relation to the real. The reality of subjection was symbolized as legal necessity and misrecognized by the subject as the freedom of choice (Althusser 1971). This attribution of a structural significance to law led to the formulation of critical legal studies as a critique of the form of law: the radical analysis of the legal form was one which most clearly evidenced or exposed the underlying contradictions of the legal form such that each substantive discipline could be shown to rest upon contradictory premises although, perhaps not surprisingly, the law of contract was the most frequently cited example (Kennedy 1976). Contract, of course, was the emblem of a particular species of legality and was synonymous with the regulatory conception of the rule of law. Sociality was itself a contract, it was established by an originary or hypothetical agreement and was maintained by the continuance of a general consensus or volition which now resided in the sovereign as the embodiment or representative of popular will. The model of contract preceded all subsequent forms of legality, it was the structural basis of the legal form and the exemplary justification of the rule of law. Two further features of this structuralist phase of critical analysis deserve attention.

As a jurisprudential enterprise the critique of the form of law took as its starting point contemporary positivistic theories of law and criticized the self-proclaimed objectivity of their accounts of legal processes. More specifically, critical legal theory was concerned with the manifestations of legal categories and institutions, with disciplinary demarcations and with the hierarchy, practices and places of law, rather than with global or totalizing negations of the value of law or similarly extravagant denials of the possibility of justice (Kennedy 1983). The task of theory was to evidence, at the level of structure, both the impossibility of liberal versions of the rule of law and the ideological content of all supposedly scientific or positivized accounts of legal practice (Unger 1983). The conceptualization of law as a system of rules or as a strictly normative order was displaced by conceptions of law as power and more specifically by the politicization of all aspects of legal practice. Legal education, textbook and treatise writing, the substantive categories, classifications and divisions of legal subject-matter, legal judgment writing, law application and enforcement, even scholarly self-discipline and legal subjectivity as such (Gabel 1984) were now analysed through and for their political effects. Critical legal studies was to make the legal political in a sense very close to the feminist representation of the personal as political.

The final phase of critical legal studies, to which the chapters in this book form a direct contribution, involves a reorientation of the politicization of law and legal practice. In a rather loose sense it can be observed that history to some degree overtook the politics of critique. The failure of socialism engendered a renewed uncertainty as to the political role of the intellectual and most particularly as to the historical lifespan of the legal order and the western conception of the rule of law. The politicization of law became both more pluralistic and more substantive: the critique of law and of legal studies now rehearsed its own history and theoretical origins and adapted its political goals to the more modest and more immediate environment of institutional reform. To the extent that historical narrative simply indicates the ageing of desire or the relative permanence of institutional forms, it would seem appropriate to conclude this brief survey by listing certain of the tenets and consequences of the ambivalent survival of critical legal studies within the institution and even the emergence of a critical legal school of thought. While many features of the third phase are shared with earlier contributions to critical legal literature, and while critical legal studies remains broadly committed to political radicalism, the sphere of influence of critique is conceptualized increasingly and perhaps more modestly in terms of the institution (Tushnet 1991), while the mechanism of domination is perceived to be the legal text (Douzinas *et al.* 1991) and its avenue of transmission the law school, the casebook and the treatise, the specific domains and disciplines, categories and judgments of law (Goodrich 1990).

The function of the school is variously to systematize, to teach and to transmit the law. The purpose of doctrine is to turn a letter, a decision, an event or a text into law. While critical legal studies is ambivalently aware of its own status as a school and so also as a body of doctrine or teaching, the political implications of this position are only obscurely and rarely discussed. In so far as critical legal studies recognizes its own status as a school it may be caught in the potentially inauthentic position of both propounding and denouncing the law, as it must both teach the law and dismiss the value and complicity of this act of transmission. It may preach an escape from law but must also recognize – if only implicitly – that escape is impossible. In response to this crudely drawn dilemma of criticism, which is arguably the main facet of the failure of the political and legal left, critical legal studies has both expanded and contracted its claims to institutional radicalism. In theoretical and existential terms this may be termed the anxiety of closure: it adverts to the conflictual coupling of belonging and the desire for escape. The history of a closure is always dual and duplicitous: our language, institutional practice and scholarship inevitably belong to the tradition while at the same time seeking its decomposition. The desire for escape, for a transcendence which would go beyond the institution or the positivized system of governance is an impossibility. The recognition of this impossibility, the double bind of belonging and estrangement, the unhappy consciousness of this boundary or limit opens the domains of ethics and justice as the distinguishing feature of the contemporary politics of critical legal scholarship.

At a political level, the critical school has come, perhaps belatedly and inadequately (Delgado 1992), to incorporate, or affiliate itself with a diverse grouping of disaffiliated and disaffected minorities. The ontology or being of opposition, of resistance and disaffection is diverse, and the place of critical legal studies is to provide a space within the institution for such diversity. Justice should be done to those whom the institution would otherwise exclude (Williams 1991). Justice necessitates recognition of otherness but faces also the risk of incorporating or annexing difference in the name of a liberal consensus or some new and as yet inexplicit universalizing political creed. It can be argued also that the political affiliations of critical legal studies – and so also its ideological and moral solidarity with racially, sexually or economically excluded groups or other minorities – are less critical than hypocritical in the sense of some ill-defined though largely pragmatic version of oppositional orthodoxy or inversion of the dogma and hierarchy of the legal institution. It is not certain that the perpetual fragmentation and splitting-off of critical legal discourses, the restless and unsatisfied pursuit of new theories, of the latest importations or the most fashionable subcultures, is an essential rather than accidental feature of critical legal studies. The theory of contingency around which the present work is based may entail a diversity of practices but it does not ineluctably lead to the uncritical adoption or absorption of every 'pattern of dissonance' or of an endless stream of dissent. While critical legal studies may well be marginal, the pursuit of marginality is not an end in itself nor is the status of outsider the only possible or even plausible existential fatality left to the critic of law.

At an institutional level, the issue is precisely that of responsibility for the making, remaking and transmitting of law. The critical legal scholar teaches the law and is responsible for its transmission. The third phase of critical legal studies, occasionally and variously termed deconstructionist, textualist, poststructural, postmarxist, postmodern or simply pluralist, is concerned both with the role and the possibilities of critical scholarship in the reproduction of doctrine and of law in the academy. A critical apprehension of legal knowledge, it is argued, should pay direct and scrupulous attention to the moment and the means of transmitting law as law. The concern with the textuality of law is both political and ethical. The law is made, written and re-written, produced and reproduced, through the writing of judgments, the reporting of cases, the systematizing of doctrine and the publishing of casebooks and treatises. The politics of law is both literally and figuratively a politics of texts, an ethics of writing, a critique of discourses. It is as a text that law is both preserved and transmitted, it is as writing that law is taught, disseminated, revised and reproduced. It is in and through the discourse of law that the legal subject is both constituted and defined, captured, circulated and judged. Critical legal studies faces a double task. First, the focus upon the textual moment of transmission as the moment of writing law, imposes a task of reading and rewriting the texts of law. If, in institutional terms, critical legal scholars simply teach and reproduce the categories and classifications of the casebook and textbook, if not necessarily their conclusions, then critical legal studies has added little if anything at all to the critical project of changing, rewriting and transmitting the law. It has been no more than critique without copula, criticism unattached to any institutional action, ressentiment rather than resistance.

In specific terms, the project of rewriting the texts, classifications and institutions of law recognizes that the tradition carries side by side the orthodox and the heterodox, luminous and dark words, conscious and unconscious significations. The return to the institution and its histories is also a return to and recovery of those silenced and repressed voices of lawyers, visionaries, outsiders and rebels that inhabit the boundaries of the institution. There was never law without a genuine – or hypocritical – appeal to justice and concomitant critique of existing institutions. The critical rewriting of legal textuality includes tracing the history and the repeated failures of this appeal and occupying again the internal borderline between law and justice, between tradition and its negation. The second project is thus that of recognizing that in rewriting the law, critical legal studies not only indulges in a critical exercise in institutional politics, it becomes itself a school or body of both doctrine and rule, teaching and law. The question to be posed of such a moment in the development of critical legal studies is that of the specific ethics of this rewriting: what kind of legal subject does the critical project constitute? What law would be appropriate to a postmodern world? What ethics would seem significant to those that apply a legality of the contingent?

The trajectory of critical legal studies has been that of an inexorable motion towards the institution and towards its practices, doctrines and texts. Whether this movement is signalled in terms of 'deviationist doctrine' or 'postmodern manifesto' it places a renewed emphasis upon the practice and product of the legal academy. While such an emphasis has at times seemed to be a retreat from politics to the institution, it has been recognized by others as a politicization of the institution and a return to the politics of the subject. The centre has shifted or has been displaced. Where the politics of jurisprudence was previously conceived as a question of epistemology – it was sufficient to know that this rule or norm was law – it has now been faced more directly with the question of ontology or of the social and institutional being of law. The politics of legal texts, of writing, interpreting and applying law, is not simply a question of institutions, it is also a question of inhabiting the text and living the meanings attributed the status of law. The return to the question of the text and of the law of the text is not only an aesthetic or literary endeavour. A concern with the figures of the legal text or with the symbolic structure and context of law applying acts is a concern with a series of highly political yet largely unquestioned aspects of legal governance. The critical scholar attends to the marginal, the peripheral or the surface precisely so as to recapture the politics which has escaped the text, or has been hidden beneath its ritual paraphernalia. The critical concern is with the reappropriation and rewriting of the fantasies and images, the narratives and visions, that prompted yet were excluded from the law applying and law following act. To understand the relation of law to experience or of legal subject to legal institution is to recapitulate a series of repressed meanings and hidden, failed or residual forms. It is through the analysis of the text, through the talking cure or symptomatic reading that critical legal study can approach the emotion, the image, fantasy or story so as to indicate not only the provenance of law but also the immanence of law, the unfolding of the legality of the contingent in each affect, gesture and perception of everyday life.

ETHICS AND LAW

The contingencies of law – its errors, its weaknesses, its shifts of position, its subordination to policy and its flagrant miscarriages of justice – are perhaps its most manifest contemporary feature. The critical perception that 'things are not going well' either in doctrine or in practice, the historical sense that the legal system has failed, that lawyers are masking the reality of their practice and the politics of their decisions, can be formulated most acutely in terms of the distance between justice and law. The problem of modernity was the problem or antinomy of law, the *quaestio quid iuris* or question of which law, which rule, which governance (Rose 1984). The defining feature of modernist legality was the separation of legality and morality: a wholly positivized conception of juridical phenomena was predicated upon the exclusion of ethics, morality, value and indeed substance from questions of law, legality, validity and form. The analysis of questions of justice, opposition to power, despotism or the 'arrogance and abuses of wealth', had to be found outside law in disciplines such as philosophy, politics, psychology, sociology and aesthetics. The legality of modernity was represented variously as a necessary science, as a species of black-letter discipline, a purely formal set of normative constraints without any deeper justification than the validity of its law-applying institutions. It was a blind justice, a geometry of rules (*more geometrico*) without the sensibility of proportion, perception of place or understanding of harmony or even principle that the critical tradition had required of the practice of law.

Modernity, to adopt and adapt MacIntyre's parable, is an era of profound 'moral catastrophe', an era that has witnessed the radical breakdown of ethical understanding and the systematic annihilation of communities of value and traditions of virtue (MacIntyre 1981: 1–5). Law – both in its practical and theoretical facets – has been the field in which this catastrophe has been carried out in the most radical sense, while at the same time it is law that has been presented as the substitute for the denuded value consensus. As lawyers we are well aware of this de-ethicalization of law, this banning of morality from legal operations. For the bulk of modern jurisprudence, the law is public and objective; its posited rules are structurally homologous to ascertainable 'facts' that can be found and verified in an 'objective' manner, free from the vagaries of individual preference, prejudice and ideology. Its procedures are technical and its personnel neutral. Any contamination of law by value will compromise its ability to turn social and political conflict into manageable technical disputes about the meaning and applicability of pre-existing public rules.

Morality, on the other hand, is subjective and relative; it is about values, norms and preferences which are in principle incommensurable as no general value agreement exists. Indeed even this mutilated and publicly worthless morality is treated as a second-order legality. Morality is about moral codes and the following of rules and principles posited either by a divine authority whose claims to universality in a multi-religious society are defunct or in the various neo-Kantianisms by the autonomous and free subject who must discover in himself the laws of his universal subjection. Moral responsibility is measured according to a heartless subjection to law and moral success according to criteria of instrumental rationality and conformity to the dictates of utilitarian calculations. Where we are concerned with law, morality as much as politics must be kept at a distance; indeed the main requirement of the rule of law in its contemporary version is the exclusion of all subjective and relative value from the operation of the legal system. This insulation of law makes the exercise of power impersonal and guarantees the equal subjection of citizens and state officials to the dispassionate requirements of the rule of rules as opposed to the rule of men. And just as adjudication is presented as the paradigm instance of law, the demand for justice is identified with the moral neutralization of the judicial process. In formal terms justice is identified with the administration of justice and the requirements and guarantees of legal procedure. In substantive terms justice loses its critical character and acts not as critique but as critical apology for the extant legal system. The lawyer counts for nothing and offers nothing: the lawyer has neither personality nor morality, can neither choose, nor decide nor act because his [*sic*] role is administrative and procedural; it is the law which chooses, the law which has discretion, morality and integrity already inscribed or established within it. The lawyer cleans up the refuse left by morality, politics and other forms of social action. The radical gap in the normative universe created by the strict separation between legality and morality and the reduction of ethics to the relative and subjective is filled by the abstract discourse of law as a purifying symbol leading the way to an imaginary realm of universal and objective truth. Individual responsibility as reaction to moral stimuli is seen as a matter of private and subjective value to be kept away from the operation of the law.

As it could be expected this process of de-ethicalization was fully acknowledged and on occasion expounded by the canonical texts of modernist jurisprudence. For Austin, law was the command of a sovereign habitually obeyed because of the threat of sanctions. Austin's model of normativity as fear of punishment applies not just to the laws of the state but to law *tout court*: even divine law based its obligatory character and effectiveness on coercion. When Hart announces *contra* Austin that the law is not commands but rules, the main characteristic of which is their normative character, the transition from a morality of personal responsibility to a morality of heteronomous legislation is complete. Hart's concept may have lost the brutal realism of Austin's recognition of violence, of the role of power and force in the success of law, but it has achieved the final transition from a morality of value to a legality of norm. The 'internal point of view', the characteristically ethical response of obligation towards the law, is now accorded to the valid accretions of state power in the form of rules which are carefully separated and immunized from all ethical content. Morality has vacated the normative universe which is now exclusively inhabited by the prescriptions of the legislator and the decrees of the institution. The transition from status to contract is supplemented by a parallel passage from value to norm and from good to right. The foundation of meaning and value has been firmly transferred from the transcendent to the social but in this transition normativity has forfeited its claim to substance and value and has replaced them with blanket certifications of source and conformity with form.

This attitude is taken a (sophisticated) step further in the writings of Dworkin. The law is no longer just about rules in the manner of Hart and certainly it is not the outcome of the unlimited will and power of the omnipotent legislator as Austin had argued. Law's empire includes principles and policies and its operation involves the interpretative acts of judges who are invited to construct the 'right answer' to legal problems creatively, by developing and applying political and moral theories about the legal system that would present the law in the best possible light and create an image of the community as integrity. Morality (or moral philosophy) now enters the law and is properly recognized as an inescapable component of judicial hermeneutics. But its task is to legitimize judicial practice by showing the law to be the perfect narrative of a happy community. Morality is no longer a set of subjective and relative values nor is it a critical standard against which acts of legal and judicial power can be judged. Conventional morality, as found by the judge, and moral philosophy have now become the guarantors of the law's perpetuity. If a right answer exists and can be found in every case through the mobilization of morality, judges are never left to their own devices. The dreaded supplement of judicial discretion (in other words the individual morality of the judge) that Hart had reluctantly admitted at the cost of endangering the rational completeness, coherence and closure of law is firmly kept outside the system.

The jurisprudence of a positivized system of law is a morality of celebration, an apology for the law and its mouthpiece the judge. At the risk of stating the obvious, a morality that functions so explicitly to legitimize the legal enterprise, to establish the intelligibility of law and the validity of its judgments can scarcely be used as the basis of moral criticism of such laws and the judgments which apply them. The morality and justice of law are not identical with legality nor can they simply be reduced to the following of legal principle and procedures. Acts of power cannot be criticized solely according to other acts of power. Justice is either a critical concept or it is totally redundant if not positively harmful for jurisprudence in that it encourages an unquestioning attitude to law. The collapse of modernity, or at least of the ideologies that variously sustained the stupid belief of the 'moderns' in the superiority of the contemporary, throws open again the question of ethics. Critical jurisprudence supposes the injustice of modern legality and yet fails to make explicit its conception of justice and the criteria upon which the inequity and intolerance of law are denounced.

The profound scepticism of orthodox jurisprudence towards morality is shared by progressive lawyers and critical legal theory. Their reservations stem historically from the rather muted approach to morality and justice adopted by Marx and Marxist theory. To put it briefly, the writings of Marx are full of outrage and condemnation of the suffering, poverty, oppression and exploitation created by capitalism. According to E. P. Thompson 'Marx in his wrath and compassion, was a moralist in every stroke of his pen' (Thompson 1978: 363). At the same time, however, Marx and later Marxism, as a self-proclaimed scientific theory of society, insisted on the transient character of morality, its context-dependence and finally its (immediate or ultimate) determination by the economy and domination by politics. This contradictory attitude led marxisant lawyers to adopt a rhetoric of moral condemnation and exhortation when faced with the well-documented legal abuses towards women, ethnic minorities or other underprivileged groups. Yet this was accompanied by an almost universal lack of interest in morality which was presented as bourgeois, Christian or simply as ineffectual liberal apologetics. Moral concerns were unflinchingly voiced on the streets and in the courts; but they were accompanied by persistent theoretical attempts to demystify their rather weak hold on political imagination. If the orthodox positivist thought and acted morally only outside the law, the radical acted politically both inside and outside, both in law and in morals.

A similar attitude was adopted by Marxism towards justice. A well-known debate amongst political theorists in the 1970s and early 1980s considered exhaustively the contradictory attitudes of Marx himself (Cohen 1979, 1981; Buchanan 1982; Lukes 1985; Geras 1985, 1992). The majority concluded that his frequent references to the unfair nature of capitalism were polemical and pragmatic and that Marx and Marxism had no satisfactory theory of justice. This attitude was also characteristic of radical lawyers. They denounced justice as 'class justice', while their struggles were aimed at achieving 'social justice'. At the practical level this led to limited successes; but theoretically the field of moral philosophy was abandoned and the few radical responses to the most influential recent theory of justice, that of Rawls, remained at the level of a general denunciation. In a curious, almost schizophrenic way, progressive lawyers were both for and against justice, fired by moral indignation but unable or uninterested in developing either a critical conception of justice or a programme for legal doctrine.

This lack of theoretical interest in questions of morality and justice was seemingly confirmed and strengthened by recent developments in poststructuralist and postmodern theory. One strand associated with Foucault emphasized the death of God and of the subject and virulently attacked the barren moralism of humanism. The subject was no longer seen as the ontologically unified centre of meaning; her consciousness could not be grounded phenomenologically in the world nor her conscience in morality. If the subject's soul was the contingent creation of the discourses of knowledge and power and her body was the pliant outcome of the operations of the disciplines, any appeal to moral codes based on the rights or unalterable characteristics and needs of human nature were *ab initio* wrong in theory and counterproductive in practice. This type of argument was particularly familiar and well-suited to the needs of critical lawyers. After all it was in law that the first radical critique of the form of (legal) subjectivity was developed and entered the left canon. The extension of this well-known critique from the legal subject to the subject *tout court*, and from Marx, Pashukanis and Edelman to Foucault and Baudrillard, seemed quite natural. In what was a rather unprecedented instance, critical theory appeared for once to follow critical legal theory. But while this convergence was welcome, it widened the gap between critical lawyers and traditional jurisprudents of the left and the right.

In recent demonology, the final attack on reason, morality and humanism allegedly came with the deconstructive and textual turn. Deconstruction sees the subject as the outcome of linguistic, semiotic and psychoanalytic codes, which are in principle undecidable and open to the free play and dissemination of the sign. As no ultimate ground for meaning and morality exists, the postmodern intellectual relishes his freedom in a release of *jouissance* and innocence and a Nietzschean affirmation of amorality. The legal proponents of these heresies are derided from the right for nihilism, self-indulgence and immorality (Duxbury 1991) and from the left for relativism and for their lack of politics or of any relevance to the concerns of the 'real world' (Geras 1987; Dews 1988). It is against this rather burdened history that a postmodern politics of law puts the return to ethics at the forefront of critical theory and practice.

There are undoubtedly many good practical reasons for rediscovering and reviving the ethical concerns of the legal enterprise and even more theoretical ones that do not allow us to return to the morality of codes, rules and forms of Kantian morality or to a community-sanctioned version of the Good. Critical legal theory cannot return to (legal) reason or to the subject as the measure or account of law. But similarly it can no longer accept with modern jurisprudence the complacent view that ethics is not a proper concern for law or lawyers. Caught between the call to justice and a lack of any determinate criteria for ethical action, critical legal studies is left with responsibility – indeed, one might say it is left with responsibility for responsibility. A postmodern ethics of law thus starts from the (Kantian) recognition that we are called to ethics before we begin its and our questioning. Before, prior to and in front of the law of the institution comes the law of ethics. The intersubjective structure of consciousness means that before I speak, comprehend or desire, another has already appeared and spoken. This orientation of openness to the world is radically ethical. In the most synoptic of terms, we may say that language and ethics precede the law in the precise sense that justice, the right to a hearing, to a day in court, to judgment, is the precondition for the appearance of law. In this ontological sense, the law only comes into being upon the presupposition of the particularities of judge, judgment and justice. Ethics precedes law, it is the precondition and horizon of the political – of the making of law – while justice is the precondition of legality. As against the moralism of maxims and codes, as against the complacency of established institutional ethics or more properly institutional ethos, the critical concern with the ethical is a return to the political and an embrace of responsibility: for the other, for the stranger, the outsider, the alien or underprivileged who needs the law, who needs, in the oldest sense of the term, to have a hearing, to be heard. It is the responsibility of all law to heed the appearance of she who comes before the law (Cornell 1991, 1992).

Ironically reversing Kant's court of reason, critical legal scholarship moves to place the law of the institution on trial in the court of ethics. The law is committed to generality and uniformity, it calculates those it judges according to their broad similarities and differences, and attempts to subsume them to a rule as instances of its application or to distribute them according to the regularities of a norm. But the justice of the judgment will depend on law's answer to the unique and singular demands of the person who comes to the law. There is an almost imperceptible but at the same time infinite distance between the law's calculation of the rule and the incalculable responsibility of justice for which we can never say in advance 'here it is, follow its demand'. If there are criteria of justice they are aporetic; they are criteria of doubt which precede calculation, rule of law, and they are only momentary (Douzinas and Warrington 1994); they arise at the point of their application, as the just decision must be both regulated and without regulation, both respect the law and 'also destroy it or suspend it enough to have to reinvent it in each case. . . . Each case is other, each decision is different and requires an absolutely unique interpretation, which no existing, coded rule can or ought to guarantee completely' (Derrida 1990: 961). These aporetic criteria are local, partial and concrete (Sarat and Kearns 1992). The task of judgment is both impossible and necessary, both risk and calculation, just and unjust. It is only the ceaseless capacity to raise the question of justice, to be open momentarily to the possibility of rethinking the law in each judgment, to doubt the existent *regulae* or rules, to question the protocols and the procedures that can give justice and the subject of justice, the subject before the law, the possibility of being seen and their cause heard (Levinas 1969: 225). It is not a question of seeing the subject of law as an essence 'without the mediation of skin', as Plato would have had it, but rather of seeing the legal subject in terms of differences, of lives composed or built up of accidents, contingencies and errors.

This openness to the concrete materiality of the other arguably enables postmodern ethics and justice to resist the totalizing influence of politics and law. According to Lacoue-Labarthe and Nancy (1982) the characteristic of contemporary totalitarianism is the total colonization of the social by politics, their complete synchronization from which there is no escape, exterior or remainder. This analysis is not without consequences for law. If all areas of the social are open to the interventions of law, if law is catching up with 'reality', the question is whether any residue of transcendence and alterity remains or whether all society has become immanent to the operations of a totalitarian discourse that allows nothing to escape. If the retreat of morality from legality is complete, we need to envisage a new type of secular transcendence which is not accompanied with a nostalgia for a lost integrity. But is there any element of transcendence left that is not a transcendental signified, a metaphysical craving for a foundational discourse or principle? A postmodern theory of justice allows otherness to survive and to become a theoretical space through which to criticize the operations of the law's ceaseless repetitions. Postmodern justice, however, cannot follow the protocols of a theory, it is not a concept and does not apply a principle, value or code. The postmodern judge is implicated, he stands in proximity to the litigant who comes before the law and hears his speech or request. Justice returns to ethics when it recognizes the embedded voice of the litigant, when it gives the other in her concrete materiality a *locus standi* or place of enunciation. The law is necessarily committed to the form of universality and abstract equality; but a just decision must also respect the requests of the contingent, incarnate and concrete other, it must pass through the ethics of alterity in order to respond to its own embeddedness in justice. In this unceasing conjunction and disjunction, this alternating current between the most general and calculating and the most concrete and incalculable, or between the legality of form and legal subjectivity, lies the ethics of a critical legal response to the material legal person, law's morality of the contingent.

LAWS OF POSTMODERNITY

The justice of contingency is a justice dedicated to failure, to escape and to the remainder, to that quotient of the thing that obstinately escapes the concept. This fraction or fracture of things that could not be reduced to knowledge or to law was precisely what forced thought to think and what turned law to justice. There is always a difference which exists between what we know of a phenomenon in advance, even before being confronted with it, and what we are to learn of it *a posteriori*, what we could in no circumstances have foreseen, anticipated or judged *a priori*. It is this difference which pertains to a real experience, as opposed to any possible experience. The empirical element in any experience – that which is contingent, that which could not have been known – marks a line of flight: of Ideas, not as essences but as events, as accidents.

Since Aristotle the accidental cannot be the object of science, since it is not possible to have a science of something which happens only accidentally, something which might always cease to be what it is, something which *is* only in so far as it is conjoined with another being, something which has the name being only in the improper sense. That part of being which eludes the concept is the space of *pathe*, a space within which various types of accidental being make themselves felt, a space of all that which occurs neither always nor necessarily nor for the most part. The history of the 'pathological' has always been opposed to the history of (being)–good–measure–limit–form– what is completed in itself. As that which has no limit and no measure, and consequently no form and no completeness in itself, an accident is an index of non-being, of that which is doomed to remain 'always undetermined', 'utterly unstable', 'never satiated' and in a permanent state of 'absolute poverty'. This classical metaphysical opposition between essence and accident, was staged and restaged in all the theatres of modernity, descending as the difference between necessary and contingent truths, true and false knowledge, right and wrong opinion, correct and incorrect judgments, good and bad objects. Even for Descartes, the great theorist of the passions, accidents – colour, shape, magnitude, extension – are not real, because they are the contingent modes of a substance, and therefore not necessary to its essence. What is real is the essence or cause of a thing, which precedes and determines its existence. Divine being is the cause of created being; the cause of a thing is more real than its effect, and therefore the divine form of being has more reality than other forms of being. One thus passes from the superiority of the cause to the superiority of its being, and then to the superiority of its reality. Beings are defined by their rank in the hierarchy, they have more or less reality, more or less being, as they are more or less remote from God, from the first cause or first principle.

For the post-Cartesian, though still 'modern', Spinoza a finite mode of being is no less real than an infinite one. We finite modes belong to the order of passions and extrinsic determinations. The order of encounters is an order of joy and sadness: we make contact with other bodies which either agree or disagree with our nature. Ethics is the art of organizing joyful encounters. A body that increases my power of action produces in me a feeling of joy; a feeling of sadness comes into any relation I have with a body that does not agree with my nature: this feeling of sadness is our only way of knowing that the other body does not agree with our nature, is not 'good' in relation with me. Evil is a bad encounter: it is of the same kind as indigestion, intoxication or poisoning. It destroys our body and decomposes our relation; wickedness and goodness do not express essences, but bodies whose relations are incompatible or compatible in a certain respect. Whatever a body does is its natural right. Legality is the renunciation of being determined by personal affections, and the submission to the determination of common collective affections (Deleuze 1990). Legality can only be expressed through the contingency of the body, its actions and passions; it has no existence outside this expression.

Here the necessary expresses itself through the contingent; the law becomes the pathos, the philosophy of law, a pathology.

Kant's Second Critique tells us that the moral law does not, and cannot, depend on the pathological: on the body, on the sensible, on the happy, on a common moral sense, on habit, on experience, religious, or political, on any pre-existent Good, on any part of the sensible world; the moral law is a pure and empty form on which the good as such depends. But it is not to the Second Critique that we must look for a theory of legality, it is rather to the third critique, the *Critique of Judgement*. Legality does not belong to the moral but to the aesthetic order. There is a validity to aesthetic judgments, but it is founded upon feeling not upon concepts. It is the legality of the felt which puts into play a subjective attachment to a particular order and organization of experience. We should not suppose that the contingency of empirical laws confers upon experience itself a contingency. The emotional conditions for the legality of law are experienced in the form of contingency, because the art of law is the art of how 'feeling comes to be exacted from every one as a sort of duty' (Kant 1952: ss. 40). It is as an art that law can account for common experience, for 'legality without concepts', for a conformity to law without law.

One might say that jurisprudence *supposes* this absence of law, this collapse of the law, either the collapse of the legality of law, its conditions of possibility, or the collapse of the effectivity of law, its social and historical functioning, its 'utilities'. For Leibniz, the collapse of the legality of law demands that the lawyer reconstruct the world, as exactly the same but on another scene and related to new principles capable of being justified – from whence jurisprudence (Deleuze 1988). But for the postmodern, the *world* which supported what Kafka called the 'being at home' (*warmes beisammensein*) has collapsed, and there is nothing left to do but reconstruct it: as collapsed, as fragmented, as *different*. As Lord Keith remarked in *Ferguson* v. *Walsh*, 'a broad and purposive interpretation may properly lead to the conclusion that demolition is embraced by the word construction' (1987 3 All ER 777, at 783).

Chapter 2 of the book takes up the specifically legal problems of the difference or contingency of judgment. Hachamovitch proposes that a theory of legal judgment must have as its basis a theory of experience. If experience is more than a series of events, it is because the processes of seduction and fascination are at work in every moment of contact with the real. What makes itself felt as experience is a small fraction or fragment of the real, a little piece of the real which has seduced us. The obscurity of the experience is repressed in the relation of judgment, which confers upon an essentially confused and indistinct moment the logic of sense. 'There is no judgment,' Hachamovitch argues, 'there is only affect, affectivity; and the problematic of the law is how this affectivity becomes normative, how it becomes practical.'

For Murphy, the notions of experience and tradition which form the two-tiered epistemology of the English common law remain largely unexamined. The set of scribal practices which constitute the common law tradition are wrongly attributed with the character of orality, while the experience of a timeless horizon of law which prompted the interpretative habits of common law judges is wrongly reduced to that of a dialogue with the past. Murphy questions whether the contemporary sense of judicial interpretation bears any real relation to the continuous series of 'adjustments' and 'adaptations' which made up the common law tradition, a tradition 'lived in a perpetual present' whose only 'guarantee' of truth was the proximity of its metaphors, its associations, its contiguities and resemblances to the nature of things. It was this responsiveness to the contingent which enabled the common law tradition to condense different ideas, ideologies, epistemic processes and institutional practices in a concrete way of being in the world.

The question that remains after experience is that of how to analyse the oneiric or unconscious logic of common law experience, its specific classifications, its substantive judgments. Goodrich suggests that rhetoric was always a tool for the analysis of emotional structures. The analysis of the figures and tropes of the surface text was important precisely because these figures betrayed inexplicit passions, obscure fealties, and unconscious and peculiarly English emotions. In three case studies Goodrich analyses slips in the language of judgments to illustrate the reservoir of emotion which underlies the conscious manipulation of legal meaning. The emotions are not transcendental illusions, they are not metaphysical accidents, they are juridical facts. The language of the court is not mere accident or ornament, it is, in a sense, a royal road to the institutional unconscious. Rhetoric assumes the legality of the emotions; to read a case through its governing rhetorical figures is to recover the emotional infrastructures of a juridical and political space.

Alain Pottage, and Costas Douzinas and Ronnie Warrington return to the central question of law, the *quaestio quid iuris*, the question of the possibility of law in a culture that has ceased to believe in foundations. It is wrong to suppose that a juridical system is supported and preserved by rationality alone; a postmodern theory of law must also consider the emotional conditions for the possibility of law, the unconscious structures of fascination, of captivation, of identification through which the subject is emotionally bound to the legal institution. Taking up the work of Pierre Legendre, Pottage examines the psychoanalytic formulation of law as 'the law of the Father', and reconsiders the sense in which the authority of law, of reason, of knowledge are supported by the *mythological* authority of the symbolic Father. Pottage argues that while the paternal metaphor may represent one particular unconscious structure of Occidental culture, it is not obvious that this representation does not itself repress other possible representations of power which have been dislodged by a quite conscious valorization of a masculine politic, a masculine desire, and a masculine ethic. The French feminist philosophy of Luce Irigaray is, Pottage suggests, the perfect foil to the theoretical claim that a paternal order of misfortune is the unconscious foundation of Occidental subjectivity. For Irigaray, the quests for God, for law, for truth are the effects of a political order constructed to confirm a 'masculine imaginary body', and to suppress the figure of the Mother who is none the less present, to mark the place of a lost (emotional) origin, for which auto-affection is but a substitute. Both systems are involved in a kind of myth-making; such mythologies are an indisposable part of the fantasy of theory.

It is possible that the spectacle is indeed the form and force of law. For Douzinas and Warrington the spectacle of Antigone is as important for the exploration of the origins of law and ethics as that of Oedipus was for the foundations of psychoanalysis. The law of law, write Douzinas and Warrington, is destiny; and the singularity of each destiny is the call of justice. If Antigone answers this (divine) call it is not without violating the (political) essence of the ethical relation; yet it is only by binding the 'I' to the madness of the 'I must' ('Yes! He is my brother . . . I must bury him myself') that the force of law as justice ever makes itself felt. What appears to be a violation is the very ground of the law itself: the impossible demand for justice, the maddening accountability to a timeless law that only ever manifests itself in the imminent appeal of the Other.

BIBLIOGRAPHY

Althusser, L. (1971) *Lenin and Philosophy and Other Essays*, London: New Left Books.

Bankowski, Z. and Mungham, G. (1976) *Images of Law*, London: Routledge, Kegan, Paul.

Bartlett, K. and Kennedy, R. (1991) *Feminist Legal Theory: Readings in Law and Gender*, Boulder, Colo.: Westview Press.

Brentano, F. (1975 edn) *On the Several Senses of Being in Aristotle* (edited and translated by Rolf George), London/Berkeley: University of California Press.

Brigham, J. and Harrington, C. (1989) 'Realism and its consequences: an inquiry into contemporary sociological research', *Int. J. of the Sociology of Law* 17, 41.

Buchanan, A. (1982) *Marx and Justice*, London: Methuen.

Carty, A. (ed.) (1990) *Postmodern Law*, Edinburgh: Edinburgh University Press.

Cohen, G. (ed.) (1979) *Marx, Justice and History*, Princeton: Princeton University Press.

—— (1981) 'Freedom, justice and capitalism', *New Left Review* 126, 3.

Cornell, D. (1991) *Beyond Accommodation*, New York: Routledge.

—— (1992) *The Philosophy of the Limit*, New York: Routledge.

Deleuze, G. (1988) *Le Pli: Leibniz et le Baroque*, Paris: Editions de Minuit.

—— (1990) *Expressionism in Philosophy: Spinoza*, New York: Zone Books.

Delgado, R. (1992) 'The imperial scholar revisited: how to marginalize outsider writing, ten years later', *University of Pennsylvania Law Review* 140, 1349.

Derrida, J. (1990) 'Force of law: the "Mystical Foundation of Authority" ', *Cardozo Law Review* 11, 919.

Dews, P. (1988) *The Logics of Disintegration*, London: Verso.

Douzinas, C. and Warrington, R. (1991) 'A well founded fear of justice: law and ethics in postmodernity', *Law and Critique* 2, 136.

Douzinas, C. and Warrington, R. (1994) *Justice Miscarried: Ethics and Aesthetics in Law*, Hemel Hempstead: Harvester.

——, —— with McVeigh, S. (1991) *Postmodern Jurisprudence: The Law of the Text in the Text of the Law*, London: Routledge.

Duxbury, N. (1990) 'Some radicalism about realism? Thurman Arnold and the politics of modern jurisprudence', *Oxford Journal of Legal Studies* 10, 12.

—— (1991) 'Postmodernism and its discontents', *Oxford Journal of Legal Studies* 11, 589.

Edelman, B. (1979) *Ownership of the Image*, London: Routledge.

Ferry, L. (1990) *Homo Aestheticus: L'invention du goût à l'âge democratique*, Paris: Grasset.

Fine *et al.* (eds) (1979) *Capitalism and the Rule of Law*, London: Hutchinson.

Fitzpatrick, P. (ed.) (1991) *Dangerous Supplements: Resistance and Renewal in Jurisprudence*, London: Pluto Press.

—— and Hunt, A. (eds) (1987) *Critical Legal Studies*, Oxford: Blackwell.

Foster, H. (ed.) (1983) *Postmodern Culture*, London: Pluto Press.

Fraunce, A. (1588) *The Lawiers Logike, exemplifying the praecepts of logike by the practise of common law*, London: W. Howe.

Gabel, P. (1984) 'The phenomenology of rights consciousness and the pact of the withdrawn selves', *Texas Law Review* 62, 1563.

Geras, N. (1985) 'The controversy about Marx and justice', *New Left Review* 150, 47.

—— (1987) 'Post-Marxism?', *New Left Review* 40.

—— (1992) 'Bringing Marx to justice', *New Left Review* 150, 37.

Godolphin, J. (1678) *Repertorium Canonicum or, an abridgement of the Ecclesiastical Laws of this Realm consistent with the Temporal* (1687 edn), London: R. Atkins.

Goodrich, P. (1987) *Legal Discourse: Studies in Linguistics, Rhetoric and Legal Analysis*, London: Macmillan.

—— (1990) *Languages of Law: From Logics of Memory to Nomadic Masks*, London: Weidenfeld & Nicolson.

—— (1992a) 'Critical legal studies in England: prospective histories', *Oxford Journal of Legal Studies* 12, 195.

—— (1992b) 'Sleeping with the enemy: an essay on the politics of critical legal studies in America', *New York University Law Review* 67, 1013.

Griffiths, J. A. G. (1977) *The Politics of the Judiciary*, London: Fontana.

Harding, T. (1565) *A Confutation of a Booke Intituled an Apologie of the Church of England*, Antwerp: Laet.

Hotman, F. (1567) *Anti-Tribonian ou discours d'un grand et renomme iurisconsulte sur l'estude des loix* (1603 edn), Paris: J. Perrier.

Hunt, A. (1986) 'The theory of critical legal studies', *Oxford Journal of Legal Studies* 6, 1.

Jacobson, A. (1985) 'Modern American jurisprudence and the problem of power', *Cardozo Law Review* 6, 713.

Jacoby, R. (1987) *The Last Intellectuals*, New York: Noonday Press.

Kairys, D. (ed.) (1990) *The Politics of Law: A Progressive Critique* (2nd edn), New York: Pantheon.

Kant, I. (1956) *Critique of Practical Reason* (trans. L. W. Beck), New York: Library of Liberal Arts.

—— (1952 edn) *Critique of Judgement*, Oxford: Oxford University Press.

Kennedy, D. (1976) 'Form and substance in private law adjudication', *Harvard Law Review* 89, 1685.

—— (1983) *Legal Education and the Reproduction of Hierarchy*, Cambridge, Mass.: Afar.

—— (1985) 'Psycho-social CLS: a comment on the Cardozo symposium', *Cardozo Law Review* 6, 1013.

Klare, K. (1978) 'The judicial de-radicalization of the Wagner Act and the origins of modern legal consciousness', *Minnesota Law Review* 62, 265.

Lacoue-Labarthe, P. and Nancy, J-L. (eds) (1982) *Rejouer la Politique*, Paris: Galilée.

Lambard, W. (1591) *Archeion or Discourse upon the High Courts of Justice*, London: Seile.

Levinas, E. (1969) *Totality and Infinity*, Pittsburgh, Pa.: Duqesne University Press.

Lukes, S. (1985) *Marxism and Morality*, Oxford: Clarendon Press.

MacIntyre, A. (1981) *After Virtue: A Study in Moral Theory*, London: Duckworth.

Maravall, J. A. (1986) *Culture of the Baroque: Analysis of a Historical Structure* (trans. T. Cochran), Minneapolis: University of Minnesota Press.

Mathieson, T. (1980) *Law, Society and Political Action*, London: Academic Press.
Murphy, W. T. (1991) 'The oldest social science', *Modern Law Review* 54, 182.
Pashukanis, E. (1978) *Law and Marxism*, London: Ink Links.
Postema, G. (1986) *Bentham and the Common Law Tradition*, Oxford: Oxford University Press.
Rabbin, H. (1992) 'Unpublished notes', Colorado College.
Rose, G. (1984) *Dialectic of Nihilism*, Oxford: Blackwell.
Sarat, A. and Kearns, T. (eds) (1992) *The Fate of Law*, Ann Arbor: Michigan University Press.
Schlag, P. (1990) 'Normative and nowhere to go', *Stanford Law Review* 43, 167.
Schlegel, J. H. (1992) 'A certain narcissism; a slight unseemliness', *University of Colorado Law Review* 63, 595.
Spinoza, B. (1982 edn) *The Ethics and Selected Letters* (trans. S. Shirley), New York: Hackett Publishing Co.
Stein, P. (1966) *Regulae Iuris*, Edinburgh: Edinburgh University Press.
Stewart, I. (1987) 'Law and closure', *Modern Law Review* 50, 908.
Sugarman, D. (ed.) (1983) *Legality, Ideology and the State*, London: Academic Press.
Thompson, E. P. (1978) *The Poverty of Theory*, London: Merlin Press.
Tushnet, M. (1991) 'Critical legal studies: a political history', *Yale Law Journal* 100, 1515.
Unger, R. (1983) 'The critical legal studies movement', *Harvard Law Review* 96, 561.
Williams, P. (1991) *The Alchemy of Race and Rights*, Cambridge, Mass.: Harvard University Press.
Wiseman, Sir Robert (1664) *The Law of Laws: or the Excellency of the Civil Law*, London: Royston.

Part I

The contingency of judgement

Chapter 2

In emulation of the clouds

An essay on the obscure object of judgement

Yifat Hachamovitch

> Why does a man walk to Megara and not stay at home, when he thinks he ought to be there? Why does he not walk early some morning into a well or over a precipice, if one happens to be in his way?
>
> Aristotle, *Metaphysics*

For there to be judgement – for it not to be mad – its order supposes a discharge, an excess, a fantasm: a pure witness of the event, a body which comes forth bearing evidence. It is on the basis of this evidence that the fragile, explosive, dissolving scene of experience which *de facto* cannot 'always again' can be judged. There must be a residue, something left over, something that remains, and this remainder must bear a resemblance, or offer a similitude, an icon of its cause. It is on the basis of this iconicity that something like an object ever makes itself felt. It is on the basis of this affectivity that a mobile, vulnerable, extremely provisional and indeterminate 'soul' – what Kristeva calls a *chora*[1] – can be inscribed with dispositions, affiliated with a particular seraglio of obligations, can come to imagine this filiation as a structure of destiny. 'Why does a man walk to Megara and not stay at home, when he thinks he ought to be there? Why does he not walk early some morning into a well or over a precipice, if one happens to be in his way?' Aristotle tells us that it is the fantasm that enables the man to guard against this because it is on the basis of the fantasm that a man 'does not think that falling is alike good and not good'. The fantasm of the good as a *cause* is what is bound in the judgement. But also the fantasm of Megara, and of home, and of a man walking.

The juridical power to bind and unbind – *potestas ligare* – is first of all a power to bind the *same* images to the juridical montage, so that the again and again of their juridical validation might be opposed to the negative validity of other images, images which are no longer faithful to the emotional guilds of a culture, images bound to no particular horizon of validity, no particular passion or affection, or, rather, images which have their territory in the space a culture has reserved for its hallucinations, its madmen, its anchorites.

This chapter attempts to show that beneath the ideal object of judgement is the slow moving history of images that collude and support the long cycles of the symbolic. These images are repressed in a tradition of judgement because they obey all the exigencies of life; they are not errors of thought 'which come from the outside', but illusions interior to judgement itself; they are subject to its laws.

If there is judgement – if one thing is better and another worse – it is because the images of the social montage come to serve as the positive and juridical supports of experience; they carve out of the emotional subject those affections which support the legality of law; they offer legal but fantasmatically equivalent substitutes for those fragile, explosive, dissolving fantasms that *de facto* cannot 'always again'. These substitutes may be called affects, in the classical dogmatic sense of *pathos* or *hexis*; they serve as a kind of emotional musculature of the juridical–political order; they pathologize the space of judgement, and then confer upon this pathological space the value of an institution. *There is no judgement, there is only affect, affectivity*, and the problematic of the law is how this affectivity becomes normative, how it becomes practical.

It is a question of a theatrical staging of the fantasm, *the first and foremost of which is the law itself*. As 'affect', the law is something that comes like fate, from the outside, an icon or image of God, of Truth or of Reason, a pure witness of its event; as affection, as *pathos*, the law is something that comes from the inside, or a fold in the soul, wrought by the law's reception. The scene of the law is thus always two scenes, implying two causalities. First, an originary scene of affection, in which the law itself is imagined as the cause of a (genealogical) seduction.[2] And second, a scene which 'draws its efficacy from its retroactive evocation of the first, by association',[3] so that it is always as a memory or as an affection that the law is first recognized, an affection always and already there, which takes the 'me' from behind, as it were, 'leaving it disarmed, unable to use defenses normally turned toward the outside, and arousing thus the *mise en jeu* of a pathological defense'.[4] For centuries, the pathological basis of judgement guaranteed a conformity to law without law.

The long-standing imperative of building into judgement an irreversibility that dissimulates the contingency, both pathological and cruel, of all that we inherit, betrays a tradition of jurisprudence obsessed by the fantasmatic text. The scene of the fantasm is the theatre of judgement, its history includes the entire symbolic machinery (*figuralia*) by means of which the laws become the structures of care – in the Augustinian sense of *structura caritatis* – the montage, the assemblage of images through which the laws make themselves loved: 'Science is like a machine, through which is elevated the construction of love' (*Scientia tamquam machina quaedam, per quam structura caritatis adsurgat*).[5] The law is this science of political love (*fidei scientia*); it fascinates and converts[6] the legal subject through images which do not die, it attaches the subject to images of itself, and through these images to a juridical and political genealogy.

An image institutes an emotional bondage to the juridical apparatus by establishing a liaison between an unconsious peopled by local '*mes*' and the images or prototypes of the social montage, which fill these selves with legal fantasms.

> That these selves are immediately narcissistic is easily explained if one considers that Narcissism is not a contemplation of oneself but the filling up of the image of the self when one contemplates someone else: the eye, the seeing me, is filled with an image of itself in contemplating the excitation that it binds.[7]

This binding is affective, that is to say, it is a structure of the ego's affectivity. For Husserl, it is not that the local 'self' has an affection for the image that it binds, it is the 'affection' of the object that obtrudes on the ego, the affection of the object to which the ego yields. Moreover, it is not as a simple transmitter of information that the fantasm produces its pathological effects, but as an object of love: before it is known, the fantasm makes itself loved – in the sense of *affectio*, in the sense of an obtrusion, or as an 'attraction which it exerts upon the ego'.[8] The fantasm displays an 'affective tendency toward the ego', which causes the ego to turn towards it. The obtrusion is not the object itself;[9] at the level of 'original passivity', the object does not yet exist. Fantasms are not-yet objects, they are 'emotional pulls' incited by external events.[10] Moreover, what obtrudes is not yet an object: it is a form of fate, a message-messenger; and what is obtruded is not yet an ego; the fantasm excites an original passivity, seduces it, makes itself felt as its *pathos*, and organizes its political pathology. The three fates – Lachesis,

Clotho, Atropos – represent the three types of synthesis[11] which build into the body itself the irreversibility of law, so that biology is bound at once to the social and to that strange knowledge of the body itself – a body penetrated by a power that Freud called the unconscious.

Judgement does not begin with the *cogito*, it is already in the primary process; it is the way '[an] animal forms an eye in fixing the meaning of the sparse and diffused luminous excitations reproduced upon a privileged surface of its body'.[12] '[T]he eye determines there what every organ determines, namely, duties.'[13] Each affectionate fantasm causes a physical change or 'affect' in the living body which is retained as its condition or *habitus*. Each time a fantasm is bound another local me is formed, but 'a passive, larval, partial me'.[14] Affects pile up; they sediment, they accumulate through repetition: they become organs. The objects of memory, of sexuality and thence of thought make themselves felt as effects of differences produced in the body itself in an economy of scarcity whose essence is this: that there not be enough places for every affection.

An organ is an organization of jealousies;[15] it binds its fantasms jealously to itself, one jealousy on the other (*utrumque jus*).[16] Thus the biological subject is always aligned with the subject of fantasms, and the subject of fantasms with the subject of truth. The entire history of judgement is the history of this pathology.

A SHORT HISTORY OF THE FANTASM

In the classical age, it is the fantasm which serves as the basis of moral judgements, of judgement as such. Aristotle's *hexis* or *pathos* is a 'sort of imprint stamped into a bodily organ', which prepares the body for memory, gives it a political disposition, an affection for the city and the good. For Aristotle, 'the *pathos* is what a sense perception causes in the soul as a kind of image, the having of which we call a memory. Since it is a physical change or "affect", a fantasm is also an "affection" or *passio*.'[17] That vast depository of legality which calls itself a body is already a jurist, excited and propelled by fantasms which are already public objects, fantasms which institute the structures of political love. The repetition of fantasms that work themselves into the nervature of the soul's voluptuous, exposed 'hyletic' surface predisposes it towards particular ethical judgements, by creating in it a memory of the good, a just pathology. If we are to look for the pathological basis of law, it is in this repeated figuration, preparation, and intensification of this jealous site, this soul that is first Roman, then Christian, then secular and territorial – a soul which takes the place of the blood as the obscure object of transmission, the obscure object of judgement, the obscure object of love.

Epicurus of Samos (342–270 BC) tells us that solid bodies emit idols which are empty and mobile and which carry the colour and form of their bodies to our sight and our thought. An image φαντασια (*phantasia*) of this body is thus impressed upon our spirit or our senses; it bears its own evidence because it bears its own cause. Lucretius reiterates the Epicurean doctrine in *De Rerum Natura*:

> there are what we call idols of things, which may be named, as it were, films or even rind, because the image bears an appearance and form like to that, whatever it be, from whose body it appears to be shed, ere it wanders abroad . . .[18]

Idols function at the limit of bodies, against bodies, they stick to bodies and protrude from them; they are 'perpetually peeled off the surface of objects and flying about this way and that through the air . . . [their impact] scares our minds . . .'.[19]

For the Stoics, the *phantasia* is an impression (*typosis*) or alteration (*heteroiosis*) in the psyche; a thing shows itself (*phantazetai*) fantasmatically, it makes itself felt as a body, dragged alongside its fantasm, as it were, which displays both itself and the body that caused it.[20] This juridical notion of a cause – of a type of evidence which the Stoics sometimes call '*enargeia*' – is already pathological: unlike Spinoza's affections, the real cause is not separate from its effect; the fantasm carries alongside it its cause; its affect upon the body is an icon of the evidence it bears. The fantasm is metabolized as an affection, a subjective fact. It is impossible to separate juridical experience from the genealogy of the imaginary, still less from the genealogy of the juridical body, the genealogy of the subject as substrate.

The blood is the first and principal fantasm invented by civilization, it descends as a legal fetish, a 'condition,' *habitus* (Greek *hexis*) or 'affection' (*pathos*)[21] of a certain finite, domesticated narcissistic-amnesiacal mode of social substance. Since what the blood signifies is the retention of *pathos*, it is the blood to which is attached precisely the memory of the social,[22] the blood which retains the law as it retained the name of the ancestors, and therefore it is the blood which must be restored in order to restore a just pathology. It is through the quantification of the blood that economic and social systems differentiate the subject and put the subject in relation to a certain order of ancestors, the legal father and the legal son, juridical reconstructions of the material of heredity.

The accession of blood to the political montage announces the subject of presence, a vitalistic, imaginary technical *gestell* which yields its image from that of the blood, as if it is the blood that descends through the juridical–political fictions which institute the body as a legal subject, as first and foremost a child of the law. The life-world language of the Roman law derived the indeterminacy of the judgement from the indeterminacy of the blood. The ordeal of judgement was detached from the living substrate so that the laws of a space of knowledge could prevail over the laws of the body, the laws of the blood. The objectification of the fact hides the ordeal of the subject within the ordeal of the decision: the blood is the ghost of the undecideable that 'remains caught, lodged . . . in every decision, in every event of decision'.[23] Thus one might say that in every originary fantasm what is repressed, and therefore repeated, is the phantom of legitimacy, and in every legitimation an *a priori* of the blood yearns to be tried and restored.

To calculate degrees of consanguinity is to calculate the limits of social substance; that is to say, what is being calculated in a genealogy is a certain type of politically organized social subject, a certain order of parental succession and thus also a certain order of inheritance. The medieval Church would adapt the Roman law of inheritance to the law of marriage: it is by deploying the blood as a religious cause that the Church could attach the reality of the blood to the *ecclesia*: so that chastity would inhere in the bone, so that the moral 'ought' would descend as a pathological object. The theatre of the blood became religious, deploying the stake of death from the scene of the ancestors, converting a political fealty into a memory of the celestial fatherland, a pathological volume into an interiority, a conscience, which sustained the body in a perpetual position of judgement.[24] The high Middle Ages uses the entire penitential apparatus to constitute an organism receptive to legal fantasms: the function of penitence is to reconstruct, within each Christian soul, a space of fiction which simulates the space of the confessional, a theatre of testimony in which idols, floating fragments of the text, the speech of the sinner and the pontifical norms endlessly rehearse a confessional scene in 'a delirious discourse of auto-accusation'.[25] What is being constructed across and through the privatization of penitence is a thought which organizes itself in the style of a veritable trial, a thought which tries itself as if it were the scene of a tribunal, a thought which communicates through 'a generalised juridism, of such a sort as to produce the effect of [public] discourse'. The object of judgement is privatized; it becomes virtual, it becomes imaginary. At the same time, the speech of the interior is 'made dull and heavy with legal beliefs and pressed through the mould of admissible rhetoric',[26] so that the trial of veridical formations within the intra-personal space of subjectivity could only ever occur in imitation of a juridical procedure. 'The penitent who receives his pardon, has acquired a second nature, until he can repeat the rule and the rhetorical statements with which it is ornamented, as if it is a question of his own thought.'[27]

This second nature is emotional, it is social, it is imaginary; it is an artificial memory system which calls itself judgement. The subject on trial is scaffolded by legalized emotions; 'what the Greeks call "phantasms" (*phantasias*)' Quintilian writes, 'we sensibly call visualizations through which the images of absent things are represented in such a way that we seem to see them with our eyes and to have them present with us. Whoever has mastered these things (*has quisquis bene ceperit*) will be very powerful in his appeal to the emotions.'[29] For Quintilian the body succumbs to being reconstructed through its memory for things (*memoria ad res*); through its retentional store of the sense or intention of a text which is continuously adapted in juridical experience, which is not equivalent to the memory of words (*memoria ad verbum*); and through the rote repetition or recitation of signs, rules, precedents, or passages of text. The transposition of a text into images (*rerum imagines*) through which it could be remembered, was first a purely mental design which served to aid in the storage and retrieval of the sense of a text. In the Middle Ages, these mental images would become painted figures, which inhabited the outer margins of the biblical text,[30] or emblematic pictures painted next to the opening words of texts.[31] The *catena* or chain of 'glosses' (authoritative commentaries) functioned as backgrounds to help fix the page as a memory-image. Albertus acknowledges Tully's twofold division of 'the *memoria* which relates to human life and justice': the natural and the artificial memory. Natural memory has a talent for remembering easily something it knew, the artificial 'is one which is made from an orderly arrangement of images and places . . .'[32] The *Rhetorica ad Herennium* likens this artificial memory to a wax tablet or papyrus, on which fantasms or images inscribe themselves; the jurist or orator then reads these impressions aloud. The background of a juridical space serves as the *mise en scène* of representation, the 'abode' of memory images or fantasms represented and arranged in a series of 'loci', commonplaces.

> The formation of the backgrounds in the mind should be done with special care and precision, 'so that they may cling lastingly in our memory, for the images, like letters, are effaced when we make use of them, but the backgrounds, like wax tablets, should abide.' One should practice daily seeing one's backgrounds and placing images on them.[33]

This notion of an architectural background, which lends to memorial fantasms an imaginary depth is taken over from theatre: the arcade screen, the centre pavilion and the side house, accompanied by a series of conventions, enabled first the dramatist and then the painter to tell a story in terms of exteriors, to present interior scenes by means of customary architectural forms into which the fantasmatic text was already inscribed.[34] The entire *mise en scène* of judgement evolved alongside such backgrounds of representation, inherited from 'the flat centuries', which played the role of perspective in painting. These scenic backgrounds framed and organized imaginary space,[35] they endowed a depth to the scene of the law, they implicated an interiority of the object of judgement.

It is on the basis of background, this *scaena*, that the fragile, explosive, dissolving scene of a fantasm which *de facto* cannot 'always again', can be staged and restaged, figured, repeated, rehearsed, dressed in religious or popular garb, and reconstructed. Judgement is nothing other than this staging of fantasms in an imaginary space which simulates the scene of a memory. This imaginary space mediates between originary fantasms, the simple certainty of belief in which they were pregiven, and the 'activity of cognition in which they receive their form and their character of legitimacy'.[36] An object of judgement is retained by attaching it to a visual image; it is the visual image which accumulates sense; and alongside sense, the image accrues a series of judgements or perceptions, it is made into a new objectivity – what Husserl calls a state of affairs – 'S is p' (which is forever breaking up into fragments). Thus a fantasm, invested with a logical sense and fixed in memory by a visual image, becomes a sedimented habituality: '[t]his means that even if the object has been given again originally, that is, perceptually, and is not only realized in memory, the new cognition has a content of sense essentially other than the preceding perceptions'.[37]

For Husserl, this voluntary establishment of a habitus involves a 'repeated running through of an explicative synthesis'[38] which throws into relief particular attributes of the object of judgement; it can thereby be distinguished according to type; a perspective is already embedded in the type. Moreover, we are back again at the *phantasia kataleptike*; what is recognized is not a fantasmatic excitation but a juridical category. This juridical and political structure of care, an image, or assemblage of images is arranged by the jurist 'in the method of a consummate painter distinguishing the positions of objects by modifying their shapes',[39] – from a distance, according to Tully, 'of about thirty feet: . . . for like the external eye, so the inner eye of thought is less powerful when you have moved the object of sight too near or too far away'.[40] It is this distance, indispensable to montages, which gives the jurist a perspective, so that the object is seen as if it were a memory, as if it were seen across the distance of lived time. A medieval optics of *perspectiva*, alongside a faculty of common sense – *sensus communis*, which decorporalized the object of sight so that it could be assimilated to thought[41] – would confer upon this perspective, this regime of perspective, the value of an institution.

The erotic, obsessive contact with the fantasm is repressed in the relation of judgement, in the relation that binds the being (*Sein*) of a structure to its being such (*Sosein*). For Husserl, the object of understanding is essentially distinguished from an object of pure passive receptivity by just such repression: what the ego produces in the activity of judging are only 'figurations of the object, not the object itself'.[42]

For the object of judgement to be reproduced without ageing and without deformation, the judgement must usurp the life-world temporality on the basis of which repetition would also and thereby implicate disfiguration. Each juridical object must descend as a perennial state of affairs, its image must have the value of a still life. This detemporalization is the basis of the irreality of judgement: 'In contrast to [the] domain of realities, states of affairs are irreal objectivities and are not bound to objective time and objective temporal points in the same way as real objectivities.'[43] The temporality of a juridical space is an omnitemporality. This omnitemporality confers upon the object an 'internal horizon',[44] a depth: the internal horizon of a thing is what secures it to a transcendental history, a genealogy, what permits 'a transcendence of sense to cling to [its] particular apperception'.[45] An object of judgement does not merely 'reappear', it descends: there is for every juridical irreality something ancestral in the air.

'The irreality of irreal objectivities', that is to say, of juridical irrealities, can 'also be interpreted in such a way that we say they are objectivities of sense . . .'.[46] This sense is the reality of the virtual. A part of the real object subtends the irreal object; but this part acquires a different nature in functioning as an object of judgement: it becomes virtual. 'Every such experience in the form of fancy is characterized not as being really present, but as being "as though/as if" (*gleichsam*) it were present.'[47] Thus an imaginary structure – an affection, a disintensified feeling, a *pathos* – is 'set up' in the ego, and it is this virtual object that serves as the substrate of judgement.

The virtual object is a partial object, it does not submit to the temporality that affects a real object.[48] It is a relic, the fragmented remains of the real object; a juridical irreality is, so to speak, a frayed or ragged virtuality. This virtuality is the essence of the juridical montage. At the level of subjectivity, it marks the divergence, the gap which separates the instinctual, vital function which aims at self-preservation and the real, corporeal objects which are its correlates, from the sexual drive which metonymizes these objects, substituting for these objects what is contiguous to them (thus in the case of the infant, substituting for milk what is directly contiguous to it – the breast), and whose satisfactions are from the start 'hallucinatory' or 'fantasmatic'. At the level of institutional reproduction, it marks a gap between, on the one hand, the world as the mythological already known and as Reference, and, on the other, what can be said about it – that is, the juridical categories, the images or topics through which it receives its form and its character of legitimacy. The imaginary 'as if' constitutes this gap, this distance which is necessary for judicative position taking; it is this distance 'from which proceeds all commentary', one might also say, all predication; and thanks to which each figuration, each legal rule, each judgement is always presented as a scaffolding of a more or less obscure text.[49]

The obscurity, the virtuality, the contingency of the object of judgement does not connote a confused or indeterminate reality, its obscurity is essential, not accidental: it constitutes consciousness of the real as 'consciousness in the mode of certainty of belief'. For Husserl, such belief in the world precedes any juridical position, any 'act of judgement which predicates existence'[50] and sustains the law as a position of faith in the world, a 'universal ground of belief in a world which all praxis presupposes'.[51]

The object of judgement is only a primer of faith; it is only ever metabolized through the imaginary 'as if' that founds a civilization of fantasms, a civilization propelled by memory, by repetition. The images of judgement are forms of fealty, forms of faith in an originary experience, the originary scene of sense, of the fantasm; the original scene authenticates the image and puts into play a logic of the as-if (*Als-Ob*),[52] a logic which authorizes a juridical and political notion of truth whose foundation lies in fiction, in the life-world as a fiction. The entire *mise en scène* of judgement revolves around this imaginary 'as if', which locks into place the positions from which the subject can experience the virtual part of the real. This implies that while reality is already implicitly 'determined' as being such an object, the 'being determined-as' is not apprehended.[53] The imaginary 'as if' which sustains the judgement as a position of sense, of common sense, of good sense, is concealed. It is as if the image took the place of the real, or better yet, held the place of the real, for the duration of the judgement. If there is judgement there is affect, affectivity; if a sound begins to designate or signify, it is because it becomes familiar or customary or conventional or artificial.[54] Moreover, the originary voices – of the law, of the ancestors, of the patriarchs or the gods – are themselves fantasms: it is only in so far as what is judged is judged again that it becomes articulate; only in so far as an originary fantasm returns that it attains its character and form of legitimacy.

From the point of view of subjectivity, it is impossible to distinguish between the irrealities of judgement and the irrealities of memory, between reality and what would pass itself off as reality, but comes from within, as a fantasmatically equivalent substitute of the real. The law, one might say, is an hallucination. It '*is or is not*, and when it is, it is absolutely useless to imagine a procedure allowing one to demonstrate to the hallucinator that he is wrong'.[55] The schema of the law comes to take the place of experience, so much so that experience itself is understood as a kind of vain, algebraic and obsessed facticity, what Husserl calls a positive validity.[56] But neither law nor logic, says Husserl, can tell us anything about the originary substrates of judgement except that they are 'categorially completely unformed'.[57] Every experience is a logical cloud, a fantasm. These clouds are the first elements of a phenomenological theory of judgement.

CLOUDS

A phenomenology of law implies that 'a crime affects the same order as the montage', so that it is the Reference itself – 'the phenomenon itself' – which is the victim.[58] Thus the problem of judgement becomes the problem of those vague, defective or obscure phenomena which bear witness to some errant or illegitimate thought, those inexact and nomadic bodies, which have no fixed, metric and formal essences, those corporealities without a surface – what Leonardo called clouds.

The cloud is an icon of the decomposition, the disintegration, which afflicts an economy of images (*oikonomia*).[59] Spinoza marked such an affliction with the name 'inadequate idea', an idea of which we are not the cause. Such an idea can only give rise to passions, to feelings that are themselves passive.[60] These passions are constantly changing, they are the cause of the body's suffering, its ageing, its illness. Moreover, all the failures of sense are reflected in this emblem of diaphaneity, this dissemblance which makes us believe that something exists when it does not exist. The cloud marks the space of non-being–evil–lack of measure–unlimited–formless–unaccomplished, which is opposed to [being]–good–measure–limit–form–what is completed in itself. As that which has no limit and no measure, and consequently no form and no completeness in itself, the cloud is an index of that which is doomed to remain 'always undetermined', 'utterly unstable', 'never satiated' and in a permanent state of 'absolute poverty'.[61]

The Aristotelian tradition assimilates the cloud to a mirror, to a figure of reflection as such. In his *Meteorology*, Aristotle writes, 'constituted as it is of a great number of elements more or less dense and aqueous, and of minute dimensions, the cloud functions in its mass like those mirrors which do not reflect figures, but only colours.'[62] The mirrors in the clouds are so small that they cannot reflect figures, but only indivisible points, colours. Its infinite divisibility is the mythological support of a theatre of refraction, of *petites perceptions* that belong to the visible order, but escape from the order of divisibility, which is the order of figuration. The cloud does not occupy a place, it does not have measures, it is not a body; rather, it produces the experience of a body which cannot be divided according to the exigencies of representation, a body which is never isomorphic with the surface of the space it occupies as an extended body.

The status of a cloud in Epicureanism is inseparable from the problematic of the simulacrum which is related on the one hand to physics and on the other to ethics: physics determines what is really infinite and what is not, and distinguishes between the true and the false infinite. Ethics teaches us to follow the true infinite and to avoid those simulacra which 'produce the mirage of a false infinite in the images they form'.[63] Clouds are not infinite approximations of real but inaccessible objects, too tenuous and distant to offer themselves to sight. Their vague projections bear witness to a space outside sense, an imaginary space whose infinite divisibility gives rise to sadness, to eternalized desire, to illusion and the myths which accompany it, to false representations of the infinite, to gods. They are a species of simulacra which enjoy a grand autonomy with respect to objects and 'an extreme inconstancy in the images they form'.[64] Deleuze tells us that fantasms may be theological, oneiric or erotic.

Oneiric fantasms are constituted by simulacra which 'are particularly subtle and agile', 'flimsier than those that provoke sight', and easily amalgamated. They penetrate the mind through the chinks of the body when the body lies dormant, and which, isolated from the senses, is susceptible to anguish and torment in the form of centaurs, Cerberus-like dogs and ghosts, 'phantoms of the dead whose bones lie in the embrace of the earth'.[65] Erotic fantasms are constituted by images which have come to stand in or take the place of the body they once *signified*. They 'are apt to be condensed'[66] and thus give the senses false evidence of an object which makes itself loved but can no longer be absorbed or possessed. 'Theological fantasms are made up of simulacra which intersect spontaneously in the sky, forming immense images out of the clouds – high mountains and figures of giants.'[67] A theological fantasm is a visual effigy;[68] it is never congruent with its optical image, but rather an effect of the clues which surround it, with which it enters in composition or in opposition, and which render it sensible by association. 'We see clouds smoothly condensing up aloft', writes Lucretius. 'Often giant faces appear to be sailing by, trailing large patches of shadow. Sometimes it seems that great mountains, or crags uprooted from mountains, are drifting by and passing over the sun. Then other clouds, black with storm, appear to be towed along in the wake of some passing monster.'[69] Here the cloud is a nomadic *nomos*, it suspends the relation of judgement, the relation which binds the being of a thing to its being-such. Our belief in the gods rests upon this mixture of theology, oneirism and eroticism, on an eternalized desire for absence, on dream images in which the mind is immersed when the body is sleeping and which it cannot refute, and on idols which 'shout at us promising eternal punishment' and seem to represent the infinite.

The cloud is a figure of disfiguration; without propriety, enclosure or measure, it is illegible, and yet it is precisely its delirium, its lack of sense, its unmeasure, which permits it to demonstrate a univocal and undivided Being, to mark, throughout the history of painting, not a space of sight, but a space of contact, with gods, angels, and saints. 'The cloud intervenes in the figurative text where it is a question not only of the relations between the sky and the earth, but between the here-below and the beyond, between a world which obeys its own laws and a divine space which no science can know.'[70]

Even a cloud which restores to space an extreme diaphaneity is draped in meaning.[71] '[F]rom Giotto's or Zurburan's Saint Francis to Madame Bovary ["the curtains of her alcove puffed up gently, around her, in the manner of clouds"] . . . the cloud is the obligatory accessory, the [dogmatic and decorous] accompaniment of ecstasy and of diverse forms of transport',[72] the first and foremost of which is vision itself. Making images is a religious exercise: the eye, the seeing me, is transported in vision, displaced in the image of a divine cloud, which yields to it its sovereignty, its law, its celestial horizon. The narcissistic ego fills this horizon in its entirety: it is not represented or figured in this other world, it is reconstructed by it.[73] For Legendre, 'narcissism is at the basis of the institutional montage', and the art of Law is the art of managing narcissistic identifications. It is a question of binding the subject with a semblance, with his semblance.[74] 'It is a question of lifting the subject and replacing his narcissistic misrecognition with a montage.'[75] The institutional montage reinvents the surface, constitutes a surface for a 'body without a surface': the machinery of paradise turns the law into a *phenomenon*.

Dimonstrare

Thus, for example, Brunelleschi writes that the sky cannot be figured, only demonstrated (*dimonstrare*);[76] in order to demonstrate it he invents a 'machine' – one machine, a painted panel, a mirror, a small hole, and then another, a spectacular theatrical machinery consisting of children garbed as angels, singing cherubs, who produce the music of the spheres with cymbals, flutes and harps; hundreds of lights circling the throne of God, and clouds, cottony clouds – deployed to demonstrate the *heavens*, to stage the problematic ascension and descent of Christ. The assimilation of these heavenly clouds to the celestial cupolas of churches would permit the painter (Correggio, Mantegna) not to represent, but to *demonstrate* the heavenly sky.

The problematic of the painterly cloud is the problematic of constructing by illusionary means, a space of judgement, a receptacle of beings or objects whose dispositions and relations are ruled by a legality itself illusionist, conceived in imitation of natural legality.

Natural law is an image of divine law; divine laws make their debut in nature, a nature whose laws proceed 'from the will of God as the Author and Ruler of nature'.[77] As Damisch shows, the clouds of Zurburan, of Murillo, or Correggio, do not only support a celestial space, but 'manifest the opening of a profane space within [this] other space, which lends it its truth . . .'[78] It is not only, as Augustine (*On the City of God*, Bk II, ch. xix) believes, that 'in the heavenly and angelic court, the will of God is law', become 'the eternal law of the entire universe'.[79] The real can only validate itself totemically, in emulation of the court of clouds, in emulation of the imaginary. The infinite cannot be the object of sense (Bruno), but the painter, and then the scientist,[80] could demonstrate the infinite, could show its laws reflected in the theatre of Nature, could convert a symbolic space into an imaginary one.

For Aristotle, 'it is by demonstration that the being of everything must be proved – unless indeed to be were its essence, and, since being is not a genus, it is not the essence of anything. Hence the being of anything as fact is matter for demonstration.'[81] Demonstration is not definition, it is to become aware of the being of a thing accidentally, 'to know thunder as a noise in clouds'. A nebulosity is *a priori* excluded from the field of geometrical representation; it cannot be figured, only demonstrated. But demonstration is itself a figure: a figure of thought which enables the orator to excite reason. Built into this figure are the rhetorical measures of demonstrative effectiveness, based upon the rendering of factual images, which deliver a 'lifelike', persuasively animated demonstration of the thing itself. Horace tells us that a horse-necked human and a woman with the body of a fish are like a sick man's nightmares; they lack *enargeia*, they do not demonstrate or describe. The Stoic *phantasiai kataleptikai* are marked in such a way that they bear their own evidence (*enarges*). They carry alongside them, as it were, their cause: 'When a matter is expressed in words in such a way that the business appears to be carried out and the very thing itself seems to stand before your eyes.'[82]

For Quintilian, the evidence (*enargeia*) wrought by a fantasm is displayed to the eyes of the mind (*Institutio* 8.3.62). An effective demonstration produces a semblance of the pathological charge with which the things themselves make themselves felt: 'the things are represented in such a way that we seem to see them with our eyes and to have them present with us' (*Institutio* 6.2.29). The life of the fantasm begins and ends with the spectator: it is he who projects upon the scattered details of a description a 'third dimension'.[83] It is he to whom the demonstration is addressed and to him falls the task of judgement.

Leonardo, in his writings on how to paint landscapes, instructs the painter to demonstrate by means of visible signs, phenomena or events which are themselves invisible – the wind, for example.[84]

Alberti tells us that painting yields its affects by reconstructing a theatre of demonstrations, of gestures of the soul which the beholder would recognize as his own.

> The *istoria* will move the soul of the beholder when each man painted there clearly shows the movement of his own soul. It happens in nature that nothing more than herself is found capable of things like herself; we weep with the weeping, laugh with the laughing, and grieve with the grieving. These movements of the soul are made known by the movements of the body.[85]

The history of judgement is solidly anchored to the discourse of the eye, with its role as the criterion of clarity and distinctness and its long-standing relation to cogitation, estimation, memory, intellect, and imagination, its ability 'to make the reality of sense not only intuitively evident but mathematically demonstrable'.[86]

As Husserl shows, it is not logic but perception that lends judgement its conceptual groundwork: 'the act of judgement which is based on external perception, on the perception of bodies',[87] serves as the exemplary case of the predicative judgement, of judgement as such. 'Perceiving and judging on the basis of perception are the *modes of pre-predicative self-evidence on which the act of predicative judgement, as this is regarded by traditional logic, is based*.'[88] Moreover, it is the self-evidence of phenomena, of the things themselves, of appearances, that furnishes us with the notion of evidence, with the very sense of evidence. Husserl's genealogy of logic is an attempt to show that the demonstrations of science, of mathematics, with its predications of self-evidence, are built on the 'domain of the pre-predicative, on practical evidence and the evidence of feeling'.[89]

Demonstration may be understood as the hinge between the symbolic and the imaginary, between logic and rhetoric, between the memory of words and the memory of things, between the space of representation and the space of feeling. For society to reproduce itself it must civilize causality itself, that which by its very nature cannot be represented.[90] The force of demonstrations lies in their elaboration of the unseen or insensible as a cause. Here, too, the cloud is epigrammatic.

The cloud authorizes a manifestation of God in proportion to its dissimulation of His visibility.[91] It demonstrates a space of objects which cannot be judged, a space of absolute unmeasure which Kant calls sublime, 'a dimension which is equal only to itself'. Like Brunelleschi's sky, this dimension cannot be figured, only demonstrated (*dimonstrare*). 'The infinite is not an object of sense; it only "excites reason".'[92]

THE MACHINERY OF PARADISE

Pictorial space imports the cloud as a theatrical prop of medieval religious dramas, where it served as part of a spectacular technical machinery – Brunelleschi's (1377–1446) term – consisting of children garbed as angels, singing cherubs, who produced the music of the spheres on cymbals, flutes and harps, hundreds of lights circling the throne of God, and clouds, again clouds, all deployed to stage the problematic ascension and descent of Christ.

The idea of the cloud is borrowed from theatre, from the *sacra rappresentazione*,[94] 'a notion of visualization of scenes of writing, . . . the repetition of moments of a sacred drama . . .'[95] In his *Vita*, Giorgio Vasari (1511–74) describes these machines (*ingegni*) which were used for performances in or in front of the churches in Florence. 'This thing was truly marvellous . . . On high was a Heaven full of living and moving figures, and a quantity of lights which flashed on and off . . . These lights looked like stars from the ground, while the beams being covered with cotton resembled clouds.'[96] The clouds, Damisch tells us, dissimulated the workings of a machinery which had been in place long before the appearance of theatrical decor in the strict sense.[97] This machinery dramatized the rule of God 'as a veritable Paradise'.[98]

This dramatic re-enactment of paradise, this repetition of the scene of the annunciation, would lend to the *mise en scène* of pictorial representation the spectacular nature of theatre: '[w]hen Mantegna, [and later Bernini] wanted to represent an Ascension, he began by reducing it to a machine of theatre, stocked with deployments of cotton which accompanied the flights of a spectacle . . .'[99] The assimilation of these heavenly clouds to the celestial cupolas of churches would permit the painter (Correggio, Mantegna) not to represent, not to figure the heavenly sky, but only to show it (*dimonstrare*). 'The spectator was unable to see the painted surface as a surface: it was impossible to determine where the ceiling surface actually was.'[100] There is always a fascination and conversion which precedes and facilitates an institution. It is a question of a symbolic machine (*figuralia*) by means of which the figures of memory can become the figures of love – in the Augustinian sense of *structura caritatis* – an assemblage of images which politicize us and civilize us: 'Science is like a machine, through which is staged a construction of love' (*Scientia tamquam machina quaedam, per quam structura caritatis adsurgat*).[101] It is a question of a theatrical staging of the law; a machinery by means of which the gods can appear to be suspended.

The staging of the sacred texts, in aerial scenes and through aerial signs, was the province of the dramatic and theological figure. It permitted the painter to yield the signifying effects of a theatrical spectacle without abandoning the rules of a painting which, as Alberti had formulated, should have as its object nothing other than visible things. The painting was a space of *istoria*, a space of figures ordered in such a way that their emotions would be projected to the observer. These emotions *are not images*. They are demonstrations.[102]

Thus, as Kolve writes, these medieval religious dramas do not invite a suspension of disbelief: 'their function is to enclose the action, whether natural or mythic, in a frame of commentary which puts the playing unmistakably at a distance from reality'.[103] This distance is produced through a complex scaffolding of belief *in the symbolic machinery*, a scaffolding stylized through the imaginary 'as if', – as if *I* loved, suffered, and died – in order to produce certain effects in the order of identification of power and of identification with power.[104]

The imaginary is instituted within this economy (*ikonomia*) of identifications, attaching to the places (*topoi*) and figures of memory as to figures of love; it does not perceive these figures, it reads them: '[m]edieval representation is developed following a discontinuous or disjunctive temporal line, the successive episodes are organized in different places (the *loci deputati*) around emblematic objects'.[105] The actor takes the place of an originary fantasm, walking from locus to locus, as Joseph, as Mary, as Christ, each place marking the scene of a biblical event, each displacement signifying a linear descent of the text, a *genealogy*. The positions of judgement are locked into place by the 'as if', so that the subject can positionally experience the Christian text, experience himself as a moveable fragment of text, prompted by dogmatic mechanisms and forms of justice which are not recognizable as such.

IN EMULATION OF THE CLOUDS

Consider for a moment a particular object, a particular pear, the pear in Bak's painting. How was it transported to this treeless terrain? How did it come to duplicate itself across the surfaces of a reflective horizon? How did it come to breed and multiply its voluptuous shape so that each cloud would bear its representation? Consider the way this seamless everyday object spills over the boundaries of a particular skin and projects its recognizable form upon the visible surfaces of a celestial horizon. It is not obvious that this genesis proceeds from the mute fixture docked on the bushes of the painting's foreground. It is not obvious that the direction of influence is from the earth to the sky – for how can we know that an object appearing on dry turf was not originally rendered in imitation of the vague repetitions of the clouds? And is it not possible that the pear-shaped clouds are themselves reflections of a deeper composition, embedded in the rocks strewn across the landscape? Their ovular forms are, after all, also typified by pears.

For Kant, the formation of the type is the first thing that the law commands. It is through the type that the law makes itself irreversible; in addition, it is through the lawful repetition and circulation of types that the law becomes an object of emulation. It is through the type that the imagination 'emulates the display of reason' and it is through the type, too, that the 'ought' is fetishized.[106]

The painting manifests an experience of emulation which is caught up in the very thing that it connects; the clouds are converted by the emulation of the pear but do not elude the movement of their 'natural' dispersion in time, their mode of succession; their deployment and rotation belong to the order of celestial objects, but their shapes conform to the prescriptions of an earthly type projected onto the horizon. Emulation both converts and fascinates its horizon; it organizes the surfaces of experience at a distance while maintaining the types, the archaisms of a territory in circulation. Moreover, emulation annihilates the distance between the object and the type; so much so that the type becomes pathological. What is revealed in the horizon of 'idealized types' are the measures of a law which is itself without measure, the 'artful' productivity of a colossus,[107] a Reference which as the absolute unmeasure can 'be equal only to itself'.

For Husserl, the legalized body does not first show itself in the ideal object of respect, but in the life-world. Even vague shapes disclose the logical commensurability of the life-world which gave them their founding: they point back not to an ecological birth, but to the conceptions of a community, to the colossus of the 'already known'; that is to say, to what Husserl calls, the 'universal passive pregivenness of all judicative activity'.[108] This mythological 'already known' plays the role of perspective in painting:[109] it guarantees that each point of view is itelf an object, or that each object pertains to a point of view. A thing is thus inseparable from the system of perspectives that renders it possible.[110] The essence of a thing is displayed not by peeling or unwinding a skin, but by revealing the narcissistic stake at the basis of its representation. As phenomena, the clouds are noematic variations; to each one belongs a noetic perspective, a tacit intentionality, a position fixed on its own idealization.[111]

The vagueness of vague objects, the mobile spaces of everyday life to which they adhere, is a vagueness suspended by the sedentary structures of representation, a vagueness fixed by concepts which remain 'essentially and not accidentally inexact', such as 'notched, indented, lens-shaped, umbelliform, and the like'.[112] For there to be judgement, for it not to be mad, each historical epoch must establish a different margin of manoeuvre for this inexactitude, and this margin must recover social space in its entirety, must circumscribe the field of visibility, must inaugurate the visible: not that which is seen, but that which must be seen, which would be seen, were the law to be sustained as a position of sense, of good sense, of a common sense which makes of itself a figure of judgement as such.[113]

The fascination exercised by the image implies that one sees always, at the same time, more and other than what commits one to an explicit intentional place.

> Things 'seen' are always more than what we 'really and actually' see of them. Seeing, perceiving, is essentially having-something-itself [*Selbsthaben*] and at the same time having-something-in-advance [*Vor-haben*], meaning-something-in-advance [*Vor-meinen*]. All praxis, with its projects [*Vorhaben*], involves inductions; it is just that ordinary inductive knowledge (predictions), even if expressly formulated and 'verified', is 'artless' compared to the artful 'methodical' inductions which can be carried to infinity through the method of Galilean physics with its great productivity.[114]

With respect to the microscopic taste for displaying these 'methodical inductions' in pictorial space, one should contrast the still life in Bak's painting, with the traditional (Dutch) practice of opening, slicing, and shattering the thing, in order to reveal to our sight the productivity 'behind' its trappings, the mechanism of its 'nature'. If the painting reveals the pathological basis of judgement, it is not by cracking open an object, unshelling it, and displaying its decretal like an open secret. The juridical phenomenon has no oyster to reveal, no internal organs, no watch-springs, no bones. Bak offers us their inferior or underside, not by cutting into the things themselves but by disclosing the dogmatic core of the experience of judgement, the rigour of the *doxa* or dogma as a cause. 'The only general characteristic of insanity', writes Kant, 'is the loss of a sense for ideas that are common to all (*sensus communis*), and its replacement with a sense for ideas peculiar to ourselves (*sensus privatus*); . . . for example, he who hears a voice which no one else hears'.[115] The privatization of sense signals a becoming-mad because it gives rise to a non-conceptual difference, a difference which cannot be identified because it cannot be identified with. Every sensible object carries alongside it its type, as a prescription, even if the types themselves belong to the world, and are forgotten as types.

> Even the physical things of this world that are unknown to us are, to speak generally, known in respect of their type. We have already seen things before, though not precisely this thing here. Thus each everyday experience involves an analogizing transfer of an originally instituted object-sense to a new case, with its anticipative apprehension of the object as having a similar sense. To the extent that there is givenness beforehand, there is such a transfer.[116]

For Freud, such a transfer is prereflexive and preverbal, and is valid in the first place for the perception of another human being, of a *Nebenmensch*, the prototype of all knowledge, whose predicates are structures of filiation to which the subject is always and already attached: thought can only ever recognize the first object of love in a series of fantasms.[117]

> An object of a similar kind was the subject's first satisfying object (and also his first hostile object) as well as his sole assisting force. For this reason it is on his fellow creatures that a human being first learns to cognize.[118]

It is only by virtue of its filiation to an originary type that an object is recognized.[119] This *affiliation* puts into play an infantile love, a love of the heights where the good object resides. Thus every act of judgement implies a kind of internal fascination: a fascination with an internalized object, the first and foremost of which is the law itself.

> Fascination (*fascinatio*) in an otherwise sound mental state is a delusion of the senses about which it is said that the senses are not dealing with natural things. The senses seem to contradict each other because the judgement that an object exists is irresistibly changed after closer attention to the judgement that the object does not exist. It is like a bird that flits against a mirror in which he sees himself, sometimes thinking that the reflection is another bird, sometimes that it is not.[120]

Isn't it a rule of the juridical gaze that it only comes to dwell upon its own reflection?, upon its own kind?, upon good copies, well-founded likenesses, pure genealogies?[121] That, short of this, it will take upon itself the task of duplication, and generate, again and again, the same images, the same clouds, the same birds?

FANTASMS

The good object, the moral object has always been an idol. 'It belongs to the heights, it holds itself aloft and does not allow itself to fall without changing its nature. We should not understand height as an inverted depth. It is rather an original dimension distinguished by the nature of the object which occupies it . . .' – a cloud, for example. The moral object belongs to the heights, not to the depths because it is not a mixture, it is always wholesome and complete, and it cannot conceal a bad piece. Along this dimension there are internal differences but no oppositions, there is the good, and the very good, the better. 'The superego . . . begins with this good object which holds itself aloft.'[122] In so far as the ego identifies with the good object, it patterns itself after it in a model of political love, what Kant calls respect. Viewed as it is, from the depressive position, the good object descends upon the ego, arrests its self-love, humiliates it, diminishes its conceit and its horizon. But this happens only when the ego cannot identify with the good object, and approaches it aggressively as something discovered, as something already there. But the moral object cannot be copied, as moral knowledge cannot be deduced. 'It concerns knowledge insofar as it can itself become the ground of the existence of objects, and insofar as reason has causality.'[123] Pure practical reason knows its objects *a priori*, because it constitutes them: it is the cause of the reality of moral objects, 'merely through the thought of the universal validity of its own maxims as a law'.[124] For the good object to confer its love upon the ego, everything must happen so that the moral object remains a floating moment,[125] not as the prototype of infinite copies, infinite idols, 'well founded pretenders, guaranteed by resemblance . . .'.

Consider in this regard Durer's *Vision of the Seven Candlesticks*, part of the Apocalypse series. It is only against the background of puffy clouds that the Good can appear. Moral objects are not images, they are 'the fantasms of a people without images (*den irrealen Phantasien und Meditationen eines bildlosen Volkes*)'.[126]

> Whereas the image is a product of the empirical faculty of reproductive imagination; the schema of sensible concepts, such as of figures in space, is a product and, as it were, a *monogram*, of pure a priori imagination, through which, and in accordance with which, images themselves first become possible.[127]

Such images, when produced to guide judgement in the application of the moral imperative to actions, Kant calls 'types'. The schema of types exceed every empirical determination, and are emptied of all empirical (pathological) content.[128] It is not a question here of either an objective validity (as in images based on experience), or a subjective validity (as in images based on perceptions);[129] rather, it is a question of the validity of the montage of reference: the Typic of pure practical judgement converts the necessity of the physical order into an analogue of the moral law.

A transcendental theory of judgement does not concern another scene, it is only, as Deleuze says, 'a superior empiricism'.[130] Hence the categorical imperative is formulated by thinking of one's actions *as if* they were subject to a law of nature. 'The rule of judgement under laws of pure practical reason is: Ask yourself whether, if the action which you propose should take place by a law of nature of which you yourself were a part, you could regard it as possible through your will'.[131] The moral law is cruel because it obeys all the exigencies of reason; it is not an error of thought 'which comes from the outside' but an illusion interior to reason itself, subject to its laws, and taking thought from within, as it were, so that thought itself is unable to turn against the force of law. The rigour of the will as a cause simulates the necessity of an order of nature.

> The difference between the laws of a system of nature to which the will is subject and of a system of nature which is subject to a will is

> this: in the first, the objects must be the cause of the conceptions which determine the will, and in the second the will is the cause of the objects.[132]

The Kantian will is the imaginary and secular cause of an order of fantasms intentionally constituted in order to project desire onto a moral plane. 'The subject, suffering from his desire, is invited to search for legal but fantasmatic substitutes, the first and foremost of which is the Law itself.'[133] To understand the law as a substitute formation is to understand how desire can find its law in itself; how, in the event of moral judgement, 'there arises an alteration in the ego, an increased sensitiveness of conscience which can hardly be called a symptom'.[134] That this alteration and the moral contentment which follows upon it is misconstrued as a motive of the moral law, as its effect or its end, is a transcendental illusion; it is that illusion we call 'happiness'. It is precisely this illusion and the montage of *pathos* to which it belongs that Kant calls diseased, and replaces with schemata: with non-pathological types that sustain the law as a position of thought, so that the question of truth is found displaced from the body. The legal fantasm does not represent the self, it takes the place of the self, and it is this displacement that effects a subjection. The process of rejecting all ideational content of law, of eliminating the wild side of subjectivity from the moral domain, of withdrawing desire from the objects of receptivity and intensifying their antithesis in objects of the will, all this is – in Freudian terms – the work of repression. The pathological subsides beneath the hammering of practical reason; it is repressed. But the repression does not hold. *Pathos* breaks through its penitential envelope, the fantasm comes back in a different form, so that it seems to come from outside . . . like fate. What is repeated, writes Lacan, is always something that occurs as if by chance. This encounter with the real calls itself destiny.[135]

> The ambivalence which has allowed repression to come into being by means of reaction-formation also constitutes the point at which the repressed succeeds in breaking through again. The vanished affect is transformed, without any diminution, into dread of the community, pangs of conscience, or self-reproaches; the rejected idea is replaced by a displacement-substitute, often by displacement on to something utterly trivial or indifferent.[136]

For Kant, a judgement resists fascination, it dislodges all the states which make us believe that something exists when it does not exist.

But from the point of view of subjectivity, symbols have a purely imaginary hold and it is precisely this subjective hold of the law and its pathological entourage of feelings – dread, fear, guilt, melancholia – that Kant excludes from the moral domain. Yet if, as Freud says, the unconscious does not have a reality – that is to say, if 'there does not exist in the unconscious any index of reality so that it is impossible to distinguish one from the other, the truth and the fiction invested with affect'[137] – there is no judgement, there is only affect, only affectivity. Reality takes place off stage; the unconscious only receives its message-messenger, accompanied by *pathos*. The subject who projects the moral law upon himself must reconstruct a universe of persecutions in order to legislate himself, to make himself a case under law. In order to become a legislator, he must become the accused because it is only as the accused that he can 'recapture a relation . . . to the people and things in the world, although the relation may be a hostile one now, where formerly it was sympathetic and affectionate'.[138] Moreover, to be pursued by the police, by the institution, by the IRS, or the BBC and to be pursued by Gorgon-like women, by Furies, is the same thing; what matters is that one is pursued, that one is desired, that one is put in relation to the gods, the government, or the clouds.

NOTES

1 See for this concept, J. Kristeva, *Revolution in Poetic Language*, translated by Margaret Waller, with an Introduction by Leon S. Roudiez (New York: Columbia University Press, 1984), pp. 25–37.

2 This seduction marks what Artaud calls the 'genitality of thought'. It aligns thought to the genealogy of the body, to the material of heredity as such, to the entire set of practices, intuitions, customs, traditions, animal instincts, and relationships which bind a historical community to its past. Historical jurisprudence, which maps out the dialectic logic of 'the people' as an organic unity is in a sense the history of this seduction. Thus for Savigny, for example, this seduction takes the form of an organic principle, a *Volksgeist*, which makes itself felt through a people's law; or for Maine, 'the huge mass of opinions, beliefs, and superstitions produced by institutions and human nature reacting upon one another'. See E. W. Jones, *Historical Introduction to the Theory of Law* (N. J.: Rothman Reprints, 1969), pp. 55–6. See also Sir Henry Maine, *Ancient Law* (London: John Murray, 1860); idem, *Dissertations on Early Law and Custom* (London: John Murray, 1883). See further R. Cotterrell, *The Politics of Jurisprudence* (London: Butterworth, 1989); D. Kelley, *The Human Measure: Social Thought in the Western Legal Tradition* (Cambridge, Mass.: Harvard University Press, 1990), ch. 13; G. Samuel, 'Science, law and history', *Northern Ireland Legal Quarterly* 41, 1.

3 J. Laplanche and J. B. Pontalis, 'Fantasme originaire, fantasmes des origines, origine du fantasme', *Les Temps Modernes* 19 (215). Translation adapted from 'Fantasy and the Origins of Sexuality', in V. Burgin (ed.), *Formations of Fantasy* (New York: Methuen, 1986), p. 9.

4 Ibid.

5 P. Legendre, *La passion d'être un autre: Étude pour la danse* (Paris: Seuil, 1978), p. 132. Legendre cites as the source of this remark, B. Fischer, 'Tamquam machina quaedam. Ein Wort Augustins (ep. 53, 39) zum Ethos der Liturgiewissenschaft', *Miscellanea liturgica in honore di S.E. il Cardinale G. Lercaro* (Paris-Romae: Desclee, 1967), II, pp. 85–93.

6 See Legendre, *Le Désir Politique de Dieu: Étude sur les montages de l'État et du Droit* (Paris: Fayard, 1988), pp. 310, 391, 407; *L'Empire de la Vérité: Introduction aux espaces dogmatiques industriels* (Paris: Fayard, 1983), pp. 110–13.

7 G. Deleuze, *Différence et répétition* (Paris: Presses Universitaires de France, 1968), p. 129.

8 Husserl, *Experience and Judgement: Investigations in a Genealogy of Logic*, translated by James S. Churchill and Karl Ameriks, edited by L. Landgrebe (London: Routledge & Kegan Paul, 1973), p. 78.

9 Ibid., p. 77. 'We must now distinguish those discontinuities (in the sensuous sphere, above all, qualitative or intensive discontinuities) which "give rise to" an obtrusion, as well as everything which, in an analogous way, is otherwise a condition of the obtrusion, from the obtrusion itself.'

10 This is the Stoic notion of fantasm, and differs from that of Posidonius for whom the passion or emotion is primary and arises from 'internal' causes, from the soul.

11 Deleuze has shown how these three syntheses, *Habitus*, *Eros-Mnemosyne* and *Thanatos*, each mobilized by repetition, constitute three different times of the unconscious, three different series of objects through which it is contracted, in both senses of contract: the object is at once a form of attachment through which the unconscious connects with the world and the locus of withdrawal, of contraction (*contraho*), of disassociation. See Deleuze, *Différence et répétition*, pp. 108–52.

12 Deleuze, *Différence et répétition*, p. 128.

13 J. Lacan, *Four Fundamental Concepts of Psycho-Analysis*, ed. Jacques-Alain Miller, translated by Alan Sheridan (New York: W. W. Norton & Co., 1981), p. 102.

14 Deleuze, *Différence et répétition*, p. 129.

15 See Alphonso Lingis, *Libido: The French Existential Theories* (Bloomington: Indiana University Press, 1985), p. 77. On the notion of an economy of jealousies (drawn from Hume's writings on the political economy of mercantilism) see Jean-François Lyotard, *Economie Libidinale* (Paris: Les Éditions de Minuit, 1974), pp. 234–40.

16 This formulation, literally 'one law on the other', refers to the complex relation of imitation between Roman Law and Canon Law. For a more detailed explanation of this principle see Legendre, *Ecrits juridiques du moyen age occidental*, XI. See also Y. Hachamovitch, 'One law on the other', *International Journal for the Semiotics of Law* 6, Spring 1990.

17 Mary Carruthers, *The Book of Memory: A Study of Memory in Medieval Culture* (Cambridge: Cambridge University Press, 1990), p. 68.
18 Lucretius, *de Rerum Natura*, IV, translated by Cyril Bailey (Oxford: Oxford University Press, 1947), vv. 46–70, p. 364; cited in V. Ronchi, *The Nature of Light*, pp. 28–9.
19 Lucretius, *On the Nature of the Universe*, IV, translated R. E. Latham (Harmondsworth: Penguin Books, 1987), p. 131.
20 Chrysipus, cited by F. H. Sandback, 'Fantasia kataleptike', in N. Long (ed.), *Problems in Stoicism* (North Carolina: Chapel Hill, 1966), p. 10.
21 Mary Carruthers, *The Book of Memory*, p. 68.
22 See on this, Paul Connerton, *How Societies Remember* (Cambridge: Cambridge University Press, 1990), pp. 85–6.
23 J. Derrida, 'Force de Loi: Le "Fondement Mystique de L'Autorité" ', *Cardozo Law Review: Deconstruction and the Possibility of Justice* 11(5–6), July/August 1990, pp. 965.
24 Gerhard B. Ladner, 'Medieval and modern understanding of symbolism', in *Images and Ideas in the Middle Ages* (Roma: Edizioni di storia e Letteratura, 1983), pp. 269–70.
25 Legendre, 'Politique des Confesseurs', in *L'Amour du censeur* (Paris: Editions du Seuil, 1974), p. 158.
26 Legendre, 'Les Maitres de la Loi', *Ecrits juridiques du Moyen Age Occidental* (London: Variorum Reprints, 1988), XI, p. 525.
27 Legendre, *L'Amour du censeur*, p. 162.
28 Legendre, *Le Désir Politique de Dieu*, p. 321.
29 Quintilian, *Institutio*, 6.2.29.
30 'One of the best written of the glossed books of Psalms was made for Herbert of Bosham, a confidant of Thomas Becket, probably in the late 1160s.' Among these painted figures is a bearded man labelled Augustinus, who points a javelin at the commentary text. Carruthers writes that these figures seem only to mark disagreement among commentators. Carruthers, *The Book of Memory*, p. 216.
31 'A figure of "ethica" holding a dove and a serpent, for instance, appears at the beginning of Psalms 4 and 11; the figure of a soul in flames, with the legend "Homo in igne, Deus in homine" is repeated at the beginning of Psalms 2, 8, 81.' Ibid., p. 216.
32 Albertus, cited in Carruthers, *The Book of Memory*, p. 70.
33 [Cicero], *Rhetorica ad Herennium*, translated by Harry Caplan (Cambridge, Mass.: Harvard University Press, 1954), III. xviii. 31; see also Carruthers, *The Book of Memory*, p. 72.
34 On the pictorial assimilation of theatrical backgrounds, perspective scenery and narrative forms see George R. Kernodle, *From Art to Theatre: Form and Convention in the Renaissance* (Chicago: University of Chicago Press, 1970).
35 See David Summers, *The Judgement of Sense: Renaissance Naturalism and the Rise of Aesthetics* (Cambridge: Cambridge University Press, 1987), p. 238, on the classical association of mechanics and fiction. 'Seneca cites the example of the stage scenery "excogitated" by "machinatores"; these dazzle the eyes of the unlearned, who do not understand how they work, so that they are made to marvel.'

36 Husserl, *Experience and Judgement*, p. 29.
37 Ibid., p. 122
38 Ibid., p. 123.
39 Cicero, *De oratore*, II, 87.358.
40 Cicero, *Rhetorica Ad herennium*, III. xix. 32.
41 On the history of common sense, its relation to optics and to judgement as such, see David Summers, *The Judgement of Sense*, ch. 8.
42 Husserl, *Experience and Judgement*, p. 253.
43 Ibid., p. 254.
44 Ibid., p. 35.
45 Ibid., p. 34.
46 Ibid., p. 268.
47 Husserl, *Ideas I* (London: Allen & Unwin, 1931), ss. 113, p. 291.
48 See Deleuze, *Différence et répétition*, p. 270: 'far from being indeterminate, the virtual is completely determined. When the work of art is reclaimed by the virtuality into which it falls, it does not invoke a confused determination, but a completely determined structure which forms its differential genetic elements, virtual elements, embryos. The elements, the varieties of relations, the singular points coexist in the work or in the object, in the virtual part of the work or the object, without one being able to assign a privileged point of view to the others, a centre which would be unifying the other centres. But how can one speak at once of a complete determination, and only a part of an object? The determination must be a complete determination of an object, and meanwhile only form a part of it. The complete is only an ideal part of the object, which participates with other parts of objects in the Idea . . . but which never constitutes an integrity as such.'
49 Legendre, *L'amour du censeur*, p. 33.
50 Husserl, *Experience and Judgement*, p. 30.
51 Ibid., p. 30.
52 On the sense of this 'as if', see H. Vaihinger, *The Philosophy of 'As if': A System of the Theoretical, Practical and Religious Fictions of Mankind*, translated by C. K. Ogden (London: Routledge & Kegan Paul, 1924). See also H. Davies and D. Holdcroft, *Jurisprudence: Texts & Commentary* (London: Butterworths, 1991), p. 133.
53 Husserl, *Experience and Judgement*, p. 208. See also Husserl, *Ideas I*, ss. 112.
54 See Gilles Deleuze, *The Logic of Sense*, translated by Mark Lester, edited by Constantin V. Boundas (New York: Columbia University Press 1990), p. 187. Thus, for Husserl, only a citizen, 'whose civic will bears within itself the national will, and who is a functionary of this will', can properly reactivate the sense of his civil constitution. An outsider can only repeat a figuration, but positive law is *ius positum*, a law constituted by a position of judgement which is only ever inhabitable through emotional identifications. See Husserl, *Experience and Judgement*, p. 266. On this point in relation to English law see W. T. Murphy, 'The oldest social science? The epistemic properties of the common law tradition', *Modern Law Review* 54, 182. 'Law was the repository of tradition and a primary bond of the community. In this sense, its knowledge was

essentially a collective product and a collective possession. Moreover, "the bank of collective wisdom, our common capital is available to us not through general theories of our collective life and its traditions but through gaining full facility with it". In this sense, prejudice was embedded in law, meaning not blind unthinking bias, but untaught intuition, preconceived and not fully self-conscious opinion and attitude, learned (or better acquired) through participation in the traditions and common life of the community.' See also P. Goodrich, 'Critical legal studies in England: a prospective analysis', *Oxford Journal of Legal Studies* 12(2), pp. 195–236.

55 Jean Laplanche, *Life and Death in Psychoanalysis* (Baltimore, Md.: Johns Hopkins University Press, 1990), p. 61.

56 See Freud, 'From the history of an infantile neurosis' [1918], SE, vol. XVII. 'Wherever experiences fail to fit in with the hereditary schema, they become remodelled in the imagination. . . . It is precisely such cases that are calculated to convince us of the independent existence of the schema. We are often able to see the schema triumphing over the experience of the individual . . .'.

57 Husserl, *Experience and Judgement*, p. 26.

58 Legendre, *Le Désir Politique de Dieu*, p. 354.

59 See Marie-Jose Baudinet, 'The face of Christ, the form of the Church', in *Fragments for a History of the Human Body*, v. I, (New York: Zone Books, 1989), p. 149. 'Economy, that is *oikonomia*, in Greek reads ikonomia. To the Byzantine ear familiar with the iconoclastic debate, the law of the icon and the law concerning the administration of goods are one and the same thing. In either case, the supreme administrator, the great economist, is God the Father who gave His essence in order that it be distributed in the visible world through His own image – the natural image of His Son.'

60 See G. Deleuze, *Expressionism in Philosophy: Spinoza*, translated by Martin Joughin (New York: Zone Books, 1990).

61 Gabriel Liiceanu, 'The limit and reaching beyond', *Analecta Husserliana*, ed. A. T. Tymieniecka, vol. XXVII, 1989, pp. 487–505, discusses this frenzy of thought around the limit; its moral intensification belongs to Plotinus.

62 Aristotle, *Meteorology*, I, 5, 342a, cited in Hubert Damisch, *Théorie du nuage: pour une histoire de la peinture* (Paris: Éditions du Seuil, 1972), p. 56.

63 Deleuze, *The Logic of Sense*, p. 277.

64 Ibid., p. 275.

65 Ibid., p. 276. See Lucretius, *On the Nature of the Universe*, IV, 695–755.

66 Deleuze, *The Logic of Sense*, p. 276.

67 Ibid., p. 275.

68 Vasco Ronchi has shown that neither ray nor wave optics account for the visual effigy, which is not congruent with the optical image. The effigy is an affect of the associations which surround an optical stimulus. See V. Ronchi, *Optics: Science of Vision* (New York: New York University Press, 1957). See also P. Heelan, *Space-Perception and the Philosophy of Science* (Los Angeles and Berkeley: California University Press, 1983), p. 91. 'The effigy is the outcome of a hermeneutical process in which the viewer

interprets the optical stimulus in the context of other surrounding clues.'

69 Lucretius, *On the Nature of the Universe*, IV, 129, p. 134.

70 Damisch, *Théorie du nuage*, p. 147.

71 See C. S. Pierce, *Collected Papers*, vol. I (Indianapolis: Indiana University Press, 1982–87), p. 171. 'The meaning of a representation can be nothing but a representation. In fact, it is nothing but the representation itself conceived as stripped of irrelevant clothing. But this clothing never can be completely stripped off; it is only changed from something more diaphanous.'

72 Damisch, *Théorie du nuage*, p. 67.

73 See André Green's article on moral narcissism in *Narcissisme de vie, narcissisme de mort* (Paris: Les Éditions de Minuit, 1983), p. 191.

74 Legendre, *L'Amour du censeur*, p. 146.

75 Legendre, *L'Inestimable objet de la transmission: Étude sur le principle généalogique en Occident* (Paris: Fayard, 1985), p. 60.

76 Manetti, in his life of Brunelleschi, writes that to represent the exterior of San Giovanni in Florence, '[Brunnelleschi] placed burnished silver where the sky had to be shown [e per quanto s'aueua a dimostrare di cielo], that is to say, where the buildings of the painting were free in the air, so that the real air and atmosphere were reflected in it, and thus the clouds seen in the silver are carried along by the wind as it blows . . .', Antonio di Tuccio Manetti, *The Life of Brunelleschi*, translated by C. Enggaass, introduction by H. Saalman (University Park: Pennsylvania State University Press, 1970), pp. 43–6. The description of this painted panel and its lentil-sized hole is of Brunelleschi's first 'experiment'.

77 Ibid.

78 Damisch, *Théorie du nuage*, p. 66.

79 Francisco Suarez, *A Treatise on Laws and God the Lawgiver* [1612], Bk II, ch. III, in *Selections from Three Works* (New York: Oceana Publications, 1964), p. 164.

80 Demonstration, resonant with evidence, and bringing the spectacular nature of theatre into the space of representation, would lend its dramatic perspective to Renaissance science. The scientist, like God, uses the heavens to demonstrate his actions (he makes the heavens move or the sun stop, Oresme tells us, as happened at the time of Joshua). Oresme, *Le Livre du ciel et du monde*, edited by A. D. Menuet and A. J. Denomy, translated by Menuet (Madison: University of Wisconsin Press, 1968); cited in F. Hallyn, *The Poetic Structure of the World: Copernicus and Kepler* (New York: Zone Books, 1990), pp. 44–5. The scientist would stage the *mise en scène* of a natural legality which was itself conceived in imitation of divine law, in order to demonstrate the infinite, to show the laws of nature.

81 Aristotle, *Posterior Analytics*, Bk II, Ch. 7, p. 92b, 12–14.

82 [Cicero], *Rhetorica Ad herennium*, 4.55.68.

83 Francis Leach, *The Rhetoric of Space* (Princeton: Princeton University Press, 1988), p. 17.

84 Damisch, *Théorie du nuage*, pp. 190–1.

85 Leon Battista Alberti, *On Painting* (New Haven: Yale University Press, 1956), p. 77.

86 David Summers, *The Judgement of Sense*, p. 167.
87 Husserl, *Experience and Judgement*, p. 64.
88 Ibid., p. 65.
89 Ibid., p. 65.
90 Legendre, *L'Inestimable Objet de la Transmission*, p. 186.
91 See Damisch, *Théorie du nuage*, p. 78. 'The glory of Yehova is only given to sight as hidden . . .'
92 G. Bruno, cited in Damisch, *Théorie du nuage*, p. 245.
93 Legendre, *L'Amour du censeur*, p. 112.
94 A. M. Nagle, *A Source Book in Theatrical History* (New York: Dover Publications, 1952), p. 41.
95 Damisch, *Théorie du nuage*, p. 109.
96 Nagle, *A Source Book in Theatrical History*, pp. 42–3.
97 Damisch, *Théorie du nuage*, p. 106.
98 Nagle, *A Source Book in Theatrical History*, pp. 42–3.
99 Damisch, *Théorie du nuage*, p. 76.
100 M. H. Pirenne, *Optics, Painting, and Photography* (Cambridge: Cambridge University Press, 1970), p. 84.
101 Legendre, *La passion d'être un autre: Étude pour la danse* (1978), see n. 5 above.
102 J. Laplanche and J. B. Pontalis, 'Fantasy and the origins of sexuality', *The International Journal of Psychoanalysis*, vol. 49 (1968), part 1, p. 17. Reprinted in V. Burgin (ed.), *Formations of Fantasy*, p. 25. See also, Burgin, 'Diderot, Barthes, *Vertigo*', in *Formations of Fantasy*, p. 93. 'Fantasy, is not the object of desire but its setting . . . the subject does not pursue the object or its sign: he [*sic*] gets caught up himself in the sequence of images.'
103 Kolve, V. A., *A Play Called Corpus Christi* (Stanford, California: Stanford University Press, 1966), p. 27.
104 Legendre, *L'Empire de la Vérité*, p. 162.
105 Damisch, *Théorie du nuage*, p. 213.
106 See Lukacs's reading of Kant in *The Ontology of Social Being: Labour* (London: Merlin Press, 1986), pp. 68–9.
107 On this concept of the colossus and its relation to Kant's notion of the sublime, see J. Derrida, *The Truth in Painting* (Chicago: University of Chicago Press, 1987), pp. 130–7. ' "We call sublime that which is *absolutely large (schlechthin gross)* (§25). The absolutely large is not a dimension. . . . It does not lend itself to any example. . . . Not being equal or comparable to anything, this magnitude remains absolutely unequal, inadequate to anything measurable whatever. Absolute unmeasure [*Démesure absolue*] of this magnitude without dimension, the unequal can here only be, as unequal, equal to itself, can be equal only to itself." That is what we call sublime, "a dimension which is equal only to itself." ' (p. 135).
108 Husserl, *Experience and Judgement*, p. 31.
109 Legendre, *Le Désir Politique de Dieu*, p. 154: 'elle procure une profondeur de champ, car il faut aux constructions normatives *un lointain* . . . c'est a cette condition, indispensable aux montages, que s'organise le necessaire eloignement permettant aux humains de décoller des choses pour

nommer le politique . . .' ['. . . it procures a depth of space, because what is necessary for normative constructions is a distance . . . it is this condition, indispensable to montages, that organizes the necessary distances which permit humans to unhinge things [from their ground] so as to institute the political . . .'].

110 See J.-F. Lyotard, *The Differend* (Minneapolis: Minnesota University Press, 1988).

111 See Husserl, *Ideas I*, ss. 78, p. 202. 'Every experience is in itself a flow of becoming, it is what it is within an original engendering (*Erzeugung*) of an essential type that never changes: a constant flow of retentions and protentions mediated by a primordial phase which is itself in flux, in which the living now of the experience comes to consciousness contrasting with its "before" and "after".'

112 Husserl, *Ideas: General Introduction to Pure Phenomenology* (London: Allen & Unwin, 1932), ss. 74, p. 190.

113 Deleuze has called attention to the 'powerlessness' of phenomenology 'to break with the form of common sense, which was clearly present in Kant, [and which] is also present in Husserl. What is then the fate of a philosophy which knows well that it would not be philosophy if it did not, at least provisionally, break with the particular contents and modalities of the *doxa*?' Deleuze, *The Logic of Sense*, pp. 97–8.

114 Husserl, *The Crisis of European Sciences and Transcendental Phenomenology* (Evanston: Northwest University Press, 1970), p. 51.

115 Kant, *Anthropology*, p. 117. The exemplariness of the realm of sound rather than sight is not insignificant, and is of special interest when considered in relation to Freud's valorization of the heard, in 'A case of paranoia' (1915). There an acoustical hallucination has as its role to activate 'the typical fantasy of overhearing, which is a component of the parental complex'. 'Such fantasies are on the contrary an indispensable part of the fantasy of listening.' The sound is an index of the primal scene, on the basis of which 'the origin of the fantasm is integrated in the very structure of the original fantasm'. Laplanche and Pontalis suggest that the privilege accorded to the heard is due to the way it cuts up the sensorium; 'the heard, when it irrupts, breaks the continuity of an undifferentiated perceptual field and at the same time makes a sign (the noise waited for and perceived in the night), which puts the subject in the position of interpellator; in this measure, it is the prototype of the signifier', and thence of the fantasm, of affectivity in its event. 'But what is heard, is also . . . the history or the legends of the parents, the grandparents, of the ancestors: the family sayings or sounds, this spoken or secret discourse, prior to the subject's arrival, within which and through which he must make his way. Insofar as it can retroactively serve as a trigger of this discourse, the little noise . . . can acquire this value.' Laplanche and Pontalis, 'Fantasme originaire, fantasmes des origines, origine du fantasme', *Les Temps Modernes*, 1964, 19, no. 215. Translation adapted from V. Burgin (ed.), *Formations of Fantasy*, pp. 18–19.

116 Husserl, *Cartesian Meditations*, translated by D. Cairns (The Hague: Nijhoff, 1960), p. 111. For Husserl, the question of the institution becomes the question of an origin, an original reference which transfers

its sense to each new object of a similar kind, through and across the viscosity of its sedimentations. 'Every apperception in which we apprehend at a glance, and noticingly grasp, objects given beforehand – for example, the already given everyday world – every apperception in which we understand their sense and its horizons forthwith, points back to a "*primal instituting*", in which an object with a similar sense became constituted for the first time.' This immemorial instituting act will reproduce itself, again and again, through and across the 'type'.

117 See P. Legendre, 'Ils s'écrivent: Entrée dans l'érudicion prototype', in *Paroles poétiques échappées du texte: Leçons sur la communication industrielle* (Paris: Editions du Seuil, 1982), p. 105.

118 Freud, *The Origins of Psychoanalysis*, p. 393, cited in Laplanche, *Life and Death in Psychoanalysis*, p. 65.

119 This filiation expresses the Freudian idea that 'the finding of an object is in fact a refinding of it'. An individual does not move from an objectless state of autoeroticism to a state of attachment to objects, but, rather, he is always attached to an object and begins to experience erotic feelings towards himself when such an object is gone. See Laplanche, *Life and Death in Psychoanalysis*, pp. 18–21.

120 Kant, *Anthropology*, p. 36.

121 So with the hysterical symptom, which is not a perception but a memory trace. One might reconsider all of the figures of artificial or legal reason as forms of hysterical symptoms, which are never objects of perception but legal things, overdetermined projections of legal substance which map out one fantasy while covering up another, more insidious fantasy.

122 Deleuze, *The Logic of Sense*, p. 189.

123 Kant, *Critique of Practical Reason*, p. 48.

124 Ibid., p. 46.

125 Michel Guérin, *La Terreur et La Pitié* (Marseilles: Editions du Sud, 1990), p. 154.

126 Max Dvorak, 'Durer's Apokalypse', *Kunstgeschichte als Geistesgeschichte* (Vienne, 1928), pp. 193–202, cited in Damisch, *Théorie du nuage*, p. 203.

127 Kant, *Critique of Pure Reason*, 'Transcendental Doctrine of Judgement', B181, A142.

128 This form of intention is not an issue of the depths, that is, of interiority or inner experience, but a phenomenon of the entire surface, an image of action which Deleuze sees as the death instinct in its speculative form. At its origin lies desexualized energy as an agency conditioning the mechanism of thought. See Deleuze, *The Logic of Sense*, pp. 205–9.

129 See Kant, *Prolegomena to any Future Metaphysics*, in *The Philosophy of Kant*, ed. Carl J. Friedrich, Modern Library, p. 71.

130 Deleuze, *Différence et répétition*, p. 186.

131 Kant, *Critique of Practical Reason*, p. 72.

132 Ibid., p. 46.

133 Legendre, *L'Amour du censeur*, p. 42.

134 Freud, 'Repression' [1915], in *General Psychological Theory* (New York: Macmillan, 1963), p. 114.

135 See J. Lacan, *Four Fundamental Concepts of Psycho-Analysis* (Harmondsworth: Pelican, 1981), p. 54.

136 Freud, 'Repression', pp. 114–15.
137 J. B. Pontalis and J. Laplanche, *The Language of Psychoanalysis* (London: Hogarth, 1973).
138 Freud, 'On the mechanism of paranoia' (1911) in *General Psychological Theory*, p. 41.

Chapter 3

As if: *camera juridica*

Tim Murphy

> . . . a being in whom the concept *precedes* the act, the design the execution, cannot *produce*, but can only form or model, matter already there, can only stamp the impress of the understanding and of purposiveness upon the matter from without. What he produces is purposive, not in *itself*, but only in relation to the understanding of the artificer, not *originally* and *necessarily*, but only contingently.
>
> F. W. J. von Schelling, *Ideas for a Philosophy of Nature*

This chapter is the continuation of a line of questioning begun in two earlier pieces, one concerned with the 'misappropriation' of critical theory in the context of English academic law (Murphy 1990), the other a preliminary investigation of the character of common law as the oldest social science (Murphy 1991). The second of these articles laboured a distinction between experience and empiricism, which was intended to stand against the more familiar distinction between empiricism and rationalism which has had a wide currency in the characterology of the history of epistemic styles. This chapter is an attempt at a further elaboration of the notions of common law tradition and experience.

Neither 'experience' nor 'tradition' is without many difficulties. So far as the former is concerned, we can say what it is not. It is not lived experience. It is not personal experience. It is not experimental or scientific experience (whether an 'experience' in terms of results obtained or of method); it is not limit-experience (cf. Foucault 1991: 31–2). For Bentham, for example, such 'experience' was literally nebulous, a 'Law in nubibus' (Bentham 1928: 99), and Blackstone, its principal apologist, was but a 'tranquil copyist and indiscriminate panegyrist' (ibid.: 174) plagued by a 'hydrophobia of innovation' (ibid.: 195), whose work was just 'a collection of shallow and insipid aphorisms' (ibid.: 164). It is clear enough that for Oakeshott (1933) it is aligned with what in his early major work he delineated as 'practical' (rather than historical or scientific) experience, and in due course he comes to represent politics, shipbuilding and the common law in similar terms so far as education, training and practice are concerned (Oakeshott 1962). But with shipbuilding, experience seems at first sight to undergo some kind of test, to be linked to what it produces. This may even be true in politics. Is it in adjudication? Put slightly differently, shipbuilding has a project of sorts, as, until recent times at least, did politics, and experience can stand in some kind of learning and developmental relation to that project. It is far from clear that something comparable can be identified in the case of law. In certain contexts and historical periods, law is connected with the defence of freedom and the limitation of arbitrary power. This is undeniable and has salience today in the struggles for civil and political human rights. But these are themselves contingent associations and ephemeral connections which a sense of history prevents us from elevating into the project of the common law. Indeed, if there is a project to be identified, then it is the ascendancy and dominance of law itself, and the 'idea' of a law-bounded, law-governed, law-like society.

As for tradition, law is old. This means that it is all too obvious to regard it as a tradition. Second, law is widespread in space as well as time. This means that it is tempting both to suppose that there is a core entity – law – and to regard 'local' variations as just that – variations on a common theme, modalities of something identifiable in general. This tendency is intensified both by the motivations of scholars concerned with theory, who inevitably tend to set their sights high, and by the universalist background of the history of law. The final difficulty concerns the relationship between law and social theory, both classical and contemporary. Largely because the most influential strands of social theory have emerged in or from continental Europe, and because such social theory has largely proved unable to resist the magnetic attraction of law in its elaboration of the forces which bind and/or constitute a society or social group, a particular set of claims about the character, form and epistemic pretensions of law tends as a result to be deposited in social theory itself. This is true of most who follow in the shadow of Durkheim; but it should be noted that Weber too, though alert to the differences noted above and explored below, to such a degree that 'law' in general was reduced to little more than a word, none the less developed a theoretical heuristic (and a historiographical problematization) closely tailored to the trajectory of post-Absolutist European state-building, with England and the common law left largely unexamined as a complex of deviations, exceptions and marginal notes. Of course, as Weber insisted, history is undertaken and told from a certain point of view, and this is why the problem with that legacy for present purposes is less its 'historical accuracy' than that point of view itself (Murphy 1993). Indeed, to the extent that Weber's heuristic locked the agenda into an antinomy between the traditional and the modern, which was in turn equated – at least on the surface and in terms of the formal structure of Weber's endeavour – with the opposition between the irrational and the rational, the further problem for legal theory in the wake of that agenda has been to reclaim rationality for the common law system. And it is highly misleading to do so on Weber's terms. This does not mean that the common law is irrational, but simply that it is not rational according to Weberian specifications.

There is another more significant level of problems, once those of rationality have been put to one side. Schematically, it is something like this. England modernized using medieval epistemology unevenly modified by incorporating small doses of Locke, large amounts of Burke, and some of the assumptions (but little else) of political economy. Continental Europe, by contrast, hypostatized the claims of reason – into the state, into codes. The medieval epistemology was rationalized into scientific history and hermeneutics. Both institutions and epistemic orientation diverged from a largely common medieval platform (where the differences were, by contrast with what came later, ones of degrees of success in institution-building and in attainment of objectives). Moreover, the common law was then exported to America. The rise to pre-eminence of America has meant that distinctive American conceptions and problematizations have increasingly assumed the role of world leadership.

One consequence of this 'history', so far as theory is concerned, is ironic. Postmodernism is largely concerned with the critique of reason in the Weberian sense of rationality, and in that sense civilian law is one of its targets. It is also the case that there is a fairly easy equation between secular codified law and the Law of the Father, as well as between patriarchy and rationality. Yet that same postmodernism not only involves a reappropriation of medieval theory but the common law already presents a curious mixture of the medieval and the postmodern.

Turning to the English common law as such, the other problem is the very status of the term 'tradition'. At one level, it self-evidently can mean too many things at once. Since much of what follows is 'about' tradition, it is appropriate to consider explicitly some of these problems at the outset. In the sense of a set of established arrangements, one can speak of the civilian tradition as well as, and by contrast with, the common law tradition, and in doing so we usually mean to draw attention to the difference between codes and cases or 'precedent'. Or one may use the term to conjure up an attitude towards the past – here, it is supposed that a 'traditional' society or institution is one which reveres or venerates the past, and common lawyers, of course, are often supposed to do just that through the doctrine of precedent or *stare decisis*, treated as synonymous expressions of ancestor-worship. This would require us, presumably, to characterize the common law as a traditional or traditionary discourse. It does possess some features of this sort, but they are not the most significant ones, and the doctrine of precedent is overinflated both in the schools and in popular culture. (The fear of setting a precedent – the 'what if' of the future – is another matter, which must be taken up elsewhere.) Then there is traditionality, which for Krygier (1988) and Bruns (1992) is something else yet again – essentially a hermeneutical position and predicament of an 'interpretive community' placed in a situation, tradition signalling not so much either the existence of the community or of the situation but rather the placing-in-the-situation as such. The problem with this hermeneutical inflection is that it is either a general ontology or it is one way of addressing the specific textuality of modern existence. The latter I shall consider shortly; the former is in itself too general to be of much assistance here.

The etymology of tradition suggests a handing over or surrender, even betrayal (as in *trahison*); Tacitus uses *traditor* to mean a traitor. This seems odd, at first sight, a reversal of meaning from Antiquity to the present. Or is it? Is it in fact the case that every delivery is also a betrayal, that ancestor-worship is also (or is accompanied by) parricide, that what we call tradition must be surrender and betrayal because these are, in the end, the work of *durée* and temporality? Tradition understood in this way is thus distant from the notion of an abject surrender to or embrace of the law of the father. No doubt this too has an air of ontological familiarity. So much the better. Understood not as an event but as a process or dynamic, we can see at once that tradition is a more complex or ambiguous notion than some of the above proposals would suggest.

Delivery, surrender, betrayal of what? For Antiquity, of a city. For the common law viewed as a tradition, the answer might be thought to be experience. But I would prefer to suggest something else at this point: the genius of metaphor. And here too I have in mind something elementary, general and processual: a carrying of something from one place to another. In this sense, tradition is not an esoteric initiation into the readings of texts nor the occult transfer of techniques, nor the transfer of keys to a set of canonical texts. Rather, it is the delivery of a template for use. If a tradition is thus the antinomy of delivery and betrayal, its presupposition is the activity of (or a continuing commitment to) maintenance (so that there is always something which can be delivered and betrayed again).

The dominant image of law in western thought is of something written down and fixed, so that, fixed, it can be the object of informed interpretation, systematic (or at least orderly) exposition, explicit critique and purposive alteration. The common law emerged from this general image and the practices it presupposed no less than did the civilian systems of modern Europe. It might also be said that each emerged in the age of print, that is, in the wake of a new technology which permitted the actualization of this dominant image – textual fixity, standardization and stabilization, authenticity (or at least authentication), a clear differentiation of text and interpretation, multiple copies, 'access to law' and so on, a process which 'culminated' in the 'enlightened' codifications of Europe from the eighteenth century onwards. During the same period, the common law, by contrast, moved further and further away from accepting such a reduction/redaction (and any such reduction quickly got what can only be called the medieval, glossatorial, treatment). The common law's world thus became (or remained) a scribal world but not a textual one in the new sense of textuality which emerged in the wake of print. Not fixed in place by printed texts, the common law had, instead, its judges and their opinions of it. Of course there had always been legislation, and with print that became fixed after a fashion. But the relationship between Parliament and the common law judges can hardly be stated with either clarity or simplicity, and the independence of the judges is in a certain sense real.

Continental codification proceeded to eliminate detail and gather up the law into general printed rules and principles. In England, the detail, the work of elaboration, continued. This persistence of detail meant that, in some polemical contexts, it was necessary to emphasize that the common law was an 'artificial' system, meaning by that something comparable to Saussure's not unambiguous emphasis, discussed below, upon the arbitrariness of language. And this persistence of detail has also meant that, in addition to the failings of most decision-systems ('to err is human' or 'even Homer nodded', etc.), the principal risk has been a tendency towards involution, the 'overdriving of an established form':

> cultural patterns which, after having reached what would seem to be a definitive form, nonetheless fail either to stabilize or transform themselves into a new pattern but rather continue to develop by becoming internally more complicated. . . . Being hemmed in on all sides by a crystallized pattern, it takes the function of elaborateness. Expansive creativeness having dried up at the source, a special kind of virtuosity takes its place, a sort of technical hairsplitting . . .
>
> (Geertz 1963: 81)

Perhaps this is why, at least from a purely legal point of view, parts of the common law framework are overhauled from time to time. 'The development of the law', regarded from the point of view of law as tradition, can be attentive to and interested in those changes which rescue the law from excessive involution or which make sense from a legal point of view. (Some distinctions may come to seem artificial or over-nice from a legal perspective.) This process can be observed in tandem, of course, with the shifting concerns of 'society' as a whole (more usually, the concerns of what today we call politics and administration) but it can neither be reduced to it (to the extent that the law remains a living, active – some might say 'creative' – tradition) nor can it be isolated from it.

And so the notion of tradition with which we are concerned here is a complex one embracing ideas, ideologies, epistemic processes and practices, as well as institutional settings, arrangements and presuppositions. In what follows, I seek to elaborate some of the dimensions and implications of the common law tradition as what Oakeshott (1962), condensing all these elements, calls a 'concrete manner of living'. If this particular adjective seems singularly inappropriate to preface what follows, perhaps I can add that even the simplest activity or 'way of life' can seem quite complicated at the point of reflection.

TEXTS

> According to the jurists of the Historical School, when the Sovereign of a country wants anything to be done by his subjects, the most effectual course that can be taken by him for that purpose is – not to tell them and let them know what it is that on the occasion in question he wants to be done, but to put it to them to enquire what it is that on occasions which appear to be similar he has ordered to be done, or judges appointed by him and acting under his authority have punished men for their not having done without having ever been bid to do it. Apply this notion to domestic life – to expression of will operating on the smallest scale. . . . Occasion suppose, that of providing for dinner. . . . What is the most suitable course for the master or mistress to take? To call up the Housekeeper or Cook and say to her, Let me have a sirloin of beef today with a plum pudding? Oh no. What then? Answer, this: Look over the Housekeeper's book as far back as is necessary, and then tell me what the dinner is that I have a mind for . . .
>
> (Bentham quoted in Dinwiddy 1984: 59)

How do we find what the law is? Observe how a question of this kind is a compacted one, a question always open to the answer in the form of further questions – What is law? Who can say? And how?

In providing its own answers to such questions, the common law stands apart from the modern scientific formalisms which aim to deploy man (the 'knowing subject') as a neutral instrument, without qualities, without 'prejudice'. Since it is now more or less conventional to oppose the instrumental to the interpretive or hermeneutical, and if we view the common law as encapsulating that epistemic attitude which this new formalism opposed and negated, it might seem that the common lawyer is necessarily positioned as a hermeneuticist. Yet the sense of tradition contained in common law experience is only partly to be characterized in this way, and in certain important respects it must be understood to be non-hermeneutical.

The issue of hermeneutics is most directly approached through the comparison of the common law tradition and civilian law. Leaving considerations of political and institutional history (Caenegem 1987, 1992) on one side, it is apparent that the codified law embeds the law as abstract, general and universal in a printed text which is always the same. The act of adjudication, if it is to be 'successful', requires the judge to place himself under or before the text, within its orient, trajectory, directionality and to bring the particular case towards its proper position under the shadow of the text. (In this sense interpretation is teleological, but it is too easy to reduce this telos to a narrow instrumental purpose, which is only one possible dimension of the interpretive process and attitude which this legal structure permits to be in play.)

In a revealing passage, Gadamer suggests that

> The way in which the interpreter belongs to his text is like the way in which the vanishing point belongs to the perspective of a picture. It is not a matter of looking for this vanishing point and adopting it as one's standpoint. The interpreter similarly finds his point of view already given, and does not choose it arbitrarily. Thus it is an essential condition of the possibility of legal hermeneutics that the law is binding on all the members of the community in the same way.
>
> (Gadamer 1979: 293–4)

This supposed state of affairs is contrasted with that where the will of an absolute ruler prevails:

> the will of the monarch who is not bound by the law can effect whatever seems just to him without regard for the law – that is without the effort of interpretation. There is a need to understand and interpret only when something is enacted in such a way that it is, as enacted, irremovable and binding.
>
> (Gadamer 1979: 294)

The hermeneutics in play here take as given the text of the law in which the law is housed, in which it is at home (it is crucial that the ruler cannot change the law, i.e. the text). Hermeneutics, pure dogmatics and some kind of judicial will-theory (cf. Kelsen 1992: 77–89) then jostle for primacy of place in establishing relations to such texts. I must postpone to another occasion an elaboration of English statutory interpretation from the general point of view developed here; but it needs to be recognized that this is not the position from which the common law tradition starts, and that, indeed, legislative texts are in a sense external to that tradition and approached in almost exactly the same way as the decree of an absolute ruler. Indeed, from the point of view of the common law, legislation is the product of an absolute power.

Hermeneutics presupposes a text. Where, then, is the text of the common law? There are of course those who suggest that the common law is like literature, or a chain novel, which, if the comparison is intended seriously, implies a certain intrinsic textuality. Yet this is an assimilation based largely on the fact that law, like literature, is an instance of what Derrida calls empirical writing, coupled with the commonplace empirical observation that the writing in question is not scientific, and the further assumption, part empirical, part ideological, that it is not historical writing and is creative writing (creation within limits of course, but then few now contend that the author is fully in possession of the text that he writes). However, this analogy does little more than remind us that, viewed as a serial or sequence, the delivery of chapters already written can be betrayed by the writer of the next (though the analogy is meant to make us think of time as a matter of the 'development of the law'). In fact, as Foucault suggested, in literature we have 'the ranging to infinity of fragmentary languages . . . the simple, continuous, and monotonous line of language left to its own devices, a language fated to be infinite because it can no longer support itself upon the speech of infinity' (Foucault 1977a: 67). And in any event, the emphasis upon the delivery of what is written so far – for safe keeping, for betrayal, for development – conceals the simple fact that it is rather as if the novel is written afresh every time.

Many of these difficulties derive from the nature of the relationship between the English common law and writing. Let me suggest (even if doing so involves an intolerable degree of simplification) that the common law operates in, with and through a medieval textuality, which means that from a modern perspective it is 'unwritten'. The literature it resembles, in other words, is medieval literature, not modern novels, chain or otherwise. Once this is grasped, it also becomes possible to identify some of the specific confusions which result when the common law finds itself under house arrest, frozen into a modern, printed, text, as has happened with the constitutional law of the USA.

These features of common law epistemology become clearer if we repeat the suggestion advanced above that the common law involves a revalorization of certain very general dimensions of medieval thought. According to Carruthers, 'few features of medieval scholarship are so distinctive as an utter indifference to the pastness of the past' (Carruthers 1990: 193).

> A work of literature was not taught in isolation, as an artifact produced by some person long dead whose intention we must now 'recover', but as an ever-rolling stream accumulating and

> adapting over time as it is 'collated' with its multitude of readers. *Collatio* means all these things: bringing together of texts, conversations about texts, and feeding upon texts as one feeds at a community meal.
>
> (Carruthers 1990: 217)

For Carruthers, the logic of medieval writing is 'expansive'; thus

> the written exemplum . . . offers a 'common place' which collects subsequent comments, glosses, references, as readers apply, adapt, restate, meditate upon it . . . it is commentary and imitation which make a text an 'auctor' – not the activities of its writer but of its readers . . . no modern reader would think of adapting and adding to the work of someone else in the way that medieval readers freely did, . . . the results plague every editor of a medieval text . . .'
>
> (Carruthers 1990: 214)

Like the common law, that is, we encounter here a set of scribal practices so different from those modern ones which become synonymous with the core idea of writing in the age of print that we attribute to them (wrongly) the character of orality. And from the vantage point of the modern printed book, the common law is a pre-text, not a text. If this seems strange, perhaps it is no more strange than the clothing worn in court, or the language used in legal documents. And it is no more than a convenient illusion or a heuristic device to suppose that social practices have a proper time.

That the common law is not a modern text (and therefore in practical terms is something memorized and handed down – see Goodrich 1991a: 246–50) is in fact entirely commonplace, but requires periodic restatement in an era of insistent formalism. Thus Holland, reworking a theme already well-worn in Blackstone, on the meaning of *lex non scripta*:

> In legislation, both the contents of the rule are devised, and legal force is given to it, by acts of the sovereign power which produce 'written law'. All the other law sources produce what is called 'unwritten law', to which the sovereign authority gives its whole legal force, but not its contents, which are derived from popular tendency, professional discussion, judicial ingenuity, or otherwise, as the case may be. . . . The Roman writers . . . give to these terms a merely accidental and literal meaning. Their 'ius scriptum' is that

> which is committed to writing, by whomsoever, at the time of its origin.
>
> (Holland 1916: 77 and n2)

'Popular tendency', 'professional discussion', 'judicial ingenuity', or, in the best legal style, lest such specific items might seem to be exhaustive, 'or otherwise': in place of a text, the common law offers a sort of commonplace book, an *aide-mémoire*, a repository, and a resource; it is a little too fashionable these days to say, also, a 'conversation'. The essential 'as if' of the common law tradition is that it offers itself 'as if' it is not a (modern) text. Writing is evidence, a copy, a record (Clanchy 1979, Thomas 1989). This is to say, the common law is not a modern text even though common lawyers have long used writing and even though much of what the common law is and was is stored in written records. Writing always comes later upon the scene.

The common law is not a text in another sense too: it is not something woven or fabricated because, like language, it is not made according to any human plan or scheme. Once a nation had to thank God or Providence if it was 'fortunate' in its language or its laws; with the twilight of the Gods, the question of indebtedness has also become obscure: is the debt owed to *nature*?

> All your sophisters cannot produce anything better adapted to preserve a rational and manly freedom than the course that we have pursued, who have chosen our nature rather than our speculations, our breasts rather than our inventions, for the great conservatories and magazines of our rights and privileges.
>
> (Burke 1987: 31)

This is of course the 'error' – or, better, the disappointment – of those who look to codification to bring to an end the process of interpretation, as they usually put it: to have law simple and direct. Thus Locke complained:

> in the interpretation of Laws, whether Divine, or Humane, there is no end; Comments beget Comments, and Explications make new matter for Explications: And of limiting, distinguishing, varying the signification of these moral Words, there is no end. . . . Many a Man, who was pretty well satisfied of the meaning of a Text of Scripture, or Clause in the Code, at first reading, has by consulting Commentators, quite lost the sense of it, and, by those

> Elucidations, given rise or increase to his Doubts, and drawn obscurity upon the place . . .
>
> (Locke 1975: 481)

I am not sure whether it is useful at this point to formulate these problems in terms of a desire for the text, for a code, for a *techne*, for law. If we did so, it would of course be necessary to stress that 'desire' cannot be satisfied, only repeated. But we would also need to distinguish whether the desire we wished to identify was a desire for the text or a desire for law. (And a desire for 'justice' seems to involve yet a further and distinct object for desire.)

Bowie has written caustically of both (what he calls) 'high' and 'low' desire, those '[p]owerful confluential currents within European and American culture have made "desire" . . . into a major conceptual nostrum of the age, a terminological tribute paid by the bourgeoisie to its own purportedly new and self-aware sexuality' (Bowie 1987: 2), concluding that, for all the insights gained along the way, desire has come to be given

> a wider currency than any one concept is ever likely to deserve. The imitators [of Freud] have turned a once provocative set of insights into an obliging semi-theoretical *ritornello* and, removing their study of human instinct more readily than Freud ever did from the sphere of social and political actuality, have discovered in 'desire' a readily marketable metaphysical gadget.
>
> (Bowie 1987: 4–5)

I tend to agree. It is easy to move too rapidly from subjectivity to the social, or from the social to subjectivity. Since Durkheim, this has been one of the central problems of social theory. In the forecourts of the law itself, however, it may be that such a perspective, which is exorbitant from a general sociological point of view, has a certain appropriateness. (Some of the excesses presented so tellingly by Goodrich (1991a, 1991b) certainly suggest this to be the case; so far as civilian systems are concerned, it may be that Legendre makes some sense at a comparable level.)

In large measure, therefore, we are probably dealing with a projection of desire by lawyers on to society, lawyers or legal glossators and commentators who desire interpretation to end, to have the question of law settled once and for all, or, in the case of the common law, to begin. Of course, at the same time, most lawyers from most legal traditions know how naïve this is; both Kelsen and hermeneutics undermine the dogmatism which assumes a definitive text does or can provide an end. Interpretation or decisionism is thus the already known condition of unsatisfied desire, of the unsatisfiable desire for a definitive – finished – text.

The common law tradition disappoints or deflects desire at an earlier stage: by rejecting or resisting graphism and formalism. The prototype of the common law sovereign is Alfred rather than Justinian:

> many of them [the laws] which I did not like, I rejected with the advice of my councillors and ordered them to be differently observed. For I dared not presume to set in writing at all many of my own because it was unknown to me what would please those who should come after us.
>
> (Coleman 1992: 572)

'Alfred's is a statement, Coleman comments, 'not about a fear of making new laws but about the consequences of writing them down' (ibid.). Does this then mean that belonging to law – or self-recognition – becomes more resolutely institutional or 'professional' if there is not a modern text? If the people cannot carry the law home in their pocket, is the alternative that living law requires the entombment and interment of its professionals in its own special space?

AUTHORS AND ORIGINS

> My criticism of *Roe* v. *Wade* is that the Court failed to establish the legitimacy of the decision by not articulating a precept of sufficient abstractness to lift the ruling above the level of a political judgment based upon the evidence currently available from the medical, physical, and social sciences. . . . Constitutional rights ought not to be created under the Due Process Clause unless they can be stated in principles sufficiently absolute to give them roots throughout the community and continuity over significant periods of time, and to lift them above the level of the pragmatic political judgements of a particular time and place. . . . The failure to confront the issue in principled terms leaves the opinion to read like a set of hospital rules and regulations, whose validity is good enough this week but will be destroyed with new statistics upon the medical risks of childbirth and abortion or new advances in providing for the separate existence of a foetus.
>
> (Cox 1976: 113–14)

That the historical Alfred had little to do with the emergence of the common law tradition is irrelevant; but the attitude to texts is exemplary, even mythic. And the crucial point of the story is the fear of writing things down, the fear of what might happen as a result: it is not technology as such but the uses to which it is put which is the decisive concern.

The most important written document to affect our view of the common law tradition is the Constitution of the USA and its Amendments, because these documents have served as an engine-house of contemporary 'Anglo-American' legal theory. Yet these documents are essentially written in the common law style; not even Oakeshottian 'abridgements' of a concrete manner of living, they are rather particularistic provisions aimed not so much at giving fixed and unalterable textual form to the dictates of a general reason as at defining a set of limitations, rather like those of a property settlement, open to (perhaps inviting) subsequent amendments remedying mischiefs which might arise from time to time. Neither in textual form nor in their modes of genesis were these documents which should necessarily derail the tradition.

Indeed, one writer has recently suggested that

> the unwritten in constitutions . . . contains far more than merely that which can be objectified into material definition . . . it is precisely those unwritten components of a constitution that represent its most integral features and its most fundamental properties. They remain integral and fundamental, . . . because of their need for protective obscurity and because of their inherent resistance to explicit expression. . . . The unwritten part of a constitution is its most significant element because it accommodates the constitution's encoded system of abeyances by which any constitution ultimately survives or perishes . . .
>
> (Foley 1989: 81)

In England, there are familiar enough examples of 'old' statutes which function in the perpetual present of the common law: compare the English case-law 'on' the Preamble to the Statute of Elizabeth 1601, or even on the more well-trodden sections of the 1925 property legislation (Murphy and Roberts 1987). American provisions like the Second Amendment ('A well-regulated militia being necessary to the security of a free State, the right of the people to keep and bear arms shall not be infringed') and the Seventh Amendment ('In suits at common law, where the value in controversy shall exceed twenty dollars, the right of trial by jury shall be preserved . . .'), both of 1791, seem to present specific requirements amenable to a similar decisional drift; the 'accident' of writing does not get in the way of 'Burkean' organic adaptation:

> Our political system is placed in a just correspondence and symmetry with the order of the world and with the mode of existence decreed to a permanent body composed of transitory parts, wherein, by the disposition of a stupendous wisdom, moulding together the great mysterious incorporation of the human race, the whole, at one time, is never old or middle-aged or young, but, in a condition of unchangeable constancy, moves on through the varied tenor of perpetual decay, fall, renovation, and progression.
>
> (Burke 1987: 30)

Yet writing and history have been combined to thematize the passage of time as a problem, by conferring specificity upon the past, by reworking the constitutional documents so as to constitute a set of origins and authors. This brings into play a quite different occidental problematic associated with codes, God and Great Legislation – the problematic of authorial creation, will and intention, aided and abetted in this case by the *Federalist Papers*, or, in other terms, rational hermeneutics and modern historical consciousness.

Contemporary disputes over the interpretation of the US Constitution are thus routinely regarded as debates between 'originalists' and 'non-originalists'. Indeed, even a critic as supposedly post-authorial as Fish takes this problematic of authors and origins for granted, writing of the debate between originalists and non-originalists that 'there cannot be a distinction between interpreters who look to intention and interpreters who don't, only a distinction between the differing accounts of intention put forward by rival interpreters' (Fish 1992: 300) so that 'originalism is not an *option* for interpreters but the name of what they necessarily do' (ibid.: 303) provided that interpretation, so understood, is distinguished from 'playing with the text' (ibid.: 302) where 'I am not trying to figure out what it means but trying to see what meanings it could be made to yield' (ibid.; cf. Eco 1992: 45–66 on overinterpretation).

In the medieval period, by contrast, '*auctores* were . . . texts, not people . . . there *is* no extra-textual authorial intention – whatever *intentio* there is is contained in the textual signs alone' (Carruthers 1990: 190). This 'expansive' mode of medieval sacred textuality is precluded or lost; the text becomes a modern text, and its 'author' is required to fulfil the function of indicating the horizon of its interpretive possibilities. A 'dialogue' of some sort with the Founding Fathers is thus enjoined, and this brings law and history into a forced co-existence. Whether or not one wishes to characterize the resulting interpretive situation as hermeneutical (or to regard hermeneutics as a recipe book containing correct or appropriate interpretive procedures), this destabilizes the basic presupposition of timeless continuity which is essential to the antinomy of delivery and betrayal central to the common law tradition. It does so in two alternative ways. The combination of law and history prevents the 'originalists' from occupying the position of Burke, who, according to Pocock, was 'not calling upon his contemporaries to return to a seventeenth-century habit of mind, but assuming that it is still alive and meaningful among them' (Pocock 1971: 208). Because they cannot do this (or because, in trying to do this, they became ensnared in the mesh of modern historical consciousness), they assume the position of curators not conservatives: they turn the Constitution into National Heritage Law.

The so-called non-originalists are equally unable to keep alive the tradition; they too are ensnared by history, but seek to combat it with an abstract universalism which is not infrequently tempted, additionally, by a historical teleology which flirts from time to time with the end of history, and which, like all such teleologies, involves a particular revalorization of the origin. The 'keynote' of this abstract universalism is the theme of 'principle':

> The Founders' Constitution of 1787–1788 proved to be, for later generations of Americans, a successful experiment. Its success is a constitutive fact of American public life and culture. Americans take pride in living under the longest-lasting written constitution in the world, and they think of constitutional argument in terms of the demands for the justification of state power associated with that constitutive fact of their life as a people. Americans think of these interpretive demands as those of a historically continuous community of principle, and thus take an interpretive attitude to constitutional law motivated by the distinctive values they ascribe to the basic constitutional structures of that community of principle. . . . It is a contingent, unusual (in comparison with other democratic peoples), and certainly pivotally important fact of American constitutional history and law that the Founders' project is very much our project: both the making and interpreting

> of the Constitution are a continuous project in which – consistent with Lockean political theory – each generation seeks a higher-order reasonable justification for the exercise of political power (qualitatively different from their roles in normal politics) in a historically continuous community of principle.
>
> (Richards 1989: 50–3)

But it is the very particularism of the limitations contained in the constitutional documents which is lost; the imprint of historical time is upon them. The postulate of continuity requires an endless project of rational reconstruction ('higher-order justification' etc.) which renders these similarities with tradition-as-flux superficial. This marks the abandonment of the traditional attitude and the institution of another kind of attitude to law, an attitude which is essentially theoretical. In America, all attempts at creative adaptation now take the form of projects, of a repetition of the origin which is already known as a historical, that is, authorized, origin.

The combined effect is that working in a tradition becomes seen as a matter of arbitrary 'interpretation' rather than 'natural' adjustment and adaptation. These problems come from history, from the historical sense of dispersal and difference, from the sense of time as a matter of series, rather than the return or replication of originals. In this way, and to this extent, America has left behind the common law tradition.

The English common law tradition, by contrast, as I have suggested, has lived in a perpetual present.

> Hale . . . despaired of knowing when any particular point in the law had originated, or of recovering its original meaning from its successive reformulations, or of establishing what the state of the law as a whole had been at any moment in time past; nor did he think that this mattered . . .
>
> (Pocock 1971: 221)

To a legal thought attuned in this way, 'originals' are a resource, and require the genius of metaphor for their successful recognition (cf. Foucault 1982: 44). A point Saussure makes about language applies here quite exactly:

> language furnishes the best proof that a law accepted by a community is a thing that is tolerated and not a rule to which all freely consent. . . . No society, in fact, knows or has ever known language other than as a product inherited from preceding generations, and one to be accepted as such. That is why the question of

> the origin of speech is not so important as it is generally assumed to be. The question is not even worth asking; the only real object of linguistics is the normal, regular life of an existing idiom.
>
> (Saussure 1974: 71–2)

THE OPERATING SYSTEM

> Nature gives itself in metaphor. Which is why, moreover, the metaphoric capacity is a natural gift. In this sense, it is given to everyone. . . . But, following a framework we regularly come across, nature gives (itself) more to some than to others. More to men than to beasts, more to philosophers than to other men. Since the invention of metaphors is an innate, natural, congenital gift, it will also be a characteristic of genius. The notion of nature makes this contradiction tolerable. In nature each has his nature. Some have more nature than others, more genius, more generosity, more seed. If 'the greatest thing by far is to be a master of metaphor', some have the genius of metaphor, know better than others to perceive resemblances and to unveil the truth of nature. An ungraspable resource. 'To be a master of metaphor' 'is the one thing that cannot be learnt from others and it is also a sign of genius'. . . . One knows or one does not know, one can or one cannot. The ungraspable is certainly a genius for perceiving the hidden resemblance, but it is also, consequently, the capacity to substitute one term for another. The genius of mimesis, thus, can give rise to a language, a code of regulated substitutions, the talent and procedures of rhetoric, the imitation of genius, the mastery of the ungraspable.
>
> (Derrida 1982: 244–5)

The formalizations of much legal theory (even in common law jurisdictions, even in the UK, without the 'project' of a Constitution) articulate ideals or aspirations ('quite rightly', some would say) which inevitably, just as in the philosophy of science, overshoot the 'defective reality' of practice. It is not my purpose here to discuss whether that means that these formalizations are 'wrong'; but working as they do with a tension of sorts between 'ideal' and 'actuality', they project a picture which is more coherent, purposive, and sophisticated than the object supposedly framed in the picture. What is underplayed as a result is the centrality, at its most particular, of analogy in 'legal reasoning', or, in more general terms, of metaphor.

In common law jurisprudence, the question of metaphor, when acknowledged, tends to be regarded as trivial, as something to be mentioned, in passing, on a journey from and towards something else which is more important. Yet in fact it is this trivial obvious point which is the essential one.

This is to use 'metaphor' as a metaphor for the epistemic organization and *dispositif* of the common law. The figurative use of tropes to be found in legal texts continues to be revealing and thus worthy of study in its own right. Indeed, it is linguistic operations on the surface which are so often at issue: 'plain English', the hostility to rhetoric, the resistance to 'jargon'; your words and my words. Such disputes about language and its proper use pose issues of group membership, of inclusion and exclusion. It may even be that they should be regarded as the constitutive mechanism through which such processes of inclusion take effect. If language is the way in which group identity is sealed, then contests of or in language may be very important (for some discussion, see Anderson 1983, Smith 1986) and on the fate of language may hinge the fate of groups (consider, at the time of writing, 'Macedonia').

By contrast, the present concern is with the metaphorical structure of the common law tradition, with the 'operating system' rather than with the programmes – the tropes – which can be run on it. Lévi-Strauss's *The Savage Mind* provides an excellent vehicle for characterizing such an epistemic attitude, given the resistance to formalism which is one of the hallmarks of the common law tradition. This is a study, as Sperber suggests, of 'untamed thinking' (Sperber 1985: 71), of 'mind in its untamed state as distinct from mind cultivated or domesticated for the purpose of yielding a return' (Lévi-Strauss 1972: 219):

> there are still zones in which savage thought, like savage species, is relatively protected. This is the case with art, to which our civilization accords the status of a national park, with all the advantages and disadvantages attending so artificial a formula; and it is particularly the case of so many as yet 'uncleared' sectors of social life, where, through indifference or inability, and most often without our knowing why, primitive thought continues to flourish.
> (Lévi-Strauss 1972: 219)

As Sperber elaborates, the contrast Lévi-Strauss seeks to emphasize is between such untamed thinking and thinking which has been domesticated in the specific sense that it has been trained and thereby tamed 'in order to increase the quality or at least the quantity of its output' (Sperber 1985: 71). This is encapsulated in a contrast proposed between the 'engineer' and the *bricoleur*: 'the engineer is always trying to make his way out of and go beyond the constraints imposed by a particular state of civilisation while the "bricoleur" inclination or necessity always remains within them' (Lévi-Strauss 1972: 19).

> [The *bricoleur*'s] universe of instruments is closed and the rules of his game are always to make do with 'whatever is at hand', that is to say with a set of tools and materials which is always finite and is also heterogeneous because what it contains bears no relation to the current project, or indeed to any particular project, but is the contingent result of all the occasions there have been to renew or enrich the stock or to maintain it with the remains of previous constructions or destructions . . . the elements are collected or retained on the principle that 'they may always come in handy'. Such elements are specialized up to a point, sufficiently for the 'bricoleur' not to need the equipment and knowledge of all trades and professions, but not enough for each of them to have only one definite and determinate use.
>
> (Lévi-Strauss 1972: 17–18)

Thus, while it is possible for legal pedagogues to teach the law 'as if' it is technique, these techniques are those of the bricoleur, and this in two senses: their acquisition and retention (or 'discovery' and 're-discovery') are haphazard and largely a matter of contingency; and they are kept in case they come in handy when the need arises, not honed and improved and experimented with for the purposes of furthering a project. This is perhaps most essential of all: there is no project, except, sometimes, that of the maintenance and consolidation of law itself.

Within anthropology (which means, for present purposes, within those social sciences ambiguously positioned between the study of the 'primitive' and of the 'traditional') Lévi-Strauss is much criticized for the artificiality of the 'great divide' he insinuates between modernity and the pre-modern (see, for example, Goody 1977). More interesting, I think, is the suggestion that in characterizing the science of the concrete in terms of *bricolage* and contrasting it so resolutely with the abstraction of modern science, he overlooks the epistemic achievements represented by geometry and architecture (Wilson 1988: 156). And as I shall try to show below, this sense of place is essential too. The *bricolage* of the common law is not that of a hunter-gatherer, of a man on the move, as it seems in a certain sense to be, paradigmatically, for Lévi-Strauss; it is the *bricolage* of man in domesticated space – in the household of the king, in the courtroom. Gadamer, following Aristotle, makes much of the space of the unsaid from which what is said is said (Gadamer 1976: 59–68). And, as Arendt reads Aristotle, political theory originates in the assertion of the need for a proper place for speaking. Mere recognition of a 'place' for speaking does not make an activity hermeneutical; rather, hermeneutics consists in a certain 'taking account' of the place in understanding speaking.

We should remember, then, that the 'unsaid' of the common law is the courtroom, and consider the epistemic implications of such domesticated, geometrized, artificial space, if it is right to suggest, as Wilson does, that a 'building is a diagram of . . . how the system works' (Wilson 1988: 153; see also Murphy 1991: 194). I suggested above that the common law is not at home in a modern printed text; but that does not leave it either homeless or 'in nubibus' if it lives, quite concretely, in the forecourts of the palaces of kings.

It is in relation to the 'unsaid' of such palaces that we can consider briefly the general structure of the process of the substitution of the concrete for the abstract which saturates the thinking of the common law. Law's experience resides in (and guarantees) the 'intuitive' link – the copula – embedded in the simile and concealed in the metaphor. Here, the process of rendering visible conceals the *modus operandi* by drawing attention to the *opus operatum*. The effect is that the resemblance is one which will have been established. It is guided by nature so that its effect is natural. Nature thus is presented as the source of the possibility of borrowing, as the 'criterion' for the need to borrow, and as the reservoir of the borrowable. Metaphor keeps the common law tradition close to, and constantly replenished by, nature, a symbolic that thus lives close to the real. As Burke (1987: 30) insists, 'by preserving the method of nature in the conduct of the state . . . we are guided not by the superstition of antiquarians, but by the spirit of philosophic analogy'. Nature has no need of artifice, one might say, but artifice has need of nature. Viewed in these terms, a somewhat different set of questions about law suggest themselves.

If analogy cannot be taught, only illustrated, disciplined through observation and imitation, then the common law itself is genius and cannot be reduced to a mechanical art. Indeed, do not the (philosophical) formalizations of metaphor, unpromising as they are, suggest that all we can get are systems of classification and not rules of application, so that analogy can only be taught or its use policed and monitored by analogy?

The metaphorical structure thus permits indeterminacy while giving the sense of determinateness. It permits discontinuity while seeming to preserve the past. It permits, most importantly of all, the very difference between surface and depth, the central 'as if' of instantiation, that, in the meantime, instances and examples, hints and suggestions, allusions and intuitions, can all be offered and set in motion, but that the 'real thing' is in a sense always deferred, kept back as a promise, held in reserve 'as if' it is at home 'somewhere else'. In this sense, the operational conditions of the common law tradition can be compared to those of classical rhetoric.

Rhetoric, Foucault suggests, was a sign of and was necessitated by the insufficiency of enunciation in relation to language, an insufficiency which was at once poverty and excess:

> Rhetoric did not enunciate the laws or forms of a language; it established the relationship between two forms of speech: the first mute, indecipherable, fully present to itself, and absolute; the other, garrulous, had only to voice this first speech according to forms, operations, and conjunctions whose space measured its distance from the first and inaudible text. For finite creatures and for men who would die, Rhetoric ceaselessly repeated the speech of the Infinite that would never come to an end. Every figure of rhetoric betrayed a distance in its own space, but in signalling the first speech it lent the provisional density of a revelation to the second: it showed.
>
> (Foucault 1977a: 66–7)

It is this 'provisional density' which is especially interesting. As a tradition, the common law lives in the saying of the language in which it has its home. Yet the saying is only, always, partial; the 'real' language of law is not so much a secret language (though it is of course esoteric) but it operates 'as if' it is an Ur-language, a language whose foundational character makes it at once accessible (to the extent that saying now, in the present, always derives from and depends upon it) and distant: it is never the language of actuality that as real individuals we are able to speak. And this is why the essential character of enunciation is metaphorical: utterance is always a play in language of substitution and resemblance, analogy of analogy. There is no final word (or thought or sentence) because there is no first word (etc.) which can be said again. To find whether it was ever said is to interrogate the first word in terms of the structure of the event. This is to bring modern historical consciousness to bear on the time and facticity of the first word. But the first word is virtual and escapes or eludes such consciousness; the first word belongs to the register of the 'as if'. Here is the source of the ever-present danger of slippage and seduction between poetry and law and science: rhetoric and its canons of appropriateness as means of containment of the power latent in the mobilization of language. And it is at this point that Aristotle generates the polemical (and fateful) opposition between the literal and the metaphorical (cf. Lloyd 1990: 14–38) in which forms of speech are linked to standards of truth. Rhetoric was once a means of training speakers to establish a particular relation to this language of infinity (in which, we should also remember, resided the destiny – because there lay the identity – of humanity as such).

Today, 'tradition' is often thought to serve as a mask for the true difficulty which arises in decision-making situations where rationality seems to fail. In the face of modern decision theory, there is something unacceptable about a decision-system which draws upon and rests upon something so elusive as tradition (cf. Elster 1983, 1989). To think about the ground of a decision-system in such terms tends to require a certain bracketing of modern preoccupations. Law is a way of being not an instrument of manipulation. In this precise sense, law does not have 'policies'; it seeks to do justice (and is vulnerable to abuses and miscarriages of justice) but not to create a 'just society' if by that is meant something more than a society in which justice is administered by and according to law. For the common law tradition, phronesis and experience are the genius of being at home in the play of connectives and associations which is the metaphorical architecture of contiguity and resemblance. It is a 'science' of the mobilization of virtual orders, a realism of the 'as if'. Its 'traditional' guarantee, at its core, was based on the insinuation that these resemblances and contiguities lived in close proximity to the nature of things. As the book of nature fades, this answer may come to seem arbitrary. But the second basis for this truth of metaphor seems more resilient. This is the optical prowess of the bearers of the tradition, a prowess sharpened and sustained by immersion in metaphoricity, in the practice of 'seeing as'.

VISIBILITIES

> In spite of her respect for Law, she was never at home with a generalization. . . . She believed in what she saw, and she acted accordingly; beyond that she would not go. . . . Years after the discoveries of Pasteur and Lister, she laughed at what she called the 'germ-fetish'. There was no such thing as 'infection'; she had never seen it, therefore it did not exist.
>
> (Strachey 1986: 155)

'In order to reduce us for a moment to being only an eye' writes Lacan, 'we had to put ourselves in the shoes of the scientist who can decree that he is just an eye, and can put a notice on the door – *Do not disturb the experimenter*. In life, things are entirely different, because we aren't an eye' (Lacan 1988: 80). The eye of the subject, the eye of law, the eye of science: are they the same? If so, how do we account for Florence Nightingale, whose self-certainty and immediatism suggest some kind of difference? What difference might this be? Is it a matter of instruments and apparatuses? Is it to do with the strategic placing of the 'as if'? For science, there are pictures of the real which function as if this real is authentic.

> To ask whether a photograph is analogical or coded is not a good means of analysis. The important thing is that the photograph possesses an evidential force, and that its testimony bears not on the object but on time. From a phenomenological viewpoint, in the Photograph, the power of authentication exceeds the power of representation.
>
> (Barthes 1984: 89)

In this sense, the thematics of representation are displaced in science, by the problematics of 'representativeness' and 'approximation', probability and indeterminism (see especially Hacking 1975, 1990; Gigerenzer *et al.*, 1989). The 'as if' of its pictoriality is legitimated by calculation – by method, rules, and formalism.

How, by contrast (if there is one) is the common law's 'as if' to be understood? What governs the movement of its eye (cf. Haldar 1991), what is the intelligibility of its own concern with visibility? Perhaps this could be suggested: visibility, for the common law, is a presupposition, not a construction or achievement. It is not simply a question of virtuality. It is always, rather, 'as if' the world is already seen. The common law does not investigate the world and so can propose no world which can be pictured as the result of such investigations.

Its 'evidence' is in no sense a matter of methods guaranteeing (or constructing) what is there to be seen, but of learning to see.

> Now if any the most refined Braine under heaven would goe about to Enquire by Speculation, or by reading of Plato or Aristotle, or by Considering the Laws of the Jewes, or other Nations, to find out how Landes descend in England, or how Estates are there transferred, or transmitted among us, he wou'd lose his Labour, and spend his Notions in vaine, till he acquainted himselfe with the Lawes of England, and the reason is because they are Institutions introduced by the will and Consent of others . . . the Positions and Conclusions in the Mathematicks have more Evidence in them, and are more Naturally Seated in the minde than Institutions of Laws, which in a greate measure depend upon the Consent and appointment of the first Institutors . . .
>
> (Hale, quoted in Pocock 1971: 219)

The 'long observation' which is presuppositionally constitutive of common law experience involves a process of introjection; over time (though not in such a way that this 'time' will itself be subjected to critical scrutiny or thematic elaboration) the world is absorbed by the eye of the law so that the visibilities of the world are contained in the tradition. Like the genius of metaphor to which this is closely related, this is not an act of individual heroism (only those enthused by projects of World Leadership could take the single, heroic judge to be a useful vehicle for understanding the common law). The law can see everything but has no desire to see, or, at least, it does not know through seeing, but in seeing or through having seen (the same) before – *noscitur a sociis* is a maxim of experience. This is not subsumption of particulars through the universal but a process combining aspects of metaphor and metonymy ('we've seen this sort of thing before'). That is, knowledge is not generated from what is seen by the law, through the process of subjection to the judicial gaze. The acquisition of truth and knowledge in that way is, by contrast, positivism, or, still more loosely, formalism. Observation, seeing, the gaze is more like practice, training, learning in . . . observation, seeing, the gaze: 'the trained eye'. In the judicial gaze, metaphor enhances clarity of vision, and the secret of its enhancement is itself restricted (not on open access; to be taught only by analogy). The structure of the judicial gaze is attuned to possibilities of contiguity and resemblance – this is like . . ., it is as if . . .

The central structural trope is thus the simile. This permits 'matters' to be presented as if they were in, or, more precisely, 'before' the judge-in-court. Mediate though its very structure is, the use of simile aims to cancel all mediation, to achieve pure visibility in a scene of the pure gaze, a gaze which is prejudiced only in the sense that it has been used – it has gazed – before. Again, a question: what, here, do you gaze at? The object – that which will have been assimilated when the work of resemblance is perfected – or the simile? Is the simile an instrument of the judicial gaze for the (of course legitimate) apprehension of the object or a substitute for the object, or a difference which precedes an identity?

Lacan is therefore suggestive up to a point when he says

> The odd thing is that an entire system of metaphysics has been founded on geometry and mechanics, as though optics has been exploited as much as it could have been. Yet it should lend itself to a few dreams, this strange science which sets itself to produce, by means of apparatuses, that peculiar thing called *images*, in contrast to other sciences, which import into nature a cutting up, a dissection, an anatomy.
>
> (Lacan 1988: 76)

But only up to a point. What is lacking is an apparatus. The common law lacks the external machinery for the enhancement and externalization both of its gaze and of the visibilities of the world which are produced in science. In this fundamental sense, law does not add in a constitutive way to world knowledge. This is the crucial difference between the visibility proper to the common law and the Panopticism of Foucauldian normalization (Foucault 1977b), which plugs the minuscule observation of the offender into a multi-stranded knowledge-circuit which generates a plurality of scientific pictures of criminality in, for example, its psychological, sociological and economic 'aspects'. Instead, the optical prowess of common lawyers, sharpened by the inheritance of previous acts of seeing, permits an immediacy of vision on each new occasion. This immediacy, to be sure, is contained in a certain way by rules governing what can be seen, or how seeing can be undertaken, and such rules of evidence can be regarded as in a certain sense lessons of experience and/or prudence. But such rules seek to regulate the appearance of the world, not the manner of knowing. This is precisely why there is no 'methodology' in the sense of an external guarantee governing the conditions of production of the visibilities of the world. Methodology presupposes a situation of distance between observing subject and object of observation, as well as between individual acts of observation and general or approximated 'calculated' pictures which assemble the wider significance of such particular investigations. The common law, by contrast, is geared to generating a situation of immediacy, and rules of evidence serve as much as anything to exclude the world if the simulation of immediacy is jeopardized.

All this is connected to – and follows from – the fact that law is a matter of judgment in a particular place from which things can be seen in their proper arrangement. These visibilities have a quite precise anchorage in the configuration of the place of the courtroom, the institution of the court and the person of the judge. It is well known that the common law elevates the importance of its judiciary to an unusual degree (Caenegem 1987). But this centrality goes beyond the judges' role as the point of 'real' historical origin, creativity, source of renewal and regeneration (the development of the law, etc.), or, conversely, beyond their role as an obstacle to democratic policy-making (their conservatism, individualism and hostility to legislation, etc.). It is in fact the importance of courts (or, to be precise, of some courts) within the political culture which is in play here, since it is in relation to, or even more particularly, simply *in* court, that judges are so important. Because what is important is not judges as such, but, almost by analogy with (or in structural counterpoint with) the Queen-in-Parliament, judges-in-court which is important. When society at large accuses judges of being out of touch, it is judges-in-court which are really in question, because in court, in this proper place, it is of little account whether the personnel shops at Safeways on its way home.

Within this epistemology, seeing has a concreteness and specificity, an awareness of the detailed surface of its object, which makes such seeing seem close to touch.

> There is evidently . . . a certain affinity and correspondence between each visible object and the precise tangible object represented by it, much superior to what takes place either between written and spoken language, or between spoken language and the ideas or meanings which it suggests. The language which nature addresses to our eyes, has evidently a fitness of representation, an aptitude for signifying the precise things which it denotes, much superior to that of any of the artificial languages which human art and ingenuity have ever been able to invent.
>
> (Smith 1980: 158)

This concern for 'immediate' visibility, where the only mediation between reality and observation is the alchemy at work in the judicial retina, also means that language cannot be accorded a mediating role of its own. In this sense language is to be seen, rather than interpreted, or 'interpreted' only by means of a kind of inner, pictorial dictionary, of the kind Locke dreamed about:

> Words standing for Things, which are known and distinguished by their outward shapes, should be expressed by little Draughts and Prints made of them . . . he that has had occasion to consult them, will have reason to confess, that he has a clearer Idea of Apium, or Ibex from a little Print of that Herb, or Beast, than he could have from a long Definition of the Names of either of them. . . . If Men will not be at the pains to declare the meaning of their Words, and Definitions of their Terms are not to be had; yet this is the least that can be expected, that in all Discourses, wherein one Man pretends to instruct or convince another, he should use the same Word constantly in the same sense: If this were done . . . many of the Philosophers (to mention no other,) as well as Poets Work, might be contained in a Nut-shell.
>
> (Locke 1975: 523)

Beyond that, practice will naturalize the artifice entailed in lawyers' use of language, and that use, where language is a pure instrument (Murphy and Roberts 1987), means that language cannot conceal 'the thing itself' which in turn means that when judges see a word they see the thing.

This 'attitude' to visibility seems to underscore the much-vaunted 'realism' of the common law. This realism is a central dimension of the legal imaginary. More than a matter of ideals or ideology, it is a way of seeing the world of sorts, but it is not something which is all conscious, explicit, 'upfront', all at once, all the time. The 'idea' of experience (and all that goes with it) is part of the legal imaginary. The activation of this experience (as well as being a rhetorical gesture) involves making explicit elements of this imaginary and putting them to use in argument and decision-making. This realism is a fantasy (cf. Duerr 1985) of touching, of contact, a realism of images, which is also an embodiment of experience in the figure of the judge. And this is 'figurative' in a strict sense, condensed in the familiar 'in my view' which punctuates judicial texts, an expression in which sight stands for immediate cognition while stressing the embodiment and (implicitly) acknowledging the perspectivism. And so a realism which insists that its images are quite particularly true, so real that they barely warrant discussion. Adam Smith sketches a portrait of such a man:

> A Plain man is one who pays no regard to the common civilities and forms of good breeding. He gives his opinion bluntly and affirms without condescending to give any reason for his doing so; and if he mentions any sort of reason it is only to shew how evident and plain a matter it was and expose the stupidity of the others in not perceiving it as well as he. . . . He is not at all sedulous to please, on the conterary he affects a sort of austerity and hardness of behaviour. . . . He despises the fashion in every point and neither conforms himself to it in dress, in language nor manners, but sticks by his own downright ways . . .
>
> (Smith 1983: 36–7)

Smith presents this as a sketch of a typical clergyman of his time, and it occurs in the course of a wider, self-consciously modern discussion about the plain speech of eighteenth-century government and the demise of the 'Old Eloquence' (Smith 1983: 196–200); but it is clear that he offers it too as a portrait of that doyen of the common law, Lord Mansfield, with whom, for many common lawyers, the modern age begins.

SIGNS

> Men do not understand one another by actually exchanging signs for things, nor by mutually occasioning one another to produce exactly and completely the same concept; they do it by touching in one another the same link in the chain of their sensory ideas and internal conceptualizations, by striking the same note on their mental instrument, whereupon matching but not identical concepts are engendered in each. Only within these limits, and with these divergences, do they come together on the same word.
>
> (von Humboldt 1988: 152)

In an elaboration of law as tradition, it is common enough to suggest that the object as well as medium of delivery and betrayal is a language. Common lawyers are familiar enough with the notion of 'symbolic delivery'; where an object is too heavy or bulky for physical transfer from donor to donee, it will suffice to transfer a symbol of the thing to transfer the title to it. The keys to the city can stand for the city in the eyes of the law. But in the play of tradition, what can 'stand for' the law itself?

In this respect it is instructive to consider briefly Saussure's elaboration of language as tradition. For Saussure, who thought of law as code, as housed in a modern text, there were significant differences between law and language, as we shall see. Those very differences, however, can serve here to bring out a further dimension of the attitudinal difference between common and civilian law and to provide a further accentuation of the engagements set to work in a system of law as tradition.

In his reflections on tradition, Saussure is primarily concerned not to trace the historical, etymological or philosophical origins of language, but to bring out an opposition between language regarded as a purposive, calculated human creation, on the one hand, and as something, on the other, which, although human, is natural-human rather than rational-human, the accidental and cumulative consequence of ordinary human activity, not the product of careful design. His anxiety over the graphic representation of language, discussed so tellingly by Derrida (1976), is no doubt marked by the western metaphysics of presence (and thus the prejudice for speech) of which Derrida's first major writings provide so sustained an *exposé*, but the more insistent problem ghosting this enterprise of a general linguistics as a branch, as Saussure puts it, of psychology, derives from the fact that Saussure – like Freud (1991: 213) or Bergson (1988) – belongs to a period where there is an attempt to bring mind and matter together (though cf. Schelling 1988: 9–42), or to reformulate the position of each, or to create a third element between mind and matter – neither matter nor mind but somehow something else, something almost only representable through a procedure of materializing mind and spiritualizing matter (see further, Glymour 1991, Deleuze 1991: 73–89).

With law as with language, once this difference is posed, then the question arises: To which order does it (law or language) belong, that of Mind or of Matter? And it is traditions which make this harder to answer because traditions seem to be a way of turning artifice into nature, of materializing the products of mind.

For Saussure, language is distinguished from law because it involves a 'collective inertia toward innovation':

> Language . . . is at every moment everybody's concern; spread throughout society and manipulated by it, language is something

> used daily by all. Here we are unable to set up any comparison between it and other institutions. The prescriptions of codes, religious rites, nautical signals, etc., involve only a certain number of individuals simultaneously and then only during a limited period of time; in language, on the contrary, everyone participates at all times, and that is why it is constantly being influenced by all. This capital fact suffices to show the impossibility of revolution. Of all social institutions, language is least amenable to initiative. It blends with the life of society, and the latter, inert by nature, is a prime conservative force.
>
> (Saussure 1974: 73–4)

But 'Language is checked not only by the weight of the collectivity but also by time' (ibid.: 74).

> At every moment solidarity with the past checks freedom of choice. . . . This does not prevent the existence in the total phenomenon of a bond between the two antithetical forces – arbitrary convention by virtue of which choice is free and time which causes choice to be fixed. *Because the sign is arbitrary, it follows no law other than that of tradition, and because it is based on tradition, it is arbitrary.*
>
> (Ibid., emphasis added)

Saussure insists that 'the arbitrary nature of the sign is really what protects language from any attempt to modify it' (ibid.: 73). What this does therefore is to establish an intimate link between tradition and the arbitrary. And this in turn raises the question: arbitrary in relation to what? – that is, the return of the natural, of the nature of things.

> Unlike language, other human institutions – customs, laws, etc. – are all based in varying degrees on the natural relations of things; all have of necessity adapted the means employed to the ends pursued. Even fashion in dress is not entirely arbitrary; we can deviate only slightly from the conditions dictated by the human body. Language is limited by nothing in the choice of means for apparently nothing would prevent the associating of any idea whatsoever with just any sequence of sounds.
>
> (Ibid.: 75–6)

Considered from the point of view of the circumstances of its creation, language is 'naturally' arbitrary; from the point of view of its ordinary functioning, however, it has a quasi-naturality (or at very least a givenness), and it is this which the graphic representation of language can disfigure. 'Though it creates a purely fictitious unity, the *superficial* bond of writing is much easier to grasp than the only *true* bond, the bond of sound' (ibid.: 25, emphasis added). And this is why graphically-induced mispronunciation (like pronouncing the *t* in *sept femmes*) is more than infelicity; it is a sort of inauthentic, alien, modification of the system's own internal dynamics, a change imposed from without:

> such phonic deformations belong to language but do not stem from its natural functioning. They are due to an external influence. Linguistics should put them into a special compartment for observation: they are teratological cases.
>
> (Ibid.: 32)

Writing distorts the 'rules' of language by making them seem like those of a legal code:

> literary language . . . has its dictionaries and grammars; in school, children are taught from and by means of books; language is apparently governed by a code; the code itself consists of a written set of strict rules of usage, orthography; and that is why writing acquires primary importance. The result is that people forget that they learn to speak before they learn to write, and the natural sequence is reversed.
>
> (Ibid.: 25)

It should be apparent how close this position is to that of the common lawyers. Thinking that law is a set of rules or instructions, amenable in principle to being wrapped up in a book, is mistaken; it is, 'in reality', a manner of living, a way of 'speaking' the pivotal moment of which is always synchronic, always 'now'. At best, the law books are abridgements of this concrete manner of living.

Reduced to books, of course, the law can atrophy and die. Consider the following recent discussion by a comparative lawyer:

> our feeling for play, rhythm, and proportion is inborn. . . . This predilection . . . is culturally reflected in alliteration [*sic*; not assonance] and rhyme, ludic features which touch the very root and core of our being. . . . Legal language causes a response in our very selves . . . we have in ourselves a receiver on the same wave-length as the sender of legal language . . . we obey the law from a consensual, inner impulse which we experience as moral duty, even as

> joy. Law resonates within us, is our own; we now want to do what we should do because we are in harmony with it. No free legal system can get on without this.
>
> (Grossfeld 1990: 104–5)

This is why, for Grossfeld, 'ancient law so often took the form of poetry'. An oral legal tradition is naturally more sensitive to language. Poetry, 'deploying the spiritual power of the word', can convince legal subjects of law's 'merits'. 'If, as happens too often today, the law does not appeal to our feeling for language, we find it alien, a flood of rules breaking over us. Unless great care is taken with language the positive law will awaken no sense of its justice' (ibid.).

This kind of approach links up far too easily with the shaky problematic of the desire for law. It is less immodest to suggest that if the law is poetry, then it is poetry for those who recite it and memorize it: the secret harmonies of the lawyers themselves. (Perhaps, unwittingly, Grossfeld is lamenting the fall into prose of the language of law itself, that lawyers can no longer hear this harmonics.)

For Tocqueville, by contrast, law flowed from the books to the people in nineteenth-century America:

> Scarcely any political question arises in the United States that is not resolved, sooner or later, into a judicial question. Hence all parties are obliged to borrow, in their daily controversies, the ideas, and even the language, peculiar to judicial proceedings. As most public men are or have been legal practitioners, they introduce the customs and technicalities of their profession into the management of public affairs. The jury extends this habit to all classes. The language of the law thus becomes, in some measure, a vulgar tongue; the spirit of the law, which is produced in the schools and courts of justice, gradually penetrates beyond their walls into the bosom of society, where it descends to the lowest classes, so that at last the whole people contract the habits and the tastes of the judicial magistrate.
>
> (Tocqueville 1945: 290)

The high rationality of continental Codes is commonly regarded as uncoupled from the language of the people, and set against the theme of living law which, as Weber caustically observed, can even seem to revalorize (from a distance, of course) the common law tradition. To the extent that there is now a theoretical turn in American law, it may be propelled in a similar direction (and encounter similar counterstrategies). By contrast, the life of the English common law tradition has involved a range of simulations which serve to obscure the incompatibility between law as tradition and law as the language of the people. Though we should not ignore the legalism of the political discourse of the eighteenth and nineteenth centuries (a legalism which has far from disappeared today), it was, all the same, less a matter of dissemination than of the enclosure of contingency. Behind the judiciary is the profession of the bar, the true and ultimate container of the English common law tradition (Lemming 1990). This is the home, seed-bed and reference point for the experience with which this essay has been concerned. And perhaps, therefore, the 'popular' criticism of lawyers registers in part a view of common law as an act of usurpation, an appropriation from both Prince and people.

> How else comes it to pass, that Princes, speaking or writing to their Servants, in their ordinary Commands, are easily understood; speaking to their People, in their Laws, are not so? And . . . doth it not often happen, that a Man of an ordinary Capacity, very well understands a Text, or a Law, that he reads, till he consults an Expositor, or goes to Council; who by that time he hath done explaining them, makes the Words signifie either nothing at all, or what he pleases.
>
> (Locke 1975: 496)

The successful combination of enclosure and contingency involved a relative openness – even responsiveness – to the contingent which enabled the common law to adapt to, to absorb, new and changing circumstances. I have suggested above that its metaphorical epistemic structure was crucial to this. Adaptation largely took place through analogy. But so, too, the genius of metaphor was protected by enclosure. The adaptations did not rely upon or appeal to processes which were genuinely esoteric. But lawyers kept their signs to themselves, enclosed. This, more than anything, is the 'secret' of the alchemy through which the contingent or the arbitrary acquires the quasi-naturality which infuses the repetitive tautology of legal self-justification, that the law is the law . . . etc. There was not, and is not today, any shortage of popular works in which law was made simple for 'outsiders', for those who stood before the law (cf. Derrida 1992), the reading public. But such works, however wide their circulation, are always ambiguous in function: they can enhance dissemination, as perhaps occurred in Tocqueville's America, or reinforce the solidity of enclosure, which, I would suggest, was the dominant, though not exclusive, pattern in England, where law, perhaps (despite the reticence exemplified in the barrister's hood) never quite shook off the perversely tainted association of trade.

The common lawyers have always been a pure instrument, servants of money and of power. Part of their so-called independence and impartiality is in fact an abstraction from this service role. As the cab-rank principle used to illustrate, lawyers will work for anyone, and this fact is itself taken to signify their freedom. And this in turn serves as the basis for suggesting that the freedom of lawyers – or the freedom which lawyers 'represent' – is one of the preconditions for the freedom of us all, an essential element in what it means to live in a free society. Yet on the other hand this is only possible because lawyers are dependent on and partial to law itself, to the tradition. And this has ways of its own, a life of its own. It is this which connects the bar to the judges, a form of subordination most clearly articulated in all its ramifications by Durkheim (1984: xxxi ff.) which we have come to know as professionalism more or less in the moment of its partial eclipse. Or, at least: recognition of the law as 'a' profession comes not far in advance (in terms of that history which as we have seen the common law denies it has) of a rather different way of thinking – ways which perhaps have acquired particular resonance in a shoeshine society of 'service' delivery. The commercialization of solicitors, the cost accounting emphasis in the administration of legal aid, the possibility of MDPs, etc., have the potential to combine to reconfigure the infrastructure and the rationale of English law.

Such a partial eclipse is not the 'end of law', not at all. But something changes if the maintenance or adaptation of the apparatus of a tradition, of its rituals and apparel, its methods of recruitment, even of its language, becomes a project, if the English bar becomes a showcase for National Heritage law and its more commercially minded members gatekeepers and guides who show the tourists around (insisting, of course, that all cameras are left outside the door of the courtroom).

REFERENCES

Anderson, B. (1983) *Imagined Communities: Reflections on the Origin and Spread of Nationalism*, London: Verso.

Barthes, R. (1984) *Camera Lucida: Reflections on Photography* (trans. Richard Howard), London: Fontana.

Bentham, J. (1928) *A Comment on the Commentaries: A Criticism of William Blackstone's Commentaries on the Laws of England* (ed. Charles Warren Everett), Oxford: Clarendon Press.

Bergson, H. (1988) *Matter and Memory* (trans. Nancy Margaret Paul and W. Scott Palmer), New York: Zone Books.

Bowie, M. (1987) *Freud, Proust and Lacan: Theory as Fiction*, Cambridge: Cambridge University Press.

Bruns, G. (1992) 'Law and language: a hermeneutics of the legal text', in G. Leyh (ed.), *Legal Hermeneutics: History, Theory and Practice*, Berkeley: University of California Press.

Burke, E. (1987) *Reflections on the Revolution in France* (ed. J. G. A. Pocock), Indianapolis: Hackett.

Caenegem, R. C. van (1987) *Judges, Legislators and Professors: Chapters in European Legal History*, Cambridge: Cambridge University Press.

—— (1992) *An Historical Introduction to Private Law* (trans. D. E. L. Johnston), Cambridge: Cambridge University Press.

Carruthers, M. J. (1990) *The Book of Memory: A Study of Memory in Medieval Culture*, Cambridge: Cambridge University Press.

Clanchy, M. (1979) *From Memory to Written Record*, London: Edward Arnold.

Coleman, J. (1992) *Ancient and Medieval Memories: Studies in the Reconstruction of the Past*, Cambridge: Cambridge University Press.

Cox, A. (1976) *The Role of the Supreme Court in American Government*, New York: Oxford University Press.

Deleuze, G. (1991) *Bergsonism* (trans. Hugh Tomlinson and Barbara Habberjam), Cambridge, Mass.: MIT.

Derrida, J. (1976) *Of Grammatology* (trans. Gayatri Chakravorty Spivak), Baltimore: Johns Hopkins University Press.

—— (1982) *Margins of Philosophy* (trans. Alan Bass), Brighton: Harvester Press.

—— (1992) *Acts of Literature* (ed. Derek Attridge), London: Routledge.

Dinwiddy, J. R. (1984) 'Early-nineteenth-century reactions to Benthamism', *Transactions of the Royal Historical Society, 5th ser.*, 47.

Duerr, H. P. (1985) *Dreamtime: Concerning the Boundary Between Wilderness and Civilization* (trans. Felicitas Goodman), Oxford: Basil Blackwell.

Durkheim, E. (1984) *The Division of Labour in Society* (trans. W. D. Halls), London: Macmillan.

Eco, U. (1992) *Interpretation and Overinterpretation* (ed. Stefan Collini), Cambridge: Cambridge University Press.

Elster, J. (1983) *Sour Grapes: Studies in the Subversion of Rationality*, Cambridge: Cambridge University Press.

—— (1989) *Solomonic Judgments: Studies in the Limitations of Rationality*, Cambridge: Cambridge University Press.

Fish, S. (1992) 'Play of surfaces: theory and the law', in G. Leyh (ed.), *Legal Hermeneutics: History, Theory and Practice*, Berkeley: University of California Press.

Foley, M. (1989) *The Silence of Constitutions*, London: Routledge.

Foucault, M. (1977a) 'Language to infinity', in *Language, Counter-Memory, Practice* (trans. Donald F. Bouchard and Sherry Simon), Oxford: Basil Blackwell.

—— (1977b) *Discipline and Punish* (trans. Alan Sheridan), Harmondsworth: Penguin.

——— (1982) *This is Not a Pipe* (trans. and edited by James Harkness), Berkeley: University of California Press.

——— (1991) *Remarks on Marx: Conversations with Duccio Trombadori* (trans. R. James Goldstein and James Cascaito), New York: Semiotext(e).

Freud, S. (1991) *On Metapsychology* (ed. Angela Richards), Harmondsworth: Penguin.

Gadamer, H.-G. (1976) *Philosophical Hermeneutics* (trans. David E. Linge), Berkeley: University of California Press.

——— (1979) *Truth and Method* (trans. William Glen-Doepel), London: Sheed and Ward.

Geertz, C. (1963) *Agricultural Involution: The Processes of Ecological Change in Indonesia*, Berkeley: University of California Press.

Gigerenzer, G. *et al.* (1989) *The Empire of Chance: How Probability Changed Science and Everyday Life*, Cambridge: Cambridge University Press.

Glymour, C. (1991) 'Freud's androids', in Jerome Neu (ed.), *The Cambridge Companion to Freud*, Cambridge: Cambridge University Press.

Goodrich, P. (1991a) 'Specula laws: image, aesthetic and common law', *Law and Critique* 2, 233.

——— (1991b) 'Eating law: commons, common land, common law', *Journal of Legal History* 12, 246.

Goody, J. (1977) *The Domestication of the Savage Mind*, Cambridge: Cambridge University Press.

Grossfeld, B. (1990) *The Strength and Weakness of Comparative Law* (trans. Tony Weir), Oxford: Oxford University Press.

Hacking, I. (1975) *The Emergence of Probability*, Cambridge: Cambridge University Press.

——— (1990) *The Taming of Chance*, Cambridge: Cambridge University Press.

Haldar, P. (1991) 'The evidencer's eye: representations of truth in the laws of evidence', *Law and Critique* 2, 171.

Holland, T. E. (1916) *Jurisprudence* (12th edn), Oxford: Clarendon Press.

Humboldt, W. von (1988) *On Language: The Diversity of Human Language-Structure and its Influence on the Mental Development of Mankind* (trans. Peter Heath), Cambridge: Cambridge University Press.

Kelsen, H. (1992) *Introduction to the Problems of Legal Theory* (trans. Bonnie Litschewski Paulson and Stanley L. Paulson), Oxford: Clarendon Press.

Krygier, M. (1988) 'The traditionality of statutes', *Ratio Juris* 1, 20.

Lacan, J. (1988) *The Seminar of Jacques Lacan Book I: Freud's Papers on Technique 1953–1954* (ed. Jacques-Alain Miller, trans. John Forrester), Cambridge: Cambridge University Press.

Lemming, D. (1990) *Gentlemen and Barristers: The Inns of Court and the English Bar 1680–1730*, Oxford: Oxford University Press.

Lévi-Strauss, C. (1972) *The Savage Mind*, London: Weidenfeld and Nicolson.

Lloyd, G. E. R. (1990) *Demystifying Mentalities*, Cambridge: Cambridge University Press.

Locke, J. (1975) *An Essay Concerning Human Understanding* (ed. Peter H. Nidditch), Oxford: Clarendon Press.

Murphy, W. T. (1990) 'The Habermas effect: critical theory and academic law', in *Current Legal Problems 1989*, London: Stevens, p. 135.

——— (1991) 'The oldest social science: the epistemic properties of the common law tradition', *Modern Law Review* 54, 182.

——— (1993) 'The bondage of freedom: Max Weber in the present tense', in A. Norrie (ed.), *Closure or Critique: New Directions in Legal Theory*, Edinburgh: Edinburgh University Press.

——— and Roberts, S. (1987) *Understanding Property Law*, London: Fontana.

Oakeshott, M. (1933) *Experience and its Modes*, Cambridge: Cambridge University Press.

——— (1962) *Rationalism in Politics*, London: Methuen.

Pocock, J. G. A. (1971) *Politics, Language and Time: Essays on Political Thought and History*, Chicago: University of Chicago Press.

Richards, D. A. J. (1989) *Foundations of American Constitutionalism*, New York: Oxford University Press.

Saussure, F. de (1974) *Course in General Linguistics* (trans. Wade Baskin), Glasgow: Collins.

Schelling, F. W. J. von (1988) *Ideas for a Philosophy of Nature* (trans. Errol E. Harris and Peter Heath), Cambridge: Cambridge University Press.

Smith, A. (1980) *Essays on Philosophical Subjects*, Oxford: Oxford University Press.

——— (1983) *Lectures on Rhetoric and Belles Lettres* (ed. J. C. Bryce), Oxford: Clarendon Press.

Smith, A. D. (1986) *The Ethnic Origins of Nations*, Oxford: Basil Blackwell.

Sperber, D. (1985) *On Anthropological Knowledge*, Cambridge: Maison des Sciences de l'Homme and Cambridge University Press.

Strachey, L. (1986) *Eminent Victorians*, Harmondsworth: Penguin.

Thomas, R. (1989) *Oral Tradition and Written Record in Classical Athens*, Cambridge: Cambridge University Press.

Tocqueville, A. de (1945) *Democracy in America Volume I* (trans. Henry Reeve and Francis Bowen, ed. Phillips Bradley), New York: Vintage Books.

Wilson, P. J. (1988) *The Domestication of the Human Species*, New Haven: Yale University Press.

Chapter 4

Jani anglorum

Signs, symptoms, slips and interpretation in law

Peter Goodrich

This chapter is predicated upon a discovery relating to the textual and interpretative protocols of reading legal texts. In unadorned terms this discovery is that rhetoric is the pre-modern form of psychoanalysis. Forensic rhetoric, the pre-modern curricular form of analysis of legal speech acts, is also a methodology of symptomatic reading or of interpretation of the unconscious of law. The argument will be developed through the rhetorical analysis of three legal anomalies: specifically the rule allowing the recovery of damages in tort for psychiatric harm occasioned by damage to property, the postal rule in contract, and the immunity of the Crown from actions for contempt of court. In each case the analysis of a specific trope or textual figure – *antonomasia*, *allegoria* and *synecdoche* – will allow for the reconstruction of the genealogy of a substantive legal anomaly. The analysis of the rhetorical form, the elocution or figuration of the legal rule will trigger an institutional memory and serve to indicate a repressed history at the source of the anomaly. In classical rhetoric both the trope and the figure of speech are linked to memory and to desire, to emotion and to the images or places that recollect or reinvoke the passions that persuade or move to action.[1] Rhetoric studies language, or the forms of bodily and verbal enunciation, as the signs of the passions, as indexes of an invisible, unconscious or oneiric logic of institutional speech. In both ecclesiastical and legal terms, 'the world itself is a certain spectacle of things invisible'.[2] Law, which reasons explicitly by images, analogies, associations and other narratives or metonymies similarly represents or dissimulates the invisible affects or unconscious desires of legal custom, judicial intention or sovereign will. It is possible to go further and to suggest that rhetoric studied the symptoms or signs of desire through which Freud and later Lacan mapped out the linguistic structure of oneiric or unconscious laws.[3]

The analysis of unconscious aspects of legal decision-making is not a new theme, either within European or Anglo-American legal thought.[4] Jurisprudential analyses of legal language in terms of its metaphoric, symbolic, narrational and ideological characteristics are a commonplace of critiques of law that range in their theoretical perspective from legal realism to feminism, from pragmatism to semiotics and from existentialism to systems theory. That history of the conjunction of the two disciplines will not be rehearsed here, for the simple reason that metaphors of surface and depth, phenomenon and structure, appearance and reality, lack sufficient linguistic or, more properly, philological detail to allow for the development of a methodology for reading cases. It was rhetoric which was the discipline that traditionally classified the forms of language use, of invention, topics, argumentative distribution, discursive (sentential) form, elocution and memory in terms of emotive effect. Psychoanalysis and jurisprudence can draw upon a common language and certain shared themes. It may be briefly noted from the existing literature that both disciplines are concerned with authority and with prohibition, innocence and guilt. The law of the father equiparates with that of the sovereign and the private self is seen as just as juridical an institution as is public legal personality.[5] In a pragmatic sense, both lawyers and analysts take cases, endeavour to resolve conflicts and more broadly to adapt the individual to the conditions of institutional existence.[6] In a more hermeneutic sense, both professions indulge in symptomatic readings of written and also often unwritten texts.[7] The surface is never an adequate explanation, but is rather to be interpreted in terms of gaps, symptoms, slips, repetitions and other indicia of repression or unconscious cause.[8] The list of coincidences, of themes or terms, doubts or desires that are shared by law and psychoanalysis could be proliferated but to little purpose. The argument here will rather concentrate upon the linguistic and specifically rhetorical interest that the two disciplines share.

Rhetoric studies language use, particularly argument, style and memory, in terms of topics, tropes and figures of speech. It studies the flawed linguistic phenomenon, the figures of enigma (*aenigma*), slip (*paracriasis*), lapse (*aposiopesis*), neologism (*soraismus*), ambiguity (*amphibologia*), paradox (*paradoxon*), repetition (*anaphora*), solecism, impropriety (*catachresis*), deceit (*ironia*) and error (*cacozelia*) as well as decorous speech (analogical *decorum*) and felicitous use (*gnome*), so as to discover the underlying emotion or affective content of language use.[9] For the rhetorician, words are inevitably signs and should thus be read as symptoms of affective states. In its classical definition, a trope was not simply the use of a word in a changed or 'non-proper signification' but it was further defined as a linguistic shift either between species or between affections: thus metonymy, irony, metaphor and synecdoche are the principal tropes of species, while catachresis (borrowing), hyperbole (exaggeration), metalepsis (cause for effect) and litotes (diminution) are the master tropes of the affections.[10] The figures of speech, the schemata, are defined as the linguistic forms of representation, as 'the apparel and ornament of the body . . . of words and speech' which allow the speaker not only to represent but equally to fashion, to carry across, to feign, dissimulate, seduce, delight and move.[11] The *gnome* or figures of sentence are thus defined by Smith as 'pathetical, or such as move affection and passion'.[12] The figures of speech are understood rhetorically as condensations of emotion, as the specific language of particular passions. In rhetorical manuals the most powerful or effective figures were thus those which carried the greatest emotional content or were deemed likely to have the greatest affective impact. Figures were therefore listed according to their potential use in different genres of speech. In most lists of figures, however, extremity of emotion was associated particularly with figures of antithesis (*oppositio*), exclamation (*ecphonesis*), emphasis (*auxesis*), recollection (*anamnesis*) or visual effect (*hypotyposis*).[13] The classical art and practice of rhetoric was that of persuasion or at least of discovery of the means of persuasion, it sought to manipulate emotion, to advocate policies, plead causes or praise civic offices by means of identification between audience and oratorical projection. The judicious use of the lexicon of tropes and other rhetorical and argumentative forms would institute a distinction, discrimination or judgment as between affect and antipathy, between identical and alien, like and unlike and finally, in terms not dissimilar to Freud's basic drives of *eros* and *thanatos*,[14] between affirmation and negation, between life and death.

The rhetorician pursued the linguistic levers of passion. The orator was always an advocate in search of the continued oratorical play (*permutatio*) of irony or allegory, of things signified 'by other words'.[15] Rhetoric was a consistent pursuit of emotive force, of some movement of the mind 'as of love, hatred, gladness or sorrow' under the general label of vehemence of affection (*pathopoiea* or *affectus expressio*).[16] This oratorical goal of affective dissimulation, of allegorical representation of the 'other scene' of human motive, desire and action, was subject to a further unconscious law. As the definition of affective expression suggests, the language of public speech, or institutional enunciation, the language of rhetorical genres, of law (forensic), politics (deliberative) and ceremony (panegyric), was antagonistically structured. Its characteristic emotional force was that of antithesis or opposition whereby the realm of affectivity was identified and separated from that of the alien, unfamiliar or simply other. One explanation for such an antinomic structure of public discourse could be that rhetoric was modelled upon its early agonistic legal uses. All institutional speech would be pleading in the context of some species of trial, the hearer was always a judge.[17] Whether the court was that of reason, taste, opinion or law, all auditors were in some measure forensic actors and would play the role of both jury and judge.[18] A further explanation might project the juridical into the social so as to suggest that the antagonistic or properly *antirrhetic* structure of discourse was a consistent form of institutional self-representation.[19] To have an effect, to persuade, threaten or otherwise move its auditor, the legal speech or text had to identify its audience or constituency and provide that audience or those hearers with such symbols, images, icons or figures as would allow communication in its classical or at least etymological sense of communion. The audience of law would identify itself narcissistically with the legal institution, with the mirror of its projected images, and would simultaneously reject its competitors, neighbours or simple alternatives, those whom the law denounced or the judge admonished. Thus the rhetoric of affectivity is coupled with that of negation, praise of the identical, the similar, the like or proportionate is accompanied by denunciation of the strange, the unlike, disproportionate or heteroclite in the same historical and political sense that orthodoxy creates heterodoxy and that doctrine defines heresy as its necessary or complementary form.[20] Two preliminary illustrations from rhetorical manuals should suffice to indicate the nature of this correlation between affirmation and negation, praise and denunciation and more broadly between unconscious intent and the figures of speech. For where rhetoric maps the emotional body of the institutional audience, psychoanalysis will subsequently equally attend to the images, figures and symbols whereby linguistic practice can be read symptomatically as representing past patterns of power, repressed emotive sources of action and the residue more generally of unconscious desire.

In an essay directly concerned with persuasion through appeal to the affections, Daniel Tuvil represents the effective orator as speaking with the 'tongue of the heart'. To capture the affection of the auditor is the principal part of rhetorical success

> and the reason hereof is not farre from hand. For passions are certain internal acts, and operations of our soul, which being joined and linked in a most inviolable, and long-continued league of friendship with the sensitive power, and facultie thereof, do conspire together like disobedient and rebellious subjects, to shake off the *yoake of reason*, and exempt themselves from her command and controllment, that they still exercise those disordered motions, in the contract world of our frail and human bodies.[21]

Rhetoric analyses, evokes or unleashes a dark and unconscious realm of vehement affection, sense and corporeal volition or will. Whether it is depicted as deceitful, irrational or simply subversive, the rhetoric of affection plainly depends upon or harbours either other reasons or the other of reason, which is variously termed the imagination, intensivity, violence or affection.

Rhetoric and psychoanalysis converge in the analysis of the conflict or cause which relates the institutional to the individual and in both disciplines law is the term used to depict the relation of the subject to patristic judgment, *patria, regia, iudex* or *pater*. The common theme of cause, conflict or disputation is most noticeable in the alignment of rhetoric with specific images of conflict, trial, demagogy and verbal war. The telos of rhetorical speech is victory rather than cure, a metaphor which is lengthily elaborated in Bernard Lamy's, *The Art of Speaking*, though other handbooks provide equally striking elaborations in terms of confutation, defeat and overcoming, as well as the more obviously forensic forms of figuration such as demonstration, self-evidence, necessity and disproof.[22] In Lamy's depiction our effect upon others is most typically a consequence of the figures of our speech, which include the bodily gestures, tears or other physical signs that accompany oratory. The necessity of figures, however, lies in the hostility of institutional environments or the adversarial contexts of speaking. Lamy begins with the language of the body and remarks how 'we find in ourselves, that our Members (without direction from our Soul) dispose themselves into postures to avoid injury. That the Body frames itself into a proper condition, either to invade or to defend.' Limbs stiffen and postures are adopted automatically or unconsciously in response to threat or to an adversary 'and this is done naturally, without reflexion or debate'. The body is here no more than a metaphor for the text as Lamy continues to argue that what is true of bodily postures or figures is true also of the figures or postures of rhetorical style, of oratorical gesture and speech.

> The Figures are [not] only Rhetorical Figments invented for ornament of discourse: God has not refused to the Soul, what he has given to the Body. The Body knows [without direction from our soul] how to move, and dispose itself dexterously, for the repelling of Injuries; and the Soul may defend itself as well: the Figures employed by her in discourse, do the same, as Postures in defence of the Body. If Postures be proper for defence in corporal invasions; Figures are as necessary, in spiritual attacks. Words are the Arms of the Mind, which she uses, to disswade or perswade, as occasion serves.[23]

The metaphor, the translation from the corporeal to the textual, from gesture to trope, from posture to the speech, is based upon a homonymy between physical force and rhetorical figure, between speech and passion. The rhetorician is always on trial or before the law. Such trial dates back historically to an 'original', which was trial by combat, by ordeal, or by physical omen,[24] and Lamy simply recollects that antagonistic and physically threatening history of pleading a cause by subsequently and lengthily comparing the orator and the pleader to a soldier fighting, suggesting if nothing else that the soul is constantly in conflict, both in directing its own passions and in defending itself from those of others. In broader rhetorical terms, the discourse of the institution manipulates figures of speech, dissimulates, cajoles, threatens, orders and persuades because these are the forms of social action. The unconscious is a jurist pleading both innocence and guilt, torn between hedonism and pessimism, desire and law. The dogma or 'delirium' of institutional speech, its insistence and its repetition, is simply a further level or reflection of the antinomy of affection and negation, praise and denunciation, approval and polemic, through which the soul, or, in contemporary terminology, identity, is instituted and prolonged.

If autobiography provides both the lexicon and the narrative structure, the affections and the antagonisms of the individual unconscious, social history is the unconscious structure of institutions. To the extent that the institution survives, in so far as it is independent of any single generation of its custodians, access to its unconscious motivations, its repressions and its desires must frequently be indirect. Access will not, for obvious reasons, be by means of the

'Royal road' to the science of the unconscious, the interpretation of dreams. The institution is delirious or uncontrolled only in its habitual procedures, standard forms and other texts. It is in the slips or figures of the text that rhetoric may attend to, recover or reconstruct certain of the antagonisms, fears, identities and desires that motivate or cause institutional enunciations. In the ensuing analysis three examples of anomalous common law rules will be used to illustrate the potential uses of rhetoric in locating an unconscious of law. The examples, which are all of contemporary legal anachronisms, will move from the analysis of textual figures to that of the emotions, conflicts or repressed histories that underpin them.

ANTONOMASIA OR HARM AND THE ENGLISHMAN'S HOME

The first example is taken from the law of torts. It concerns the recoverability of damages for psychiatric harm caused by negligently occasioned nervous shock. The anomalous case is that of *Attia* v. *British Gas plc.*[25] The plaintiff employed the defendants to install central heating in her house in Middlesex. '[R]eturning home at about 4 pm on 1 July 1981 she saw smoke coming from the loft of the house. She telephoned the fire brigade but, by the time the firemen arrived, the whole house was on fire . . . obviously the house and its contents were extensively damaged.' The defendants admitted liability in negligence for the physical damage to the house but the question remained whether the plaintiff could recover damages for 'nervous shock', the psychiatric harm occasioned by seeing her 'home and its contents ablaze'.[26] The Court of Appeal held unanimously that psychiatric damage occasioned by seeing 'her home and possessions damaged and/or destroyed' was recoverable. The decision is in some respects an obvious one and it could be argued that it simply extends the general criterion of foreseeability to a new situation. The categories of negligence are never closed. The stronger argument, however, is that the decision is anomalous both in terms of lacking doctrinal justification and in terms of failure to accord with existing precedent.

The extant law on recoverability of damages for psychiatric harm at the time that *Attia* v. *British Gas* was decided was the recent House of Lords decision in *McLoughlin* v. *O'Brian.*[27] In terms of doctrinal development, the decision in *McLoughlin* explicitly established a multiple test of proximity. Lord Wilberforce, in a judgment which has more recently been annotated and affirmed by the House of Lords in *Alcock* v. *Chief Constable of South Yorkshire*, [28] stated that three elements were inherent in any claim: 'the class of persons whose claims should be recognised; the proximity of such persons to the accident; and the means by which the shock is caused'.[29] It is clearly the first head of foreseeability that is here significant.

> As regards the class of persons, the possible range is between the closest family ties, of parent and child, or husband and wife, and the ordinary bystander. Existing law recognises the claims of the first; it denies that of the second, either on the basis that such persons must be assumed to be possessed of fortitude sufficient to enable them to endure the calamities of modern life or that defendants cannot be expected to compensate the world at large.[30]

Without discussing whether British Gas plc was a recognized calamity of the modern world Lord Wilberforce may finally be cited as authority for a methodological argument, namely that in situations of the type under discussion 'the courts have proceeded in the traditional manner of the common law from case to case, on a basis of logical necessity'.[31] The figurative use of the term 'logical necessity' deserves brief comment. To claim that reasoning by likeness, by metaphor or simile, by translation from one image to another, from one affection or experience to the next, is a procedure of logical necessity can only be understood as irony, *antiphrasis* or dissimulation. It is no more possible to 'deduce' a relation between one context and another than it is feasible to claim any strict identity between the legal reconstruction of different events occurring at different times and affecting different parties. The logical necessity of analogy is at most a subjective necessity imposed by custom and habit. While Roman law long recognized the logical weakness of such arguments predicated upon similarity, the common law returns continuously to an empiricism which claims somewhat mystically that analogy is the 'natural tendency of the human and legal mind'.[32] The analogy then suggested by Lord Wilberforce is that of the different situations in which parents can recover for psychiatric harm caused by injury to their child. Lord Scarman added laconically that 'I foresee social and financial problems if damages for "nervous shock" should be made available to persons other than parents and children . . .'.[33] The Australian case of *Jaensch* v. *Coffey*, which stipulated no specific kinship tie but a 'close, constructive and loving relation' between the parties probably hit upon a formulation that best describes the current law: the tie must be close and affectionate but need not necessarily fall within the conventional classifications of lineal or familial proximity.[34]

With the well-canvassed exception of rescue cases and the unique example of a claim based upon fear of injury to a workmate,[35] legal doctrine has consistently maintained that proximity with regard to the class of persons which is to be allowed to recover means a tie of blood or of recognized relationship. Such a relationship has always been taken to mean a relationship between persons. Even taking account of judicial paternalism or the doctrinal desire to keep the legal judgment separate from the sphere of domesticity, it is hard to see that it falls within the 'natural tendency of the human and legal mind' to perceive a house either as or as being 'like' a relative or 'analogous to' a person. Nor does precedent provide any examples of 'logical necessity' leading from person to property or from animate to inanimate. A person is not in ordinary speech nor in art nor in legal language like a house. The only precedent that could offer support of any kind for the Court of Appeal decision would be the somewhat obscure earlier decision of the Court of Appeal in the case of *Owens* v. *Liverpool Corporation*.[36] In that case the accident witnessed involved a dead relative, an inanimate person, in a coffin which was dislodged by a tram operated by the defendants. The shock was occasioned to close relatives of the deceased in close proximity to the accident. On the grounds that it is the dignity or office of the dead to be in repose, the disturbance to the coffin and the threat that it might at any moment slide out of the damaged hearse and fall to the street was sufficient ground for recovery. The court recognized that the threat of injury to the dead was a marginal if not tenuous analogy to earlier situations but suggested that what was significant was the proximity or strength of affection between the parties. Lord Justice MacKinnon went further at one point and suggested consideration of the moot case of damage caused by the death of a much loved pet dog.[37] The 'beloved' dog, of course, is the Englishman's best, most trusted and most loyal friend and it is easy to imagine that the court might well have difficulties distinguishing the family dog from other members of the family. It remains the case, however, that the subjects of injury in precedent cases extended no further than a hypothetical living non-person or a dead relative.

Returning to the decision in *Attia* it is evident rhetorically that more is at stake than a simple question of the foreseeable consequences of damage to property. There is indeed an immediate shift in the depiction of the facts of that case from the cognitive to the affective and from description to evaluation when the object of damage is renamed and becomes not a house but a home. The figure[38] in question is that of *antonomasia* or change of name. It is described by Smith as a sentential figure (*figura sententiae*), which 'is a figure . . . for the forcible moving of affections, which doth after a sort beautify the sense and very meaning of a sentence'.[39] Its rhetorical effect is depicted by Peacham as that of metonymically transferring the value of some 'dignity, office, profession, science or trade' from its proper referent to a novel *comparata*.[40] In its usual rhetorical manipulation the substitution of name is metonymic in the sense of selecting a quality or essence that is representative of the whole: Cicero for eloquence, the Philosopher for Aristotle and so on, where the substituted name elects to qualify the object or subject in either a positive or negative fashion. The attribution is the more powerful for being unmarked or tacit, its force and accuracy are simply assumed and not only is the lauded or denigrated part taken for the whole but there is also a move from passive to active, from description to qualification and in sum from object to telos or goal. Whether or not one or other term, house or home, is more properly descriptive of the structure that formed the subject-matter of the decision, it is the shift or slippage from one term to the other, from species to species or from the descriptive to the evaluative that should give occasion for rhetorical concern. The trope is an indicator of an affective or unconscious intent, it is a figure of a subtle argumentative shift and it is precisely the hidden, oneiric or repressed connotations of 'home' that the rhetorical analyst should pursue. It will be my claim that these connotations are institutional and so are largely unconscious. It is certainly the case that the legal status or meaning of a home is not addressed in the judgments, nor would it appear to have been raised by counsel in argument. The institutional connotations of the shift from one noun to another have in these circumstances to be reconstructed both in terms of the particular judgment and also in the longer-term context of the doctrinal text of which the decision in *Attia* is but a minor incident.

In the course of a preliminary judgment in favour of the defendants, Sir Douglas Frank at first instance had noted that grief and sorrow were understandable responses to 'the loss of all that is embodied in the word "home" and of one's possessions'.[41] In a statement which reversed the order of substitution, such that home became house, Sir Douglas Frank took the 'modern' view that loss of possessions and of 'one's own house' was not a foreseeable cause of mental illness. The Court of Appeal differed. It recognized that the claim broke new ground, indeed 'that no analogous claim has ever . . . been upheld or even advanced'.[42] None the less the Court managed to discover a duty of care and to deem it possible that as a matter of fact it was foreseeable that the plaintiff would suffer psychiatric harm. Lord Justice Bingham went so far as to list other objects of affection that might, if destroyed, so unsettle the seemingly restrained emotional world of their owner that recovery should probably be allowed – namely, a scholar's life's work of research or composition and a householder's 'cherished possessions' or heirlooms.[43] In the present instance the damage was not simply to contents but to the structure and place of the home itself. In cultural terms an emotional life that hinges upon things or is fixed to property is arguably degenerate. To 'fall in love' with a house is ungrammatical in law and is also not recognized as a cause of action for mental distress in either contract or tort according to the recent decision of *Watts* v. *Morrow*.[44] In the absence of any manifest legal reason, in doctrine or in precedent, for the extension of liability in psychiatric harm to cover damage occasioned by injury to things, it is necessary to follow the rhetorical *indicium*, trope or textual symptom and inquire as to the legal significance of the home.

There are two important legal connotations associated with the home and traceable to the very dawn of the modern common law. First, both in case-law and in doctrinal writing, the Englishman's home is his castle. As early as *Semayne's Case*, in 1605,[45] it was held that the home was a place of sanctity, of tranquillity and peace. It was the safest of all refuges (*domus sua cuique est tutissimum refugium*). It was a place of some sanctity, a hiding place, an escape, a castle, a fortress, a space of repose and of defence. In Thomas Wood's *Institute of the Laws of England*,[46] *Semayne's Case* is discussed and cited as authority for the rule that whereas an assembly or meeting of three or more is an offence, it is not punishable if it is 'for the safeguard of his *House*, and for the Defence of the possession thereof'. It is permissible to gather friends to prevent any unlawful entry into one's own house 'but he cannot assemble his friends for the defence of his *person* against those that threaten to beat him, while he is out of his house'. Elsewhere in the *Institute* a variety of definitions of house (*domus*) and of mansion house (*domus mansionalis*) is provided and the fact that 'a chamber in an Inn of Court, where one usually lodges, is a mansion-house' no doubt did much to aid the longevity of the profession.[47]

In later case-law, the sanctity of the home and garden is reiterated and emphasized. The most famous statement of right comes in *Entick* v. *Carrington* where Lord Camden asserted the legal protection of the home to be an 'extraordinary jurisdiction' coeval with the law itself and so without origin or evidence beyond its statement, save that 'precedent supports it'.[48] The Saxon concept of 'house-peace' and the liberties spelled out in Magna Carta are likely sources of such precedent though none is needed for so ancient a rule.[49] He subsequently remarks upon the ethical legitimation of the rule as being coincident with the end or telos of law and of society itself: 'the great end, for which men entered society, was to secure their property. That right is preserved sacred and incommunicable in all instances, where it has not been taken away or abridged by some public law for the good of the whole.' With a measure of hyperbole suitable to the occasion and the threat to this admittedly defeasible right, Lord Camden concludes with the celebrated defence of the English home and garden, stating that 'no man can set foot upon my ground without my licence, but he is liable to an action, though the damage be nothing . . . [even for no more than] bruising the grass . . . or treading upon the soil'. In later cases a similar exaggeration of an impermanent right is stated in terms of the protection of every single room in the house by separate writs of trespass.[50] The house, of course, was many things in legal terms and was certainly not free of legal and ecclesiastical interference with regard, for example, to 'good government'[51] or with respect to the proper forms of worship or the duties of husband and wife.[52]

Whether or not the common law protection of the house as home of the subject is viewed as successful or otherwise effective, the home is a legal term invested with a remarkable significance. The home is autobiographically both domesticity and family, the site of an originary law, that of paternity as also in its earliest stages it is the *gynaeceum*, or maternal domain. The home is connotative psychoanalytically of emotional security, of nurture and of the immemorial, of that which is – like common law – a record or testament *aere perennius*.[53] The home represents tradition in the precise sense that the home is external to and survives its occupation, it is the place of the ancestors and forefathers, of the image, of all that *in nuce* to which we belong. The instant that the Court in *Attia* v. *British Gas* turned from house to home or simply categorized the injury as being occasioned not by damage to property, but far more specifically indicated that the damage was caused by the burning of the home, it returned unconsciously to a category of legal tradition with an extraordinary though heavily veiled affective force. The description – by the figure of *prosographia* – of the burning home as the material cause of the harm suffered carries with it an unconscious sense of an absolute violation: to destroy a sacred place is by ecclesiastical law a sacrilege,[54] a transgression of the boundaries between species or profanation of the marks of an iconic space. In more secular terms destruction of the home is disrespectful of tradition, contemptuous of lineage, of ancestral virtue and the 'titles of antiquity' which honour and family pass on through the home. One can go further and suggest that destruction of the home connotes a challenge to the most basic law, not simply that of kinship but in legal terms that of the first *societas*, the family and its order of succession. To destroy the home is technically a 'monstrous' act because it takes away from the support of the family and threatens a situation in which reproduction is no longer reproduction of the same, in which the child is a monster because the child is not like the father or the mother.[55] It remains to be observed that the plaintiff was a woman. In *Owens* v. *Liverpool Corporation*, the Court had remarked that 'if real injury has genuinely been caused by shock from apprehension as to something less than human life (for example, the life of a beloved dog), can the sufferer recover no damages for the injury he, or perhaps oftener she, has sustained?'[56] It is not clear what weight this shift in gender would have in determining the factual outcome of either case but it should undoubtedly be observed that in affective terms the home is a gendered category. In constitutional doctrine, the household, according to Sir Thomas Smith, here following Aristotle, is the internal domain of the woman while the external world is the sphere of men.[57] In terms of the ecclesiastical law of marriage contemporary with the earliest surviving statements of the privacy and sanctity of the home, it is clear that protection of the home is protection of the vulnerable, the women and children for whom the home is the world.[58] In this respect the portrait of the facts in *Attia* again betrays an unconscious reservoir of institutional emotions or structures of value that persist over the *longue durée* of common law. The figure of *antonomasia* indicates a slip or unconscious motive, it allows for the reconstruction of 'another scene' of legal judgment, that of affectivity and desire.[59] In terms, finally, of the structure of the legal unconscious, the case of *Attia* is representative of one dimension of the conflict that constitutes the dogma, dream order or delirium of the institution. It opens up a zone of affectivity, an object amongst objects of identification and of love, a political desire towards which legal policy will inevitably be directed. It forms an inside, an identity against or to which must be compared the corresponding zone of exclusion, of alienity, foreignness or otherness with which a later example will be concerned. In the next example, however, the question of identification is again central to the rhetorical recovery of a repressed memory of the objects and meanings of a specific legal anomaly: the treatment of messages sent by post.

ALLEGORIA OR THE ERASED FACE OF THE OFFEREE

The second example is taken from the law of contract. It concerns the much remarked anomaly that while contracts are the result of consensus and thus depend upon communication between the parties, an acceptance is binding once put in the post.[60] The postal rule, or, in its American terminology the 'mailbox rule',[61] is generally accredited with an early nineteenth-century origin and is viewed at best as an arbitrary concession to the needs of business certainty and at worst as irrational by virtue of being inconsistent with the consensual principles of contract formation. Explanations for the rule are various and will only be briefly reviewed. If nothing else, the absence of any plausible – let alone satisfactory – justification for the postal rule generates continued academic debate.[62] Most commentators accept that in its original terms, covering letters and subsequently the telex, the rule is here to stay.[63] Justifications for the rule thus become secondary and less consequential save in the area of the potential adoption or disavowal of the rule in relation to more recent technologies.

Attempts to explain the postal rule range from the historical through the literary to the psychoanalytic.[64] Starting with the latter, an article by an American, Professor Nusbaum, in the mid-1930s suggested that criticism of the postal rule and of the decision in *Adams* v. *Lindsell* in particular had been extensive and was 'sufficient' to discredit the rule. None the less 'they [i.e. the judges] stick to it in England as well as in this country. An attempt should be ventured to apply some "psychoanalysis" to their actions and to look for the "complex" behind them.'[65] While Nusbaum does not himself offer either diagnosis or therapy for the Anglo-American judiciary his suggestion has considerable merit. Why repeat a discredited decision or at least a rule which even the judiciary have acknowledged to be arbitrary if not for some other reason which is either repressed, forgotten or inadmissible? Nusbaum concentrates on the idiosyncrasy of the rule and adverts to its lack of historical or comparative justification. His purpose is in large measure simply to show (arguably inaccurately) that civil law systems historically have not had such a rule and that there is good reason for that absence.

A recent commentator, Simon Gardiner, elliptically takes up Nusbaum's challenge and offers a 'deconstruction' of the postal rules in terms of their historical and social context of origin. The context is that of the nineteenth-century reform of the Post Office: the Post Office monopoly, standardized rates, prepayment of postage and the cutting of letter boxes in doors all merged in the public imagination to equate posting with the certainty of delivery: 'the thesis, then, is that the decisions of the 1840s were influenced not so much by internal considerations about offer and acceptance in contract as by way of regarding the phenomena of posting as such'.[66] Using Trollope's novels as a literary pre-text for reformulating the logic of the postal rule, the deconstruction ends by confirming the repressed or at least lost external cause of the rule: 'the postal acceptance . . . thus stands alone as an exception to a general requirement for full communication . . . [the] rule may be regarded as something of a museum piece'.[67] The fiction or 'artificiality'[68] whereby the act of posting is treated by simulation 'as if' it were communication of acceptance is here viewed as anomalous or as 'compulsive' and thus arbitrary if not necessarily evil. Gardiner also recognizes that like repression itself the postal rule is likely to return: 'it is worth noticing, however, that there is a chance of history repeating itself'.[69]

Where Gardiner introduces history and literature to provide an indication of the 'real reason'[70] for the rule, it is arguable that his analysis of the rule does not take the logic of deconstruction – or Nusbaum's suggested psychoanalysis – far enough. As other contributors to the debate over the rule have pointed out, the postal exception may well be more significant than the standard rule.[71] While the rule of full communication suggests a linguistically unrealistic ideology of consensus, the postal rule introduces the objective possibility of the non-arrival of the letter, and faces the consequences of that failure of delivery or non-communication which constantly threatens to undermine the subjective theory of contracts. The narrative of the non-arriving letter would be similar to Poe's popular story of the purloined letter: the repetition or the 'sticking' of the postal rule would serve to recollect or even to cure a general theory of contractual communication which represses the mechanisms, the grammatological but also linguistic means whereby the letter, the *ipsissima verba* of the contract, circulates or finds its destination.[72] The rule of full communication would be part of the blindness of law, the exception would be conceptually anterior and liberatory:

> the exception comes before the rule in order to put the rule into circulation. The post comes before the prior, the letter before the *phone*, endless circulation before the wealth of tradition, the postal relay before the fixity of meaning and the order of politics and law.[73]

What one commentator views as being an inappropriate extension of the ideology of the metaphor of 'meeting of minds' – namely, that the offer is made continuously as it travels to the offeree[74] – is represented deconstructively as the precondition for the possibility of contract as such. Where psychoanalysis would assert the priority of the postal rule because it privileges the signifier over the signified, deconstruction would support the postal rule on the basis of a similar inversion of the hierarchical opposition of writing to speech: the written is anterior to the spoken, the post thus represents the 'destinal of Being' and the postal rule would be the emblem of the discipline of contract as a whole.[75]

There is support in the history of contract, and particularly in the early formbooks such as West's *Symbolaeography*, to support both the psychoanalytic and the deconstructive readings adverted to above.[76] The earliest forms of contract were written obligations adopted and adapted from precedent writings provided by means of

> the [notarial] trade of the making of evidence, and terms thereof, which as they be most ancient, so without doubt are they the surest, and [of] most vailable effect, and a great danger it is for those not exactly learned in the laws to alter or vary from the same.[77]

The contract, *symbolon*, creed or record, is in legal principle immemorial and immutable: the language of law is in Coke's terms *vocabula artis*, an 'unknown grammar',[78] which circulates perpetually within its own professional genre. The language of legal record, as the 'language of memorials' was destined more for posterity than for secular receipt.[79] The written obligation, *assumpsit*, or consensual bond circulated in the external language of durable legal forms. The contract is here a trace or vestige of a structure, of a prior and external agreement, of a code or language of law which precedes and survives its momentary intentional or temporal use. The postal rule, which recognizes precisely the priority of the signifier, of the letter, over the sense or content, directly expresses the logic of common law history. It would be presumptuous in the extreme to suppose that there were any single explanation – historical, literary, philosophical or psychoanalytic – to this rule. Too much has condensed around the continued metaphor or, properly, allegory, of the post and the rule of posting. That the fiction continues to return, that letters bind without being read, that the law treats writing 'as if' it were speech – in short, the allegorical narrative of contract by letters necessarily suggests another scene or unconscious place of judgment.

The postal rule can be traced to the *Digest*, which in 18.1.1.2 rules that 'sale is a contract of the law of nations and so is concluded by simple agreement; it can thus be contracted by parties not present together, through messengers, or by letters (*per nuntium et per literas*)'. In the reception, as Gordley has shown, the glossatorial interpretation of this passage frequently addressed the question of when the contract by 'bare messenger' or letter was complete. Accursius, in the *Glossa Ordinaria*, thus takes the view that if the offeree's letter or message of acceptance has been sent, an attempted revocation by the seller before receipt of the acceptance would not be effective.[80]

> To Petrus, Cinus, and Bartolus the obvious difficulty with this position is that the seller becomes bound to a contract to which he did not consent at the moment it was formed. The issue in Accursius's mind, however, was not whether the seller had consented but the moment at which a communication is effective.[81]

In terms of the post-reception development of civil law, the issue raised by correspondence was that of the status of messengers or other agents in communication between absent parties. The question became that of whether a simple or bare messenger could represent a continuing condition or consent to the transaction. The letter, in Alciatus's definition, was a silent messenger (*tacitus nuntius*) and so out of the power of the sender it communicated in its own right. By this logic, the offeree was entitled to rely upon the continuing validity of the offer.[82] Gordley mentions one other significant circumstance in which letters are effective even if not received. It is that by C 5 17 6 a marriage can be dissolved by a document that never reaches the other spouse.[83] This last example will prove to be of the utmost importance.

The glossatorial reception of the law of sale has an indirect impact upon English law.[84] Historical accounts of the development of modern contract doctrine make it clear that the elaboration of indigenous rules governing assumpsit and covenant were as significant as the earlier inheritance of Roman law.[85] While it is evident, not least from Gordley's discussion, that the common law of contract had significant Roman borrowings and further that nineteenth-century developments were borrowed almost entirely from civil law,[86] the most significant – yet least discussed – area of reception of contract doctrine was in the law on 'spousals' or marriage contracts. In pre-modern English law, the use of the term contract was often synonymous with marriage and it was in relation to the law of spousals that many of the doctrines later developed as part of the modern law of contract were first developed. In particular, rules relating to capacity, to duress, to consideration, to offer and acceptance *in praesentia* and *in absentia*, to present and future intent and to the plea of *non est factum* all had their earliest development in relation to the law of marriage.[87] It should also be emphasized that the law of marriage was subject to the jurisdiction of ecclesiastical courts and judges trained in civil law and it is that Roman inheritance that the common lawyers admitted subsequently into English law.

The specific point to be made is both simple and surprising. The postal rule, the allegory of the privileged offeree, is the allegory of the law's admittedly limited protection of women. Henry Swinburne provides the most succinct annotation of the law governing spousals contracted *inter absentes*, by messenger or by letter. Swinburne offers a relatively complicated analysis of the formation of spousals. The contract is to be inferred from the words or from manifest intentions: 'what are words but the messengers of men's minds? And wherefore serve tongues, but to express men's meanings?'[88] The word is already, in this analysis, a species of letter, a symbol of intent which can, however, be corrected or referred to its precedent cause, the intention of the author or sender, for if

> the Parties did *intend* to contract matrimony, then although the words import no more than spousals *de futuro* [i.e. engagement], the contract is no less matrimony; but when the meaning doth appear, then, howsoever the Rude and Vulgar sort do often abuse their terms, and speak improperly, we must be directed by the [rule which says] we must not otherwise depart from the signification of words, but in case it be manifest, that the speaker meant otherwise.[89]

With the stated exception of a manifest dissonance between word and intention, the meaning of the utterance and of its sending is to be construed by law and not by reference either to illocution or subjective states. The analysis of the contract made *inter absentes* thus begins by taking up the glossatorial distinction between proctor and messenger and following Alciatus defines the messenger as without warrant or authority but 'imployed only about the expedition of a bare fact, as the delivery of a mere message, or a sole postage of a letter . . .'.[90] It is thus the instrument, the symbol, messenger or letter that is the object of analysis: between whom can the letter legitimately circulate, who can send and who receive these messages? The question concerns the circulation of the 'deed', obligation or fact, the movement of the signifier and not of the signified. It is a question initially of whether the woman has the capacity to utilize a particular form of acceptance. The question Swinburne addresses next is therefore that of 'whether the woman may contract matrimony by a special messenger or letters, as well as the man?'[91] Deciding that by canon law she can in principle, Swinburne is then faced with the question: 'what if the party to whom the message or letter importing consent of matrimony, being delivered, do immediately upon the receipt thereof express the like consent, whether is the contract hereby finished?'[92] The answer is that at the instant of responding to the messenger or letter, 'there is mutual agreement at one instant . . . because the party which did first consent is still presumed to continue and persevere in the same mind, until the time of the others consent'. In short, the contract is 'perfect' or finished the moment that the woman to whom the offer of marriage was sent, expresses consent. The offeror cannot, in other words, revoke the offer between the time of consent and the time of receipt of consent. The manifest fiction cited by Swinburne relates to the offeror's continued offer, *idem est non esse et non apparere*, which is to say that not to be and not to appear is all one in the construction of law: if the revocation has not been received it is taken not to exist. Underlying this figure of consent is the relation of man to woman. It is the woman that benefits from the fiction of continued assent or continuing offer, it is the woman who is protected by the 'artificial' or fictive operation of the postal rule. If in later common law it seems anomalous to protect the offeree this is only because of the erasure of the face of the offeree, it has been forgotten that it was a woman who put a letter of acceptance in the post.

The question of gender lurks unrecognized in the background of the early development of the modern law of contract. It is certainly not the only unseen influence but it should be noted that it is not only the postal rule which survives as a memory of contracting women, the bulk of rules governing what is now termed the 'policing of the bargain' had their early operation developed around the regulation of marriage contracts. It is beyond the scope of the present argument to examine the rules of contract that develop around domestic relations and primarily concern the wife's lack of will and so of capacity,[93] but the unconscious memory of marriage contract can be seen in the judicial use of hypotheticals drawn from the law of spousals to explain the rules of offer and acceptance. What if a soldier on leave offers marriage by post just before returning to the front? What if a man shouts a proposal of marriage across a river and the offeree's answer is drowned out by a passing steamboat? Baron Bramwell, in *British and American Telegraph Co.* v. *Colson*,[94] thus asks 'if a man proposed to a woman and the woman was to consult her friends and let him know, would it be enough if she wrote and posted a letter which never reached him?' The answer which Lord Bramwell offers is of less significance than the continued presence of the female offeree. The example is not insignificant nor merely hypothetical, it recollects an institutional history, an unconscious structure within which it would be ethically absurd to allow the man to escape his duties and dishonourable in the extreme to leave a woman in suspense or unprotected. The spiritual exemplar of contract had always been that of marriage. In ecclesiastical law the order of marriage ran from that of the Church to Christ, that of the Priest to the Church, that of the christian to the creed, that of woman to man. The hierarchical order of marriages was not only a symptom of the necessary permanence of the contracted institution, it was also a sign – symbol or credo – of an order of communication, of the places of communication in a dialogue in which the sovereign father, parent, priest or male suitor or proposer would ask a question or make an offer to which the offeree could only say yes or no. The offeree in this model of contract is powerless in the sense of being brought to speech in a formulaic place, in being subject to no more than an elective rite. If the law recognized the minimal duty of protecting the offeree's election it should not be supposed that this granted the woman offeree any very great or very real right.

METONYMY: AEGYPTIANS, ALIENS, OTHERS AND THE CROWN

The example of the postal rule is again an instance of the long-term movement of law across considerable distances of institutional time.[95] The trope, figure or anomaly in the text, in many senses contradicts the legal maxim that what does not appear does not exist. It is precisely through these figurations, through slips, lapses or displacements from one institutional category to another, that the unconscious of law can be glimpsed and its reconstruction attempted. The examples argue persuasively that the survival of the institution is intimately linked to a dogmatics which appears arcane or obtuse in part by virtue of relying upon an unconscious reservoir of institutional connotations, metaphoric structures, long-term deployments of meaning which develop in the indefinite time of precedent. As Fortescue once remarked, 'we have several set forms which are held as law, and so held and used for good reason, though we cannot at present remember that reason'.[96] Rhetoric was explicitly the art of memory as well as of civil speech. Like psychoanalysis it sought not only to classify the places or *topoi* of memory but also to map the dialectic of memory and its erasure, of repetition and forgetting, and to provide some significance both to that which surfaces in memory or dream and to that which is conspicuous or marked by its absence.

The two examples so far given (of the law relating to a woman and the home, and to the anomaly of the postal rule) both imply a certain legal politics of the sexes or more properly of gender. There is more at stake in these legal examples than is immediately apparent. In the example of the home, it should be recollected that the anomalous ruling reverts to a history in which the woman is in several legal contexts treated as property while the home and garden, the spheres of domesticity, are now treated as persons. With regard to the postal rule, the example of the law's patronage of women offerees should be placed in the context of a law of marriage in which the marriage contract is often the last contract that the married woman ever makes. She is subsequently incapable either of contracting or of making a will because she is *plene in potestate viri* – namely, in the complete power of the husband,[97] or, in Bracton's phrase, not simply not *sui iuris* but further *sub virga* or under the rod.[98] It may not be inappropriate to recollect in this context that the primary and 'simplest' division of the law of persons is not between male and female but between slave and free.[99] It is that stake, the distinction between freedom and slavery, which is the subject matter of the final example to be canvassed here – namely, the law of contempt of court and the prerogative of the Crown as opposed to the right of aliens, asylum seekers and others belonging to the category of *peregrinus* or foreigner. By way of link to the previous examples it may first be noted incidentally that the earliest foreigners to emerge within the western tradition were women, the Danaides, female and Egyptian.[100]

The distinction between slave and free is cross-cut in classical Roman law by that between citizen and foreigner. Similarly one of the oldest and most venerable of common law rules relates to the distinction between members of the community and strangers. If we start with the commonality of lawyers itself it is not insignificant that one of the first rules learned by those that joined the archetypical community of the Inns of Court was that they were prohibited from inviting 'forraigners, discontinuers . . . [and] strangers' into the Inn.[101] Other legislation of the Inns was concerned directly and unremittingly with maintaining the specific physical appearance of community. Not only were foreigners and strangers excluded from the ironically titled Inns of Court, but it was forbidden to look like a foreigner, to dress like a foreigner or to behave like a foreigner. Thus it was forbidden to have a beard or long hair; foreign colours and cuts of cloth, continental caps and ruffs were prohibited; exuberant behaviour, games, tobacco, alcohol, noise and ungodliness were also debarred.[102] While it is true that the rules governing the exclusion of foreign fashions and continental mores had a peculiar and distinctive urgency in the Reformation, the principles of patriotism and xenophobia involved are of much longer standing.

Commencing with Bracton, the legal term Englishry (*Englecerie*) refers generically to being an Englishman and also to certain consequences of such a designation in cases of murder. The antithesis of Englishry was *Francigena* or being a Frenchman, which term was taken to include all foreigners or aliens, 'all outlandish men and women and especially Danes'.[103] To be a foreigner was a synonym of being outlandish, uncouth or simply dangerous. So too by the earliest common law, again reported in Bracton, to be a stranger (*extraneum*) was equally opprobrious and suspicious and 'it was because of this suspicion that it was established that no one receive a stranger into his house or permit him to depart except in broad daylight'.[104] The legal image of the foreigner is already quite precise: she was alien, other, outlandish, extraneous and suspect. The condition was also infectious, those that travelled with foreigners or Aegyptians were likely to become not simply like them but of them.[105] In later legislation the foreigner is linked both to the stranger and to the Aegyptian. An Act of 1540, *An Act Concerning Strangers*, simply expelled foreigners, while legislation as early as 1350, *An Act Touching such as be born beyond the Seas*, specifically defined the rights of succession and of property of those born outside the 'faith and ligeance' of the English Crown.[106] It is in relation particularly to the break with Rome and with the principles of a universal church that the fear of foreigners becomes most extreme.

Rastall's *Collection in English of the Statutes in Force*, in its 1603 edition, lists five Acts of the Realm in force specifically concerning Aegyptians, foreigners and vagabonds. The associations of the stranger are insidious in the extreme and the definitions of foreignness and its consequences are multiple. Thus Aegyptians are defined as 'divers and outlandish people . . . using no craft nor seal of merchandise . . . [and who] use great subtlety and crafty means to deceive the people . . . of their money'.[107] The foreigner would take away fortune and wealth by deceit. The Aegyptian was however an amorphous or spreading category and not simply an economic and ethical threat. Later legislation defined Aegyptians further as 'foreigners – come from abroad' and continues to include 'vagabonds' who were inhabitants of England who had fallen into the ways or company of Aegyptians.

> Be it enacted . . . that every person and persons, which . . . shall within this realm of England or Wales, in any company or fellowship of vagabonds, commonly called, or calling themselves Egyptians, or counterfeiting, transporting, or disguising themselves by their apparell, speech, or other behaviour, like unto such vagabonds . . . and shall or continue to do so . . . for the space of one month . . . shall be deemed a felon.[108]

The extent of the legislative drive against the stranger, foreigner, nomad, Egyptian or vagabond suggests an extreme fear, not simply of external danger but of internal decay. Even at the level of self-representation or appearance any suggestion of foreignness had to be abhorred and legislation too frequent to tabulate governing 'apparell' was concerned as much as anything else with the avoidance of foreign cloths, cuts, fashions and colours of dress, in the interest both of recognizability but also for the avoiding of foreign vices – namely, that 'inordinate excess of apparel' associated with strangers who neither knew their place nor their degree.[109]

The fear of the strange and outlandish – Egyptian or foreign – repeats itself historically through differing institutional forms that range across Jew, barbarian, intellectual, witch, coloured, unclean, heretic, poor, ill, communist, hedonist, homeless, woman and nomad. While qualities or properties of strangeness become conflated with the terroristic exclusion of the spectre of the other as such, it is possible to trace an institutional delirium concerned with the imaginary essence of the immigrant, the alien and the foreign. Such a chorography or, in rhetorical terms, *topothesia*,[110] the feigned description or illusory mapping of the threat of foreignness against which community defines itself, has been attempted in various forms by political theory. Attempts also have been made to trace the concept of the foreign in common law, the antirrhetic or anti-portrait of those outside the 'ligeance' of social legitimacy, kinship or common identity.[111] The final example borrows from that obscure or repressed history of exclusion and examines the figure of synecdoche in the law of the land. It is by means of this metonymy, by means of a tellurian contiguity or contagion that makes the law of England the law of the land or *lex terrae*, by means of proximity (*Englecerie*) and insularity, inhabitation and domicile that alienity, foreignness and nomadism more broadly can be both defined and by definition excluded. The contemporary law, in other words, still manipulates antithetical affections. It nurtures identity and sacrifices those beyond the pale or geography of common law.

The case in question stems from an application for asylum in the United Kingdom. In *M.* v. *Home Office and Another*,[112] the letter M. marks the place where the applicant would have stood. It concerns again the circulation of a letter, an alphabetical character, M., between Zaïre, Paris and London in a case concerning a refugee. It ends with the return of the letter and the revocation of a possible contract. The letter is the letter M., a terrifying textual metonymy, a synecdoche, a minimalist monument for an asylum seeker who died so as not to confuse the cartographic fictions or heraldic symbols of common law. The letter M. is all that remains, it is the trace of a being, M. for murder, the stop mark after the letter by convention noting that further letters are missing. For the narrative purposes of the case, we pick it up in September of 1990 when the applicant originally sought political asylum in Britain. The applicant was a union organizer in Zaïre where he had participated in organizing anti-government strike action. He had been arrested and had escaped from Zaïre to Nigeria and from there to Britain. M. applied for asylum in Britain under the Geneva Convention relating to the Status of Refugees and was refused by the Home Office. The Home Office did not regard M.'s story as credible and the letter of 16 November informing M. of the decision concludes by stating the all-encompassing discretionary power of the Home Office in such cases:

> The Secretary of State recognises that a person fleeing persecution may not be able to provide documentary or other proof to support his statements . . . however, allowance for such a lack of evidence does not oblige the Secretary of State to accept unsupported evidence as necessarily being true.[113]

Although the conclusion lacks logical force – its two propositions are not connected – the issue of writing, of text and body, re-emerges in the subsequent stages of the case.

M. sought leave to apply for judicial review of the decision to refuse him asylum and his application was refused on 25 March 1991. He promptly sought to renew his application and while that application was pending he was examined by a doctor provided by the Medical Foundation for the Care of Victims of Torture. The doctor reported that

> [t]he scars he bears are entirely compatible with the causes he ascribes to them. He is suffering a degree of deafness and spinal trouble quite likely to have arisen from his mistreatment. Psychologically he describes symptoms very likely to arise from the experiences he describes.[114]

The skin was and is the first site of writing: not only was the letter (M) a brand on the forehead of the slave but inscription upon the body and the pain of mutilation were the archetypes of a memory which later became attached to writing. In the instant case the bearer of this writing was about to depart the jurisdiction: his text was about to circulate elsewhere in that pending further appeal M. was to be repatriated on 1 May.

At 5.30 p.m. on 1 May, a further application for review was made to Justice Garland, who was apprised also of the fact that M.'s plane was due to leave Britain at 6 p.m. for Paris and from there he would be transferred, still in custody, to an aircraft bound for Kinshasa, Zaïre. Justice Garland 'did what any justice would have done in these circumstances. Having concluded that the application was not frivolous, he sought to obtain an undertaking from Mr. Gordon on behalf of the Home Office that M. would not be flown out of the jurisdiction and *thus the protection* of the courts of this country' (emphasis added)[115] until after the application had been heard. The Home Office was informed of this request but, for reasons that are unclear, failed to respond in time to prevent M.'s departure to Paris from whence he was flown to Zaïre. The solicitors for M. contacted Justice Garland later that night and informed him of M.'s plight. Justice Garland responded by issuing a mandatory order for the return of M. to the jurisdiction of the court and, second, ordering that pending M.'s return he be kept in the custody of servants or agents of the Crown in Zaïre. This order was communicated to the Home Office, and the British Embassy in Zaïre was informed that M. should be placed in protective custody and returned to Britain.

M. arrived in Zaïre at 7.30 a.m. and was taken to the British Embassy pending return to Britain. In the meantime the Home Office considered the case. At a meeting later that day, the Home Secretary took advice and decided to revoke the order to return M. to the jurisdiction. The Home Secretary revoked the order, first on the grounds that the underlying decision to refuse M. refugee status was correct and would be affirmed, and second that Justice Garland had exceeded his powers in making an order against the Crown: a mandatory order against the Crown was outside the jurisdiction of the courts. The consequence of this decision was that M. was informed that his appearance in London was no longer required and he was released from the custody of the Embassy. M. was never heard from again. The question before the court, on this set of facts, was whether or not the Home Secretary, a Minister of the Crown, was in contempt of court in refusing to comply with the mandatory order issued by Justice Garland.

At first instance, before Justice Brown, it was held that the court had no power to issue a prerogative order (mandamus) against the Crown. The reason given was that the relationship between government and judiciary is one based upon 'trust'[116] and has no greater status than that of a request. We may note, somewhat ironically, that the word 'trust', coming from the old Norse 'traust' meaning 'strong' is a perhaps unwittingly appropriate description of the *de facto* relation between Crown and law but it is hardly an appropriate depiction of a legal value. On appeal, on the specific issue of contempt, the Court of Appeal found no reason to deny the court's power to issue a prerogative order, such as mandamus or habeas corpus against the Crown. While the word of the Crown 'is its bond'[117] and such orders are to be viewed as largely unnecessary, the High Court is none the less in principle a Court of unlimited jurisdiction and so is capable of issuing any orders it wishes so long as they are not illegal.

The ensuing question, whether or not the Crown could be held liable for contempt of court, has not only a symbolic significance as a form of atonement for the treatment of M., but a more considerable importance for the fate of all those that subsequently seek remedy or justice in matters of asylum. Can the Crown be made to listen to the alien, the other or the refugee? It is, after all, an age-old principle stemming from Roman law, that *in fictione juris semper est aequitas*.[118] The Court of Appeal made no reference to such a principle but rather argued that actions in contempt could only be taken against 'a person or body with sufficient legal personality. As neither the Crown nor the Home Office has any legal personality, no such proceedings can be brought against them.'[119] The logic of this decision requires careful reconstruction. The Crown, Rex or Regina, is a legal fiction without personality, it is a metaphor, and as a 'symbol of royalty, "the Crown" was no doubt [historically] a convenient way of denoting and distinguishing the monarch when doing acts of government in his political capacity from the monarch when doing private acts in his personal capacity'.[120] In this context neither 'the Crown' nor its equally fictitious substitute 'the Government' can be imbued with either natural or juridical personality. Thus, while the Home Secretary, as a Minister of the Crown, was in honour and in trust obliged to comply with the order of mandamus, no action for contempt of Court could lie if he did not. Further, it would be absurd to attempt to enforce contempt proceedings, its sanctions being *in personam*, against the Crown or government. The three remedies available, imprisonment, fine or sequestration of assets, would be each and alike ineffective. It would be impossible to imprison 'some body or thing which, whatever else it may be, is not a natural person. It would be largely futile to fine a department . . . it would be impossible to sequestrate all the Government's financial assets . . .'.[121]

What chance then does an alien or foreign natural body have against such an icon of social presence? How can a single letter be the means of holding an office and dignity in contempt and so bound to act? The 'deliberate decision'[122] to ignore an order of the Court had as its consequence the probable death of M., the sacrifice of a natural body, a refugee, a person, to the cause of preserving the symbol – the icon – of an imaginary unity and community, the mystic body of the realm, this England. As in any act of sacrifice, the symbolic was held to have priority over the real. Further, the imaginary here determined that the symbolic, the 'political body', the realm as represented in the Crown, was beyond the law. There could be no retribution against nor legal accountability for the acts of fictitious persons, non-natural bodies or imaginary juridical beings. The life of one implied the death of the other. The silence of one was the speech of the other. The incivility or alienity of one was the propriety of the other. The Court proceeded latterly to distinguish 'contempt' from more serious offences, and cited approvingly the following elaboration, 'the phrase contempt does not in the least describe the true nature of the class of offence with which we are here concerned. . . . It is not the dignity of the court which is offended – it is the fundamental supremacy of the law which is challenged.'[123] The Secretary of State for the Home Department, as a Minister of the Crown and as one 'mutually recognised' element in the 'unwritten constitution', could not be said to be in contempt either of the supremacy of law or of the dignity of its administration.[124]

At one level the example of *M.* v. *The Home Office* is a simple, though important, instance of the ultimate stake of legal fiction. The representation of legal acts, and more specifically the figures of the legal text, have striking and violent consequences. This is not to differentiate legal interpretation from other species of interpretation and enforcement, nor the community of law from other political or social forms. The issue is rather that of reading the rhetorical figure, the synecdochic letter M., the diminutive or vanished part for the whole, the disappearing sign of a deeply embedded and dramatically implemented unconscious form and conflict, that of antirrhesis or here antinomy, in the production and life of the legal text. The singular letter, the lone syntagma, the 'undocumented' stranger or outsider comes before the law and is made to wait. His testimony is disbelieved by the Home Office, yet no attempt is made to verify or falsify his narrative. He is expelled contrary to an express order of Court yet it is held that this defiance of the law is not contempt and is not punishable, at least in so far as such an action would have to lie against the other synecdoche in the case, the symbol of our unity, the icon of our presence, the Crown.[125] On one side of the conflict of this particular case, the affectivity of law holds to an image of inviolate unity, of fictive presence and of imaginary trust or honour. This affectivity constitutes that most significant of images, that of the body of the realm, of the constitution and the jurisdiction of law. On the other side of this affectivity lies a relatively silent anti-portrait, a refusal to listen, a void or absence of speech in which the other is characterized not simply as without jurisdiction but as mendacious, demanding, inconsistent and without credibility or right to any further appeal. This was an Egyptian or 'outlandish' person, *Francigena* or vagabond, not merely potentially a felon but unconsciously always already fated to being disbelieved, unknown, untruthful and eventually silent.

CONCLUSION

The example of *M.* v. *The Home Office* is a striking instance not only of the latent violence of textual interpretation but also of the rhetorical forms that constitute the *indicia* or signs of structure and not simply the surface of legal texts. The analysis of the rhetoric of the antirrhetic, of the polemical or agonistic structure of the legal unconscious, indicates a series of oppositions, antitheses or simple contradictions in the organization and force of legal thought and its corresponding forms of textuality. The legal text constitutes a visible material surface, a 'terranean' screen, a body of law whose figurative function is that of representing an invisible order, a spiritual coherence, a dogma or unity which will both identify and direct the thought or the vision of the subject of law to its licit mythic image or source. The text is only ever a sign of apparent juridical community, of a mixture of visual and epistemic control, of the combination of image and word. It is the visible surface or icon of a more complex source and belief, order and unity. The unity and identity of law experienced in and through the figures of the text are pitched against – and mark the boundaries of – an outside or externality which is both heteroclite and dispersed, confused and dissembling. The incidence and continuance of such an oppositional or antinomic argumentative structure, the explicit study of law as an instance of the dogmatic genre of an unconscious antirrhetical structure, deserves a final comment.

It might be said that the case of *M.* v. *The Home Office* represents an instance of empty speech, of a speech which has lost its subject yet cannot mourn. The text erases a letter and kills a person; it removes one possible and existent gloss and thereby it blots out a child of the text. It negates – denies, rejects or annihilates – that which is excluded from the text yet it simultaneously represses and so incorporates that other of the law. Repression drives within. Negation accepts or at least takes account of that which is repressed, and repression thereby is paradoxically symptomatic of the persistence of that which doctrine or orthodoxy would seek to exclude.[126] In the literal sense of negation it is easy to observe that the antirrhetic establishes over time an imaginary – or indeed a bestiary – of lost objects, exiled subjects, illicit images and condemned words. It peoples the text with orthodoxies, the *iuris vincula*, of dogma and faith while establishing an unconscious lexicon of the voiceless, the silent, the exiled and the excommunicated. The jurisdiction is the sphere of legal affectivity as well as the site or institutionally authorized place of its enunciation. Yet a speech which has lost its subject, a speech which represses its 'other scene' or unconscious bonds cannot mourn its losses and so cannot recognize either the death of the subject or the unconscious of the text implicit in the violence which legal discourse does to things. A final brief narrative of the symbolization of legal violence will serve as a conclusion.

It is ironic, both in relation to the last analysed case of *M.* v. *The Home Office* and in relation to current debate on the reform of legal dress, that the violence of law was traditionally recognized in the wearing of wigs. It is ironic that at a time when the legal profession and judiciary have had to face considerable criticism by virtue of miscarriages of justice, archaism and elitism, that the Lord Chancellor comes upon the idea of abolishing the wig, the emblem of the lawyer's fear of criticism. The wig, the coif, rings, robes and dinners are all significant symbols of an internal community or affective 'brotherhood' of the law. The wig and its more elaborate forerunners are mentioned in many descriptions of investiture ceremonies for Serjeants at Law.[127] 'Hoods and Coyfes' were placed on the heads of new Serjeants. The question of why is answered in terms of the 'Quoyff' being a symbol of two things:

> *videlicet*, it is a Helmet or Sallet, that they should not feare having that on to speake bowldly the Law, and *est sicut vestis candida et immaculata*, and they might weare it in [the] place of justice before the King's presens; and their partye garment and hoodd betokeneth prudence and temperancye.[128]

Again, the emblem or symbol can be reconstructed according to a historical genealogy: the coif becomes in less aggressive circumstances the wig or *perruque*, a symbolic helmet, a memory of the need to protect the learned head from attack in times when that attack would be verbal or political rather than physical. Consciously, or more probably unconsciously, the legal institution no longer wishes to recollect the sudden and surprising criticism that was formerly meted out to the sagacious cerebellum. It does not wish to look behind the symbol but rather seeks to smooth out the surface of the institution, to deflect criticism, to forget, to repeat and so to further repress.

NOTES

1 On the rhetorical art of memory, see for example the forensic rhetorical manual of T. Wilson, *The Arte of Rhetorique* [1553] (London: Garland, 1982), at 413–30, on *memoria*; and on specifically legal memory, see J. Doderidge, *The English Lawyer* (London: I. More, 1631), at 12 and 200 ff., arguing that memory is the first legal art and record its most permanent practice. On the schemata of memory see P. Ramus, *The Logike* (London: Vautroullier, 1574), at 13–14, on memory and argument. For an excellent recent study see M. Carruthers, *The Book of Memory* (Cambridge: Cambridge University Press, 1990).

2 James Calfhill, *An Answere to the Treatise of the Cross* (London: H. Denham, 1565), fol. 169 b.

3 The classic texts on language, symptom and unconscious, are S. Freud, *The Interpretation of Dreams* (New York: Avon Books, 1971); S. Freud, *Psychopathology of Everyday Life* (Harmondsworth: Pelican, 1942 edn); J. Lacan, 'The function and field of speech and language in psychoanalysis', in *Écrits: A Selection* (London: Tavistock, 1977). For discussion, see J. Lacan and A. Wilden, *Speech and Language in Psychoanalysis* (Baltimore: Johns Hopkins University Press, 1981).

4 In an Anglo-American common law context, there is a very varied history of jurisprudential recourse to psychoanalysis. See J. Frank, *Law and the Modern Mind* [1930] (Garden City, N.Y.: Anchor, 1963 edn); A. Ehrenzweig, *Psychoanalytic Jurisprudence: On Ethics, Aesthetics, and Law* (Leiden: Dordrecht, 1971); C. G. Schoenfeld, *Psychoanalysis and the Law* (Springfield, Ill.: Thomas, 1973); F. R. Beinfenfeld, 'Prolegomena to a psychoanalysis of law and justice' (1965), *California Law Review* 53, 957, 1254; Robin West, 'Law, rights and other totemic illusions: legal liberalism and Freud's theory of the rule of law' (1986), *University of Pennsylvania Law Review* 134, 817; P. Gabel, 'The phenomenology of rights consciousness and the pact of the withdrawn selves' (1984), *Texas Law Review* 62, 1563. For an important review of recent and critical works on psychoanalysis and law, see D. Caudill, 'Freud and critical legal studies: contours of a radical socio-legal psychoanalysis' (1991), *Indiana Law Review* 66, 651. In continental terms, the most important work has been that of the Lacanian lawyer, P. Legendre. His first and in many ways most influential works on psychoanalysis and law were P. Legendre, *L'amour du censeur: Essai sur l'ordre dogmatique* (Paris: Seuil, 1974); *Jouir du pouvoir: Traité de la bureaucrate patriote* (Paris: Minuit, 1976). For an introduction to his work, see P. Goodrich, 'Law's emotional body' in P. Goodrich, *Languages of Law* (London: Weidenfeld and Nicolson, 1990); N. Duxbury, 'Psychoanalytic theory and Roman law in modern continental jurisprudence' (1989), *Legal Studies* 9, 94; Y. Hachamovitch, 'One law on the other' (1990), *International Journal for the Semiotics of Law* 3, 187.

5 This theme is central to J. Lacan, *Écrits: A Selection*, and see also Lacan, *The Four Fundamental Concepts of Psychoanalysis* (London: Pelican, 1978). See further, Lacan, *Le seminaire IV: L'Ethique de la Psychanalyse* (Paris: Seuil, 1990). On the educational significance of this theme, see P. Rush, 'Killing me softly with his words' (1990), *Law and Critique* 1, 21; P. Goodrich, 'Psychoanalysis in legal education: notes on the violence of the sign', in R. Kevelson (ed.), *Law and Semiotics* (New York: Plenum Press, 1987). More broadly see P. Gabel and D. Kennedy, 'Roll over Beethoven' (1984), *Stanford Law Review* 36, 1.

6 On which theme, see particularly P. Legendre, *Le Crime du Caporal Lortie: Traité sur le père* (Paris: Fayard, 1989); A. Papageorgiou-Legendre, *Filiation: Fondement généalogique de la psychanalyse* (Paris: Fayard, 1990). For a discussion of the former work, see A. Pottage, 'Crime and culture: the relevance of the psychoanalytical' (1992), *Modern Law Review* 55, 421.

7 This theme is addressed directly in D. Caudill, 'Lacan and legal language: meanings in the gaps, gaps in the meaning' (1992), *Law and Critique* 3, 165.
8 See S. Freud, *The Psychopathology of Everyday Life* (Harmondsworth: Pelican, 1914); G. Obeyesekere, *The Work of Culture* (Chicago: University of Chicago Press, 1990): J. Derrida, *Writing and Difference* (New York: Routledge, 1978); P. Ricoeur, *Freud and Philosophy: An Essay on Interpretation* (New Haven: Yale University Press, 1977).
9 These figures are drawn primarily from G. Puttenham, *The Arte of English Poesie* (London: Field, 1589); Henry Peacham, *The Garden of Eloquence conteining the most excellent Ornaments, Exornations, Lightes, Flowers and formes of Speech commonly called the figures of rhetorike* (London: H. Jackson, 1593). Further useful lists and discussions can be found in T. Farnaby, *Index Rhetoricus* (London: R. Allot, 1633); J. Smith, *The Mysterie of Rhetorique Unvail'd* (London: E. Cotes, 1657).
10 See, for this particular classification, Smith, *Mysterie of Rhetorique*, at fol B 1 b.
11 See particularly Puttenham, *Arte of Poesie*, at 155–61.
12 Smith, *Mysterie of Rhetorique*, at fol B 4 b.
13 Quintilian, *Institutio Oratoria* (on *enargeia*); B. Lamy, *The Art of Speaking* (London: Godbid, 1676); and more broadly, J. Derrida, 'The white mythology', in Derrida, *Margins of Philosophy* (Brighton: Harvester, 1982); P. Goodrich, 'We orators' (1990), *Modern Law Review* 53, 546.
14 See S. Freud, *Beyond the Pleasure Principle* (London: Hogarth Press, 1961 edn).
15 Puttenham, *Arte of Poesie*, at 155–6; Smith, *Mysterie of Rhetorique*, at E 6 a.
16 Smith, *Mysterie of Rhetorique*, at S 5 b.
17 In most of the curricula manuals hearer and judge are synonyms, as, for example, in Puttenham, *Arte of Poesie*, at 189.
18 This Aristotelian dictum is discussed in B. Vickers, *In Defence of Rhetoric* (Oxford: Clarendon Press, 1988) at 77.
19 *Antirrhesis* is defined by Henry Peacham, *The Garden of Eloquence*, at sig N iv b–N v a, 'Antirrhesis is a form of speech by which the orator rejecteth the authority, opinion or sentence of some person: for the error or wickedness of it . . . this form of speech doth especially belong to confutation and is most apt to repell errors and heresies, and to reject evil counsell and lewd perversions.' For an extended analysis, see P. Goodrich, 'Antirrhesis: the polemical structures of common law thought', in A. Sarat and T. Kearns (eds), *Rhetoric and Law* (Ann Arbor: Michigan University Press, 1994).
20 This argument is made most forcefully by M. Foucault, 'The discourse on language', reprinted as an appendix to M. Foucault, *The Archaeology of Knowledge* (New York: Pantheon, 1982). For an interesting example of this thesis, see J. Godolphin, *Repertorium Canonicum or, An Abridgement of the Ecclesiastical Laws of this Realm consistent with the Temporal* [1678] (London: Atkins, 1687 edn), especially ch. XL, 'Of Blasphemy and Heresy'.
21 Daniel Tuvil, *Essaies Politike and Morall* (London: M. Lownes, 1608), fols. 15b–16a.

22 As for example in Dudley Fenner, *The Artes of Logike and Rhetorike* (Middleburg, 1584); Richard Sherry, *A Treatise of Schemes and Tropes very profytable for the better understanding of good authors, gathered out of the best Grammarians and Orators* (London: Day, 1550).
23 Lamy, *The Art of Speaking* [1675] (Carbondale, Ill.: University of Southern Illinois Press, 1986 edn), at 226.
24 See J. Davies, *Of the Antiquity of Lawful Combats in England* [1601], in Grosart (ed.), *The Works* (Private Circulation, 1869).
25 *Attia* v. *British Gas plc* [1987] 2 AER 455.
26 Ibid., at 456 g–j.
27 *McLoughlin* v. *O'Brian and others* [1982] 2 AER 298.
28 *Alcock and others* v. *Chief Constable of the South Yorkshire Police* [1991] 4 AER 907.
29 *McLoughlin* v. *O'Brian*, at 304 f–g.
30 Ibid., at 304 f–h. Cited and approved in *Alcock*, at 912–13.
31 Ibid., at 302 f–g.
32 For discussion of this issue, see W. T. Murphy and R. W. Rawlings, 'After the ancien regime: the writing of judgments in the House of Lords 1979/1980' (1981), *Modern Law Review* 44, 617; P. Goodrich, *Reading the Law* (Oxford: Blackwell, 1986), ch. 6. More broadly, see W. T. Murphy, 'The oldest social science? The epistemic properties of the common law tradition' (1991), *Modern Law Review* 54, 182; and P. Goodrich, 'Poor illiterate reason' (1992), *Social and Legal Studies* 1, 7.
33 Ibid., at 311 e.
34 *Jaensch* v. *Coffey* [1984] 54 ALR 417, at 457 (per DEANE J).
35 On rescue see *Chadwick* v. *British Transport Commission* [1967] 2 AER 945; on workmates see *Dooley* v. *Cammell Laird & Co Ltd* [1951] 1 Lloyd's Rep 271; and for an Australian example see *Mount Isa Mines Ltd* v. *Pusey* [1970] 125 CLR 383.
36 *Owens* v. *Liverpool Corporation* [1938] 4 AER 727.
37 Ibid., at 730 f–g.
38 It should be noted that for Peacham, *Garden of Eloquence*, at E iii b, *antonomasia* is listed under 'tropes of words', while for Puttenham, *Art of Poesie*, at 168, it is listed under figures. While it is properly a trope, *antonomasia* can also be a figure of speech where it is used argumentatively rather than simply as an 'improper' or 'borrowed' sense.
39 Smith, *Mysterie of Rhetorique*, at B 4 a.
40 H. Peacham, *The Garden of Eloquence*, at sig E iii b. See also John Smith, *The Mysterie of Rhetorique*, at F 1 b; and B. Lamy, *Art of Speaking*, at 215.
41 *Attia*, at 461 c–d.
42 Ibid., at 464 c–d.
43 Ibid., at 464 e–f.
44 *Watts and another* v. *Morrow* [1991] 4 AER 937, where mental distress occasioned by a negligent survey of a 'second home' could not be recovered either in tort or in contract, despite the fact that at least one of the appellants had 'fallen in love' with the house.
45 *Semayne's Case* [1605] 5 Co Rep 91.
46 Thomas Wood, *An Institute of the Laws of England* (Savoy: Sare, 1720 edn), at 735–6.

47 Ibid., at 652.

48 *Entick* v. *Carrington and three others*, 1765, in *State Trials* (London: Hansard, 1813), vol. xix, at 1066.

49 See, *Magna Carta with short but necessary observations by Lord Chief Justice Coke* (London: Atkins, 1680 edn), particularly fol H iv b, K i a.

50 See *Bruce* v. *Rawlins* [1770] 95 Eng Rep 934; *Ratcliffe* v. *Burton* [1802] 27 Eng Rep 123.

51 See *An Act to retain the Queen's subjects in obedience*, 1593, (35 Eliz. cap I).

52 See *Queen's Injunctions*, 1559, extracted in G. Prothero (ed.), *Select Statutes and other Constitutional Documents illustrative of the Reigns of Elizabeth and James I* (Oxford: Clarendon Press, 1894), at 185–7.

53 See C. Jung, *Memories, Dreams, Reflections* (London: Collins and Routledge, 1963 edn), especially 221 ff.

54 See Sir Henry Spelman, *The History and Fate of Sacrilege* [1632] (London: J. Hartley, 1698 edn), at 22–5.

55 John Selden, *Titles of Honour* (London: W. Stansby, 1614), at fol b 4 a. For extensive discussion of this theme of genealogical legitimacy, see P. Legendre, *L'inestimable objet de la transmission* (Paris: Fayard, 1985), and more technically, see P. Legendre, *Le dosier occidental de la parenté: Textes juridiques indésirables sur la généalogie* (Paris: Fayard, 1988).

56 *Owens* v. *Liverpool Corporation*, at 730.

57 Sir Thomas Smith, *De Republica Anglorum* [1583] (Cambridge University Press, 1982 edn), at 58–9 ('The first sort or beginning of an House or Familie called Oikonomia').

58 See J. Godolphin, *Repertorium Canonicum*; H. Swinburne, *A Treatise of Spousals, or Matrimonial Contracts* [1686] (London: D. Brown, 1711 edn); and on the common law, see Anon., *Baron and Feme: A Treatise of the Common Law concerning Husbands and Wives* (London: Walthoe, 1700). On the duties of women, see W. Perkins, *Christian Oeconomie: Or a Short Survey of the Right Manner of Erecting and Ordering a Family* (Cambridge: Cantrell Press, 1609); J. L. Vives, *The Instruction of a Christen Woman* [1523] (London: H. Wykes, 1557 edn), and R. Allestree, *The Ladies Calling* (n.p., 1673).

59 On the use of this metaphor, see P. Legendre, 'Analecta' in Papageogiou-Legendre, *Filiation*, at 216–18 (on Freud's concept of *l'autre scene*).

60 *Adams* v. *Lindsell* [1818] 1 B & Ald 681; *Henthorn* v. *Fraser* [1892] 2 Ch 27; *Holwell Securities* v. *Hughes* [1974] 1 WLR 155.

61 For a useful and extensive American discussion, see *Morrison* v. *Thoelke* [1963] 155 So2d 889, District Court of Florida, and, more broadly, Dawson, Harvey and Henderson, *Cases and Comments on Contracts* (New York: Foundation Press, 1987), pp. 424–5. See further E. A. Farnsworth, *Contracts* (Boston: Little, Brown and Co, 1990), at 180–5. Also of interest is K. Llewellyn, 'Our case law of contract: offer and acceptance' (pt 2) (1939), *Yale Law Journal* 48, 779, especially 792–8.

62 Simon Gardiner, 'Trashing with Trollope: a deconstruction of the postal rules in contract' (1922), *Oxford Journal of Legal Studies* 12, 170; also P. Goodrich, 'Contractions: a linguistic philosophy of the postal rule', in P. Goodrich, *Languages of Law: From Logics of Memory to Nomadic Masks*

(London: Weidenfeld and Nicolson, 1990): C. Douzinas and R. Warrington, 'Posting the law: social contracts and the postal rule's grammatology' (1991), *International Journal for the Semiotics of Law* 4, 115.

63 G. Treitel, *The Law of Contract* (London: Sweet and Maxwell, 1991), p. 24; P. Atiyah, *An Introduction to the Law of Contract* (Oxford: Clarendon Press, 1989), p. 77; *Brinkibon Ltd* v. *Stahag Stahl und Stahlwarenhandelsgesellschaft mbH* [1983] 2 AC 34.

64 See additionally, A. Nusbaum, 'Comparative aspects of the Anglo-American offer-and-acceptance doctrine' (1936), *Columbia Law Review* 33, 920; P. Winfield, 'Some aspects of offer and acceptance' (1939), *Law Quarterly Review* 55, 499; M. P. Sharp, 'Reflections on contract' (1966), *University of Chicago Law Review* 33, 211.

65 Nusbaum, 'Offer-acceptance doctrine', at 922. That Nusbaum, in a paper that originated as a seminar presentation to Karl Llewellyn's contracts class, refers to psychoanalysis should not come as a surprise, granted the influence of Freud upon the realists in the 1930s. For a discussion of this point see particularly N. Duxbury, 'Jerome Frank and the legacy of legal realism' (1991), *Journal of Law and Society* 18, 175. See also D. Caudill, 'Freud and critical legal studies', at 662–7. The major realist discussion of psychoanalysis and law is probably J. Frank, *Law and the Modern Mind*.

66 Gardiner, 'Trashing with Trollope', at 184.

67 Ibid., at 192.

68 *Holwell Securities* v. *Hughes* [1974] 1 WLR 155, at 157 (per RUSSELL LJ).

69 Gardiner, 'Trashing with Trollope', at 192.

70 Ibid., at 176.

71 See Douzinas and Warrington, 'Posting the law', at 123–5; Goodrich, *Languages of Law*, at 150–2.

72 The 'Purloined Letter' is much discussed within psychoanalysis and also increasingly within law: J. Lacan, 'Seminar on the Purloined Letter' (1972), *Yale French Studies* 48, 39; J. Derrida, 'Le Facteur de la Vérité', in Derrida, *The Post Card From Socrates to Freud and Beyond* (Chicago: Chicago University Press, 1987); S. Felman, *Jacques Lacan and the Adventure of Insight* (Cambridge, Mass.: Harvard University Press, 1987), ch. 2; Caudill, 'Lacan and legal language', at 200 ff.

73 Douzinas and Warrington, 'Posting the law', at 124. The argument comes directly from G. C. Cheshire and C. H. S. Fifoot, *Law of Contract* (London: Butterworth, 1991), at 53: '[the rule] is perhaps less surprising if we attend to the history of the matter. *Adams* v. *Lindsell* was the first genuine offer and acceptance case in English law and, in 1818 there was no rule that acceptance must be communicated. As so often happens in English law, the exception is historically anterior to the rule.'

74 This argument is suggested by E. A. Farnsworth, 'Meaning in the law of contracts' (1967), *Yale Law Journal* 76, 939, at 945.

75 J. Derrida, *The Post Card*, at 65.

76 W. West, *The First Part of Symbolaeography, which may be termed the art, or description, of Instruments and Presidents, or the Notary or Scrivener* [1590] (London: T. Wright, 1603 edn), particularly sig A 8 a.

77 T. Phayr, *A New Boke of Presidents, in manner of a Register* (London: Whytchurche, 1554), at fol ii a.
78 Sir Edward Coke, *The First Part of the Institutes of the Laws of England. Or, a Commentary upon Littleton* (London: J. More, 1629), at sig C 6 a.
79 Doderidge, *English Lawyer*, at 51.
80 Gloss to D 18 1 1 2 (*et per literas*), discussed in J. Gordley, *The Philosophical Origins of Modern Contract Doctrine* (Oxford: Clarendon Press, 1991), at 45–6.
81 Gordley, *Modern Contract Doctrine*, at 46.
82 A. Alciatus, *De Notitia Dignitatem* (Paris: Cramoisy, 1651 edn), at 190.
83 Gordley, *Modern Contract Doctrine*, at 46.
84 On the position of Roman law in England during the reception, see F. de Zulueta and P. Stein, *The Teaching of Roman Law in England around 1200* (London: Selden Society, 1990). H. de Bracton, *On the Laws of Customs of England* (Thorne, Cambridge, Mass.: Harvard University Press, 1968 edn), vol. II at 62–5 and 283–90, evidences a clear knowledge of glossatorial discussion of the *Digest*, on gifts, contracts and obligations.
85 See particularly A. W. B. Simpson, *A History of the Common Law of Contract: The Rise of the Action of Assumpsit* (Oxford: Clarendon Press, 1987).
86 See particularly Simpson, 'Innovation in nineteenth century contract law' (1977), *Law Quarterly Review* 91, 247; Gordley, *Modern Contract Doctrine*, at 161–214.
87 I shall concentrate here upon H. Swinburne, *A Treatise of Spousals, or Matrimonial Contracts* [1686] (London: Browne, 1711 edn); J. Godolphin, *Repertorium Canonicum*; Anon., *Baron and Feme*; Thomas Wood, *An Institute of the Laws of England* (Savoy: Sare, 1720 edn). I deal with some aspects of this in more detail in P. Goodrich, 'Gynaetopia: an essay on early legal feminism' (1993), *Journal of Law and Society* 20, 276.
88 Swinburne, *Treatise of Spousals*, at 63.
89 Ibid., at 63–4.
90 Ibid., at 178.
91 Ibid., at 180.
92 Ibid., at 181.
93 On which see Anon., *Baron and Feme*, at 4–6, 214–17. Thomas Wood, *Institute*, at 96–103. For interesting discussion in the case-law, see *Copland* v. *Pyatt*, Trinity Term, 6 Car. 1 Roll 687, 79 ER 814. For discussion of the political implications of these rules, see C. Pateman, *The Sexual Contract* (Cambridge: Polity Press, 1988).
94 *British and American Telegraph Co* v. *Colson* [1871] LR 6 Exch 108, at 118.
95 On the *longue durée* and social science, see F. Braudel, *On History* (Chicago: University of Chicago Press, 1980), at 25–55.
96 FORTESCUE J., in *Anon* [1458] YB 36 Hen. VI 25–6.
97 The rule is elaborated in Glanvill, *Tractatus de Legibus et Consuetudinibus Regni Angliae qui Glanvilla Vocatur* [1187–1189] (London: Nelson, 1965), at 59. See further, Anon., *Baron and Feme*, at 4–7. On testaments, see further H. Swinburne, *A Briefe Treatise of Testaments and Last Wills* [1590] (London: Society of Stationers, 1635 edn); J. Godolphin, *The Orphan's*

Legacy or A Testamentary Abridgement in Three Parts (London: Wilkinson, 1677).

98 de Bracton, H., *De Legibus* (ed. S. Thorn) (Cambridge, Mass.: Harvard University Press, 1978, 2 vols), at 35.

99 This classification derives from Gaius. See F. de Zulueta (ed.), *The Institutes of Gaius, Part I* (Oxford: Clarendon Press, 1946 edn), at 4 ('omnes homines aut liberi sunt aut servi'). de Bracton, *De Legibus*, at 29, repeats the definition.

100 On which point, see J. Kristeva, *Strangers to Ourselves* (Hemel Hempstead: Harvester/Wheatsheaf, 1991), at 42: 'it is noteworthy to observe that the first foreigners to emerge at the dawn of our civilisation are foreign women – the Danaides.'

101 William Dugdale, *Origines Juridiciales or Historical Memorials of the English Laws* [1666] (Savoy: Newcomb, 1671 edn), at fol. 192 a–b, referring to legislation of the Middle Temple of 1631 and 1635. This literature is commented on in P. Goodrich, 'Eating law: commons, common land, common law' (1991), *Journal of Legal History* 12, 246.

102 See Dugdale, *Origines Juridiciales*, at 148–55, 191–5.

103 de Bracton, *De Legibus*, at vol. II, 381–3. See also J. Cowell, *The Interpreter or Book containing the Signification of Words* [1608] (London: Shoanes, 1637 edn).

104 de Bracton, *De Legibus*, at vol. II, 387.

105 For an excellent analysis of this metaphor of the alien as viral, drawing upon J. Baudrillard, *La transparence du mal* (Paris: Fayard, 1990), see P. Minkkinen, 'Otherness and difference: on the cultural logic of racial intolerance' (1992), *Law and Critique* 3, 147.

106 Respectively, 1540 32 Hen. VIII cap 16, and 1350 25 Edw. cap 2, which was confirmed in 1386 in 42 Edw. III cap. 10.

107 Master Justice Rastall, *A Collection in English, of the Statutes now in Force, continued from the beginning of Magna Charta . . . untill the end of the Parliament holden in the three and fortieth yere of the reigne of our late soveraigne lady Queene Elizabeth* (London: T. Wright, 1603), at 144c–145c.

108 Ibid., at sig 145b.

109 Ibid., at 12a–14c. For a contemporaneous discussion of wanton excess of dress and of the insidious character of appearing like a foreigner or a woman, see William Harrison, *An Historicall Description of the Island of Britaine, with a brief rehersall of the nature and qualities of the people of England* (London: n.p., 1586), at fols 172a–173a, stating that 'nothing is more constant in England than inconstancy of attire. Oh how much cost is bestowed nowadays upon our bodies and how little upon our souls.'

110 Peacham, *Garden of Eloquence*, at fol U iii a.

111 For an interesting discussion of this theme, see C. Douzinas and R. Warrington, 'A well-founded fear of justice; law and ethics in postmodernity' (1991), *Law and Critique* 2, 115; D. Cornell, *The Philosophy of the Limit* (New York: Routledge, 1992).

112 *M.* v. *Home Office and Another* [1992] 2 WLR 73.

113 Ibid., at 81.

114 Ibid.

115 Ibid., at 84.

116 Ibid., at 80.

117 Ibid., at 92.

118 Translation: 'fiction in law is always toward just ends'. See, for example, *Wilkes* v. *The Earl of Halifax* [1769] 2 Wils KB 256 (95 ER 797).

119 *M.* v. *Home Office and Another*, at 94.

120 *Town Investments Ltd and Others* v. *Dept of Environment* [1978] AC 359, at 380, per Lord Diplock.

121 *M.* v. *Home Office and Another*, at 95.

122 Ibid., at 98.

123 *M.* v. *Home Office*, at 98, citing *Johnson* v. *Grant* [1923] SC 789, 790.

124 Ibid., at 99.

125 The majority in the case held that an action could lie against the Home Secretary, Mr Kenneth Baker, in person. In person, however, while Mr Baker could in principle be held in contempt, he would not be regarded as being in any great measure culpable and in consequence the action would have no significant effect, nor would the then Home Secretary be personally liable for any fine consequent upon a ruling of contempt.

126 See S. Freud, 'Negation', in S. Freud, *General Psychological Theory* (New York: Collier Macmillan, 1963). For further discussion of negation, see J. Kristeva, *Revolution in Poetic Language* (New York: Columbia University Press, 1984); on 'empty speech', see Lacan, *Ecrits*, ch. 3; M. Borch-Jacobsen, *The Freudian Subject* (London: Macmillan, 1989).

127 See Dugdale, *Origines Juridiciales*, fols 118a–122b. See also J. H. Baker, *The Order of Serjeants at Law* (London: Selden Society, 1984).

128 The source is Sir Christopher Wraye, Lord Chief Justice, cited in Dugdale, *Origines Juridiciales*, sig 120a.

Part II

The law of law

Chapter 5

The paternity of law

Alain Pottage

> A master at last. It is good that men should have a master who can make them feel the fierce omnipotence of God, the inexorable steel of the law.
>
> Pierre Drieu la Rochelle, *Memoirs*

THE USES OF PSYCHOANALYSIS

An infamous science

The appeal of psychoanalytical theory was spectacularly enhanced through Jacques Lacan's elliptical 'return to Freud'. Lacan's shamanism conjured away our 'naïve' image of Freud as the *bourgeois rangé de Vienne*, and made way for a rather more irreverent, cosmopolitan – and, significantly, a *francophone* – figure. Lacan adjusted Freud's recipe for psychoanalysis so as to emphasize its muted hints of myth, poetry and irony. In doing so, he fashioned a distinctive model of the 'scientific' nature of the enterprise: 'One might say that, although [the *discours analytique*] is not altogether a discourse of science, it is conditioned by it, in the sense that the discourse of science has no place for man' (Lacan 1991: 171).

'Man' as the 'self' conceived by Reason is for this science an impossible fiction, haunted by the unsayable – or unspeakable – horrors of the unconscious. The discourse of the analytic scene has no place for this 'self', only for the desire that speaks in its place. From this vision, there emerges a deeply pessimistic rendering of that vital question: what makes our world *interesting*?; or, quite simply, what *makes* our world? The 'world' as we would see it is simply a projection of phantasmic representations stitched together in an attempt to make an insufferable lack sufferable.

For law's 'postmodern' critics, this other-worldly sorcery has evident attractions. The *other scene* addressed by the psychoanalytic conversation offers one arena for the exploration of the repressed attachments of law. And – precisely because it expresses the delirium of a domain which exceeds and precedes the Reason of law – it is almost of the essence of this discourse that it should be a 'hysterical' discourse of aimless fluidity, and hence a ready vehicle for the *linguisterie* that characterizes so much of the 'postmodern' critique. Perhaps too, desire – as a substitute for so many discredited stories of ideology and power – supplies a more malleable metaphor for the agency that holds the subject to the machinery of 'domination' or 'alienation'. This might refresh some jaded critical sensibilities, but there are dangers in such an assimilation or 'application'. Most of all, one may be too readily seduced by the attraction that, in any disagreement, the psychoanalyst-as-master has already (anticipatedly) had the last word.

The stakes in these uses of psychoanalytical theory are more problematic than such appropriations might recognize. The 'true' *lacanien* would have to be as waywardly respectful as Lacan the *freudien*: the *style* of the psychoanalyst is his most enduring legacy (Lacan 1966: 458). By that standard, Pierre Legendre seems a fitting heir to the shaman's mantle. Legendre's *Lecons* (for an introduction see Goodrich 1990: ch. 8) are a work of juridical thought, but, precisely because they slice so brusquely across what is conventionally – or critically – treated as 'law', and into a more extensive domain of mythical productions, they reveal an almost Lacanian capacity for stimulating and disrupting thought. Unfortunately, the word 'style' has in this context become rather overworked and under-productive: here, it refers to a unique work of thinking, in which the presentation of the text produces an effect which problematizes the text itself, catching the reader in a peculiar sort of double bind. How can one speak *of* or read *about* desire when everything is spoken in the voice of desire?

The problem of psychoanalytical theory is that the figure of desire only subsists *in* our desire for it. Desire, communicated through the medium of textual performance, is only meaningful because the search for a Master – the *belief* in the mastery of the text – projects a meaning onto it. How else could something as insubstantial and as frankly impossible as the *signifiant-maître* – the master signifier: an emblem which simultaneously represents 'pure' lack and 'pure' plenitude – be taken as religiously as it (sometimes) is? In the case of Legendre's *Leçons*, this double bind is as knowingly and teasingly exploited as it is in Lacan's texts. Only our implication in the regime of Law – in the expansive sense signalled by Legendre's use of the capital 'L' – enables us to recognize the regime of Law which the texts relay. This is not a work of explanation, but one of 'showing'. Perhaps for that reason, to write about Legendre is almost immediately to write *against* Legendre. However, in what is doubtless a betrayal of that point, this chapter addresses the association made in the *Leçons* between L/law and a function of 'paternity'.

Law, according to Legendre, is a far more pervasive and obscure phenomenon than our conventional learning allows. Indeed, Law in his sense is not especially the province of lawyers; lawyers deal with Law quite unwittingly. They are, for Legendre, the practitioners of a sophisticated sort of 'imbecility'. Legal reasoning is a sort of folly, or a work of repression which, in a style characteristic of the discourses of Management and Reason, allows us to forget who and what we are. The business of reasoning, classifying, putting in order, makes of lawyers the 'refuse collectors' of industrial society, whose function it is to sweep the embarrassing debris of myth or unreason away from the edifice of the industrial order. However, as participants in this *volonté moderne d'ignorer* – the modern will to ignorance – (Legendre 1985: 180) lawyers work despite themselves to perpetuate the very condition which their efforts are supposed to exorcise. The attempt to repress unreason or myth is in effect the realization of the truth of a particular myth: that of Reason in the juridical style. Rather than the label 'law', one should adopt Legendre's revitalized notion of the 'dogmatic'. Through the twists of a quasi-Heideggerian exercise in constructive etymology (see Legendre 1983: 25–33), we arrive at a sense of the dogmatic which connotes the lyricism of a shadow zone which is neither psyche nor soma.

Dogma – according to this etymology – connotes the state of one who is in the thrall of visions or dreams. Dogmatism is the juridical art of enticing and fascinating the desire which makes the unconscious so susceptible to the enchantment of the image. Law is therefore steeped in a *zone d'ombre* – in the sense of Freud's *anderer Schauplatz* – which relays the desiring subject to the montages of culture. The dogmatic function is that of weaving representations which seduce and ultimately fascinate the desiring subject, holding it in an erotic attachment to the figure of the Absolute as represented in an appointed montage. This style of representation requires something quite different from what is conventionally taken to be 'speech' or 'communication'; this is the realm of the unsayable. To experience it, according to the *Leçons*, we must learn to make thought less of a matter for speech (*'apprenez à penser en parlant un peu moins'* – Legendre 1983: 17). The underside – or 'margin' – of speech is the province of ritual, or a sort of theatricality which conveys the pure charisma of the Absolute, giving form and expression to the emptiness of pure power. The language of Law is nothing other than this poetry of power.

Law in this extended sense is *everything*: desire according to the juridical style so thoroughly monopolizes the discourse of belief that the *Corpus Iuris Civilis* prescribes for the unconscious a code of its engagement with the world. This has one quite startling quality: in giving a historical or cultural shape to the unconscious it fashions a work of history which makes of the present something just as fantastic and absurd as the more recondite disputations of medieval theology. The emblems of the past speak for themselves, or for the sensuality which they once gripped, but through Legendre's unique history of the present we are confronted with our own implication in this style of representation (notably through the liturgical imagery of advertising). We acquire a sentiment that our own sensibilities are just as absurdly or irrationally susceptible as those of our ancestors. This vitality is quite priceless. Studies of law and myth are much in vogue, but none approaches the erudition and verve of this exercise in twisting our tradition back to front, making the present as unsettlingly unfamiliar – or as horrific – as a mythical past.

Law, paternity and the bonds of belief

Law is the patron of certain traditional arts of fascination and seduction, which work to symbolize and legitimate a fiction of absolute power. In Legendre's terms, this emblem is the 'Reference'; a principle which guarantees the truth of a culture's symbolic order. If the styles of Law, religion and myth seem to replicate each other, it is simply because each is a mode of manufacturing and manipulating bonds of *belief*; of forging unconscious identifications with this 'Reference'. In industrialized society as much as any other, causation – or more accurately the Cause of the world – remains mystical: in Wittgenstein's terms, even the 'calculative' mode of thought rests on a 'normative' foundation. Here, it is apposite to recall the sense in which for the *Année Sociologique* school the question of Cause invoked the category of magic, the sacred, or *mana*. For us as much as for 'primitive' man, our world picture, our world, depends upon the communication of a 'Reference': God, the state, the Constitution, or some such representation of mystical origin.

According to Legendre's etymology, communication connotes a process of 'making common' (Legendre 1988: 402) as much as it does a style of address. And, what is 'made common' through the 'innoculation' of the Reference is a corpus of cultural material which serves as the foundation for each and every individual human identity. Law's aesthetic captures and institutionalizes the vital energy of human life, securing the raw material which sustains the social order, and at the same time offering a viable, liveable, identity for the desiring subject. Quite simply, outside the symbolic order, 'life cannot live': 'The vital issue for the social order is to ensure that life is not stifled, but made to live; not only must human flesh be produced, it must also be instituted' (Legendre 1985: 10). Law then supplies an answer to that vital question: what is humanity or human being?

Indeed, Law supplies more than an answer; it constructs the thing itself. Subjectivity and subjectification are essentially juridical. The *persona* or simulacrum with which the desiring subject identifies – the role which is assigned to the subject by the logic of the symbolic order; or, to be more specific, the *name* and the functions, duties and attachments which it symbolizes – is constructed and valorized according to a characteristically juridical aesthetic of Reason. The system of western culture is a sequence of texts, ordered and interpreted according to a juridical logic of textual practice. The cycle of life as the succession of birth and death is symbolized in juridical terms. The classical Roman law categories of *persona* and *res*, or *potestas* and *dominium*, construct for the subject an identity within an order of legitimate descent:

> Designation according to the juridical style – according, that is, to the categories of Roman law and its successors – serves to assign the human subject a status within the reproduction of species, not only so as to identify the subject and catalogue it as one of an indefinite number of replications of the category of the *person*, but also so as to allow this latter category to function as a conduit for the unconscious identifications which structure the subject's confrontation with death, and which have to do with the notorious question of incest.
>
> (Legendre 1985: 29)

One might say that these juridical categories are not only cognitive categories – ways of *knowing* the world – but also existential categories

– ways of *being in* the world. Subjectivity is defined, communicated and *lived* through a language of law and lineage.

Juridical reason is then the progenitor of institutional lives, and thus claimant to a status of 'paternity' in the psychoanalytical sense of that term. The second birth – or the *instituting* – of the subject is attributable to the paternity of the Reference. This model of a second birth is a reference to the transfer of desire and to the balance of origin and transcendental destiny in the economy of subjective desire. The juridical *persona*, which is a sort of symbol of the Absolute, functions as a substitute for the womb as irretrievable origin.

The moment of (first) birth is a moment of loss; to be more precise, a loss of dwelling. The womb is the originary *lieu*, an envelope, receptacle, or vessel for the self (Irigaray 1984: 41–94); and this dwelling, symbolized according to the nostalgia of masculine desire, is retrospectively constructed as a state of total self-containment. The womb as the house of man is then a sort of enveloping skin which through its contiguity and exteriority imparts a sense of unity. To be in one's place, in one place, is to be limited, bounded, and so assured of an identity. At the moment of birth, when the subject is cast out of its 'proper' place, the consequent separation from the primal dwelling inaugurates a dynamic of attraction, which is mediated by the desire for an ideal. This ideal incorporates a dual reference, symbolizing two impossible states of self-containment: the lost womb and an unattainable God. According to Legendre, the subject first seeks compensation in the figure of the mother, or rather in a narcissistic fascination with its own image reflected in the mother. The moment of the 'second' birth, of entry into the order of culture, is dependent upon a transfer of desire from this image to that of the transcendental Reference – namely, the image of the Father. Law's paternity consists in generating an identity cast in the image of the Reference, and enticing the desiring subject to identify with this substitute dwelling in the kingdom of the Absolute. As Roman law had it, *Mater certissima, pater semper incertus* (cited in Legendre 1983: 110); paternity is always uncertain, and the legitimacy of the claim is measured in the norms of culture rather than according to the mechanics of biology.

However, for Legendre, the West has, since the rise of Nazism, witnessed the dissolution of the classical juridical techniques of subjectification, the legal arts which wove the delicate bonds holding the desiring subject to the *corpus mysticum* of the Absolute. In place of the stories of penitence and sacrifice through which these discourses of Law represented the transcendent power of God, the regime of

Management and Science has installed an instrumental, biogenetic, account of subjectivity. Human reproduction as a question for religious or cultural interpretation has been replaced with a technology which makes of it scarcely more than the production of meat (see Legendre 1988). In appointing Science as the guarantor of the institutional order, western culture has 'de-metaphorized' the field of Law – replacing the enchanted words of the Law as interpreter with a form of brute accountancy. Power is not registered as something mythical – to be represented but never apprehended – but is instead projected as something knowable and tractable.

Modern industrial culture repudiates the classical juridical approach to reproduction and subjectivity, and instead constitutes Science as the ultimate normative authority. And Science, as the master of an infinitely manipulable Nature, duly affirms that nothing is either impossible or forbidden. The only recognizable limits being the bounds of scientific competence, the classical juridical fictions are apt to be treated as nothing more than obsolete ramblings. So, there emerges the psychotic figure of the unlimited subject, expressed in a sort of liberalism according to which each person is a sovereign state in miniature. The subject of liberalism and science is a subject *hors la loi*, one whose relations with others are predicated upon an *if I so wish* – namely, an operational denial of any authentically juridical (contractual) relation. What is so dangerous about this displacement of juridical reason is that it offers no resistance to the megalomania of incestuous desire. The virtue – indeed, the whole point – of the classical techniques was that they opposed and manipulated unconscious desire. Juridical reason interprets in the sense of being an intermediary; it functions as an agent of separation, distancing and limiting the subject *vis-à-vis* the Reference, and so constructing viable relations between self and other. The classical juridical fictions established a distinctive and indispensable relay between the symbolic order and unconscious desire. In disregarding those fictions we disregard the essential and effective nature of our culture: 'The question is not: what is the industrial system to do with this tradition whose contents are so outdated? Rather, we should ask: what can the contemporary legal order do with its constitutive style of questioning?' (Legendre 1985: 352).

There is a high price to be paid for this derogation (which is itself a mythical construction). The classical fictions of the *ratio scripta*, or the Reason of Roman law, manipulated a *logic* of reproduction, a logic which was based on the need for the subject to be introduced to a phantasmic representation of the Absolute. This is a logic of *paternity* because it expresses the need for desire to be awakened from the 'anaesthesia' of narcissistic attachment to the mother (see Legendre 1985: 51–68) and transferred to the father as agent of the Absolute. In our era, this manoeuvre has been derailed: we are faced with 'a new form of de-humanization' (Legendre 1989: 52). This is not to say that the past was a better – or less murderous – place than the present, but simply to diagnose a 'debilitating infirmity' in western industrial culture (see Legendre 1989: 170). This is represented as a crisis of paternity. The inability to think human being in anything other than technicist terms sets in train a perversion of the western institutional order. The modern incarnation of the Absolute – the icon of Science – has not altogether undone the traditional patterns of subjective becoming. Rather, it has colonized the *structure* of the classical techniques, so instituting a paradoxical and subversive opposition of form and content. So our cultural heritage persists despite and through our denial of it.

The limits of desire

It is now quite routine to propose, or rather to suppose, that the law of the Father, and its articulation through the narrative of western culture, has unravelled:

> [T]he master discourses of the West are increasingly perceived as no longer adequate for explaining the world: words and things no longer coincide, and all identities are thrown into question.
>
> (Jardine 1984: 99)

A great deal of the 'postmodern' enterprise consists in an attempt to colonize and valorize the space of the 'Other', the repressed specular (and *feminine*) substance upon which the patterns of modern thought were reflected, and upon which they depended. The practitioners of this art of transgression seek to elude, or to subvert and negate, the order of metaphysics. As Jardine points out, the spectacle of 'Post-modern Man' writing on the body of 'woman' is highly problematic, not least because it seems simply to weave another male story of (and on) woman. What is significant for present purposes is that this story of woman exposes the gaps and silences in the master discourses, the unsaid or unsayable upon which they depend, yet which they deny or, quite simply, metabolize. Legendre is not a participant in these movements of 'transgression', nor, apparently, does he recognize these discursive limits. He discerns in the unravelling of the symbolic order not the figure of the fallen Father, but that of the psychotic son. We are witnessing – and indeed *living* – an unfolding of the Oedipal logic on an institutional scale. It is not that the Father has lost his place as the guarantor of our world, but that his authority is denied in a gesture whose futility simultaneously offends and confirms Fate.

Our debt to the Father remains outstanding, and is recovered in full, according to a relentless and remorseless logic of Fate. Both sexes are equally inscribed and subjected in this paternal logic of debt and guilt. And that logic is affirmed and retrenched in an account of the Fates of modernity, according to which the institutional narrative of industrial culture, which speaks (for) each subject in advance, so committing it to a given role in the symbolic order, can be denied only at the price of psychosis. So, the machinery of culture functions silently but efficiently to impose a mode of fabrication of subjectivity which is inescapable. The positivity of the tradition constructs what is Legendre's own version of the 'iron cage' of modernity. This essay asks whether the limits perceived by the genealogical critique are not simply an exteriorization of its own methodological limits and assumptions. Two questions in particular will be pursued. First, whether the intrications of psychoanalytical theory and a feminine gender do not pose more problems than Legendre recognizes. The second (and related) question is whether Legendre's diagnosis of our present condition, and his testimony to the authority of the Father, are as disinterested as his abstractions might suggest.

THE KNOT OF LANGUAGE

Legendre's vision of subjectivity owes a good deal to Lacan's presentation of the subject of desire as the victim of ever-disappointed anticipation. For Lacan, desire – as the quest for an elusive object which is as much everywhere as it is nowhere – was the truth of the subject. Legendre's turn of phrase may express the implications of this condition rather better than any of Lacan's own aphorisms: '*il faut apprendre à manquer à soi-même*' (Legendre 1985: 305). To convey this notion, Legendre does without Lacan's complicated mathemes and topographical illustrations. A single image suffices, that of man as a standing question – a *qu'est-ce que?* – an indestructible and unanswerable question addressed to the world. Man as question is effectively man as lack, for the question – '*pourquoi soi?*' (Lacan 1966: 450) – seeks the unattainable: a respondent who might answer for the subject's very existence. In Legendre's *Leçons*, this model of being-as-desire develops through an unravelling of Lacan's 'paternal metaphor' – the *Nom-du-père* – which was for Lacan a way of describing a process of subjectification; namely, the construction of a subject according to language.

Subjectification in this sense is not the construction of a singular *identity*, but a process of *identification* (see Clément 1981: 108) in which the subject is torn in two, split between the subject 'itself' and a culturally constructed *imago*. The story is summarized in the scheme of the *stade du miroir* (see Lacan, 1966, 1977). The interpretation of this scheme is highly problematic, but, to put it perhaps all too briefly, it recounts the unconscious attachments made by the subject to a pre-cast identity prepared for it within the symbolic order of language and culture. The scene describes the encounter of an infant with its mirror image. The child, which is at that stage an incomplete human, sees in its reflection the image of an integrated and co-ordinated body. The mirror offers the infant an 'orthopaedic' image of itself, an image which – in contrast to the dislocated instances of bodily functions which had so far made up its 'self' – projects a model of unity and totality. It holds out the promise of a felicitous state of co-ordination and independence, which the child embraces with a 'jubilant laugh' of anticipation and recognition.

To set this in terms of Lacan's peculiar neologisms, the mirror image is constructed in the realm of what Lacan calls the *imaginaire* – namely, the layer of phantasmic representations which the desiring subject projects as the 'reality' of its world. This 'reality' functions as a screen insulating the subject from the horrors of the *réel*. The *réel* in Lacan's scheme is not 'real life', but a condition of radical lack occasioned by the impossibility of the Mother, a condition in which there could be no world simply because, in the absence of a narrative temporality or coherence, nothing can be *anticipated* or *ready-to-hand* (see Juranville 1984: 85). The attachment to the image purportedly secures a remedy to this originary lack in the *réel*: however, there is an unfortunate irony to the laugh which marks the child's recognition. The desired image is 'orthopaedic' in the sense of being a sort of corrective device which moulds and supports the desired identity; however, the defect of that virtue is that it ultimately becomes a rigid, restraining and imprisoning structure. To be oneself one has to be not one self, but another. In short, the 'I' is an alienation of the 'foreclosed' self: '*Je est un autre*' – I is an other – (Lacan 1966: 118).

So, this recognition is a fundamental *mis*recognition. The basis of the misapprehension is an inability to recognize the otherness of the image. In the realm of the *imaginaire*, the mirror image is not apprehended as the deception that it is (see further, Weber 1991: ch. 7). Although it is precisely because the image is *other* that it is desirable – in that there can be no movement of attraction and appropriation towards that which is truly identical – the imaginary identification narcissistically denies this difference that makes of recognition a cause for celebration. The tensions of this deception are expressed in a paradoxical love–hate relation with the image. The otherness of the image attracts because it is what one desires; by the same token, however, its alterity is a reminder that one is indeed *not* what one desires. Hence, identification with the mirror image cannot truly deliver the plenitude that it promises, so that the move to remedy originary lack in the *réel* simply draws the subject into a secondary sort of lack.

So the story continues. The child, unsettled by this imperfection, turns around to seek out the approving gaze of another. It seeks a recognition which can validate its experience retroactively. Its jubilation is therefore conditional and anticipatory. Here, one gets closer to a sense of Lacan's version of subjectivity. His story of the subject is, as Samuel Weber points out, a story written in the future anterior tense: the mode of the 'what will-always-already-have-been' (see Weber 1991: ch. 2, and Zizek 1991). The subject lies in anticipation of something that is perpetually deferred, but which, paradoxically, has always-already-been there. The significance of the *tense* of the story is that the subject's *anticipation* of plenitude assumes that the validation of its image will always-already-have-been accorded. So, to sustain the edifice of imaginary attachments which make our world we need to make a supposition. Again, the attempt to remedy lack simply transfers it to a further register: the *symbolique*, or the realm of *desire*. Desire is founded in an impossible attempt to suppress the potential between two temporal moments without eliminating the difference that creates this very potential (see Irigaray 1984: 53). This impossibility testifies to the absence of the Other as addressee of the '*pourquoi soi?*'

The story does, of course, become rather more complicated than this. However, with Legendre in mind, what matters is the role of a function of *paternity* in the construction of this subject in the future anterior. This function may be introduced by noting that the paradoxes of the subject's relations with its representation in the *imaginaire* arise because it seeks in its image an image of plenitude (or, to use the jargon, the Phallus). The mirror exercises its fascination and repulsion because it suggests and denies such plenitude. So, lack in the third register – *desire* (for plenitude) – was always-already-there. The supposition which the temporality of anticipation imposes is a commitment to the possibility of plenitude, and that commitment is a condition of the subject itself. This is evident in Lacan's identification of the subject as the subject of a speech act: in the mode of the future anterior, it is what will have been shown upon the conclusion of a speech act. To embark upon an enunciation is to have assumed a speaking position which is every bit as precarious as the child's mirror image, and just as much in need of anticipated recognition. Every speech act rests upon this anticipation. To borrow a phrase from Hegel, in language 'we ourselves directly refute what we *mean* to say' (Hegel 1977: 60). We *mean* the addressee of the statement, but our *saying* addresses the Other, or the *sujet supposé savoir* – subject supposed to know – who might guarantee our place in language. So, the horizon of intersubjectivity – or, according to one fashion, communicative rationality – that makes language possible is a horizon of desire, or belief in the Other.

To adopt a speaking position is therefore to subject oneself to an image (of the Phallus) which at once opposes and entices. This process of subjection to the law of the Other is expressed in the psychoanalytical reference to symbolic castration. The subject is symbolically 'castrated' because the anticipatory appeal to the desired Other for recognition is an acknowledgement that it does not have the Phallus which the figure of Father represents. The office of paternity is the task of communicating this figure of plenitude so as to engender desire or belief. For Lacan, this function of generating belief is represented through the operation of metaphor according to the recipe of 'one word for another' (Lacan 1966: 890). The substitution of one word (*any* word) for another prompts the interpreter to make sense of what appears as nonsense, and this projected 'meaning' hangs on the value to be accorded to the unknown quantity. This search for meaning betrays submission to the law of the Other, or to belief in the possibility of meaning or plenitude somehow. The use of language – and therefore accession to subjectivity – depends upon this structure of belief. And, every speech act – the montage of the subject-as-signifier – repeats the prototypical operation of metaphor in its demand that this investment be made. So with the name of the father: the proper name calls the subject to speak because it is the symbol of the Name of the Father, the Phallus. As a symbol of plenitude, it lures the subject into a movement of anticipation which condemns it to speech, to a speaking position, and therefore to desire.

THE INSTITUTION OF JURIDICAL REASON

Ratio scripta and the law of desire

Legendre illuminates a similar dynamic of unconscious identifications, but tracks it through the elements of an order of Law rather than one of language (as the play of signifier and signified). For Lacan, the subject's identification with a name binds it to a speaking position, and thereby subjects it to the convoluted deceptions of language. For Legendre, on the other hand, identification with or by a name is not primarily an attachment to an identity within language. This is not so much a denial of the role of language as the excavation of the linguistic chain to uncover a more extensive sensibility: indeed, one of the most suggestive aspects of Legendre's work is the more expansive picture of language that it develops in illuminating this other scene (see Legendre 1978). The *Nom-du-Père* describes a paternity of *law* rather than language because the name with which the child is identified is a structure defined and valorized through juridical techniques. As with Lacan, the 'institutionalized' subject is identified – and the unconscious secures its own identification – not *by* its speech acts but *with* its speech acts. However, the 'I' illuminated by each speech act is essentially a juridically constructed artifice. The name is indeed a proper noun, caught in the flux of the signifying chain, but, according to Legendre, it is also, and more importantly, a term in a language of lineage. The system of lineage and kinship forms a symbolic order with its own principles of combination and association. Those principles are essentially juridical, or, quite simply, *rational*: for Legendre, the schemes of lineage in which the proper name is caught mobilize a peculiarly western principle of Reason. Reason, in this sense, has a juridical character which is traced to the *animus* of the *Corpus Iuris Civilis*. Even these introductory comments reveal a more exorbitant understanding of law: as we shall see, 'Law' becomes a cipher for the conditions of our (unconscious) aesthetic susceptibility, or the 'glue' which holds the unconscious to its prefabricated montage.

This interleaving of law, kinship and reason involves marrying the stories of the unconscious to some version of Lévi-Strauss's model of kinship and culture. Lévi-Strauss's principal limitation was, according to Legendre, his reluctance to make use of psychoanalytical insights: '[H]is hesitancy over psychoanalysis led contemporary anthropology to adopt an impoverished view of what I term the domain of social artifices, by which I mean juridical artifices deeply rooted in the unconscious character of the *qu'est-ce que*?' (Legendre 1985: 124).

Some of the problems with this reception of the stuctural anthropological view of the world are evidenced by Legendre's attempt to negotiate a path through such hazards as the nature–culture divide (see Legendre 1985: 113). However, the upshot of it all is that the play of desire is identified as the dynamic of an order of kinship rather than one of language. Unconscious desire is essentially incestuous desire, but 'incest' here refers to something more than a problem of family rivalry or the perversion of a biological scheme of things. Desire is 'incestuous' in the peculiar sense that, for the unconscious, there are no boundaries between self and other, and no world other than or beyond the subject itself. This refusal to recognize otherness (the 'narcissism' referred to in Lacan's *stade du miroir*) expresses a radical will to omnipotence, a will to recognize no limits whatsoever, and especially not those ordered family relations which demand that one should occupy the singular status of father, son, or mother. So, in *Oedipus Rex*, Oedipus's incestuous relations are taken to express this more extravagant sort of tyranny: in occupying the places of son and husband to the same woman, Oedipus confounds the order of lineage, an order to which even the gods conform. His unconscious desire projects itself as a quest for the impossible:

> Incestuous desire . . . is a challenge to the gods, a desire for the absolute. Desire is just that – the affirmation of the impossible: to embrace the absolute, to possess what is most elusive, to raise oneself to an unattainable level. . . . [It] is in the nature of desire to desire the impossible. . . . [We] are born to want the impossible. (Legendre 1985: 79)

The impossible object in question here is a substitute for the total envelope of the maternal womb, the experience of complete containment which is forever lost, and which the (masculine) subject-to-be is destined to pursue (unsuccessfully) through the labyrinth of the symbolic order (see, generally, Irigaray 1984).

Legendre, playing on the image of the *Wort-Denken* ('*la pensée dans l'éclair du mot*' – see Legendre 1983: 23) is content in this to communicate a certain *idea* of desire, so that the word itself illuminates an understanding, or vision, of the driving principle of subjectivity. In that sense, the nature of the exercise may not be so different from Lacan's elliptical style of 'clarification'. Legendre, however, leaves us with a series of rather cryptic elaborations, which do not so much complicate the picture, as re-present it in successive layers. Of course, this is quite appropriate to the style of showing that characterizes Legendre's presentation. Desire, according to Legendre, is not primarily a sort of explanatory principle (indeed, the whole thrust of the writing renders the idea of explanation problematic – see Legendre 1985: 11). So, the invocation of desire is an attempt to make us experience – or to make us *feel* – the movements of a certain sort of sensibility. In this sense, it is quite appropriate to speak of Legendre's 'poetry' as a play on a memory that makes the present possible.

However, desire *does* ultimately function as a sort of 'explanatory' principle: the sensibility of the unconscious is for the theory a medium traversed by a function of subjugation – namely, the function of paternity. This function binds unconscious desire to a symbolic order which speaks (for) each of us in advance. There is a remorseless logic of Fate, according to which the subject must either cleave to its prefabricated identity or drift into madness. So, for the theory, desire is the glue which sticks together two suppositions of the theory: the subject of desire (which, given Irigaray's critique of 'masculine' desire, is far from unproblematic), and a version of the structural anthropologist's reading of the symbolic order. Desire is incestuous *because* the symbolic order is one of lineage and kinship. The unconscious is *juriste* (Legendre speaks of '*l'inconscient dogmaticien par nature*' (Legendre 1983: 81)) *because* that order of lineage is juridically constructed. This may suggest a compounding of a difficulty which affects the work of both Lacan and Lévi-Strauss – namely, that a given cultural arrangement is simply taken for granted, and fixed as an immovable symbolic order.

Legendre constructs a desiring subject and a symbolic order which are essentially incongruous (Legendre 1988). To be a functional human being one must be 'born again' into the order of culture. The reproduction of human beings properly defined is not a reproduction of flesh but the reproduction of speaking beings – the construction of civilized subjects of culture. The fit between subject and institution must be manufactured. In Legendre's presentation, this is a matter of knitting together the biological, the social, and the unconscious (Legendre 1988). This involves capturing desire through much the same techniques as those which prise the subject of the speech act from its fascination with the mirror image, obliging it to turn around and seek the Other as guarantor. So, we are returned to the dynamic of Lacan's paternal metaphor.

Paternity, according to Legendre, is an act of faith (Legendre 1983: 68). Here, the notion of 'faith' is to be negotiated with some care. To say that paternity mobilizes 'faith' is to invoke the manoeuvre through which Lacan's *Nom-du-Père* institutes the horizon of belief which makes language possible. For Legendre as for Lacan, symbolic castration consists in instilling in the subject a sense of irremediable lack – a sense that it has not got what it once thought it had. In Legendre's version, this is accomplished by notifying the subject of its insignificance in the grand scheme of things; or, quite simply, of the fact of its mortality compared to the immortality of the species. In the relationship between Man and men, Man always has the last word. This introduction to the Absolute demands a subtle play on the radical distinction between plenitude and lack because the aim of the exercise is not to stupefy or anaesthetize unconscious desire but to preserve its essential vitality. The symbolic order is entirely dependent upon the native dynamic of unconscious desire to fuel its attempts to capture and hold new clients.

Paternity is a question of Law because of the way in which this function of castration is managed in western culture. According to Legendre, our juridically attuned unconscious is most effectively seduced by a peculiarly western discourse of *legitimacy*. Truth and reason, for the *inconscient dogmaticien par nature*, are grasped through the medium of techniques of representation based on the principles of Roman law. Hence, the capture of unconscious desire and the construction of subjectivity is essentially a task for the institutions of law and government, most notably the juridical order of kinship. The general proposition here is that there is a privileged relationship between Law and Reason. Juridical reason is the paradigm of all reason, so that each of the techniques which capture unconscious desire is a variation upon a theme which found its original expression in the *Corpus Iuris Civilis*. Indeed, according to Legendre, it is a neglected fact of history that the foundation of scientific reason – the principle of objectivity – is itself derived from the principles of Roman law:

> It is significant that the supposedly human and social sciences, fascinated as they are by the phenomenon of science, by the relation between knowledge and truth, and by the structures of

> scientific regulation, should have almost completely excluded from their fields of investigation the fundamental problems contained in the law of procedure, that is to say the science of the trial, and more particularly the law of evidence. From the point of view of these prevailing ideas, modern procedure, which has been constructed almost entirely from the elaborations of Roman law synthesized by Justinian (and supplemented by the scholastics), is doubtless inhospitable territory. [However], the law of evidence is the archetype of what we in the west call the scientific approach. (Legendre 1983: 178)

The Roman law of evidence is, according to this view, responsible for instituting the objectivist approach that is characteristic of modern science: as the medieval French lawyers had it, '*rien n'est dans l'intellect qui n'ait d'abord été dans les sens*'. More significantly, the truth of the knowledge gathered through this approach is established according to the mechanisms of articulation of legal truth. The juridical construction of the question of legitimacy is, from the point of view of the unconscious, so favoured that Science's demonstrations of truth and Reason are bound to repeat and valorize a legally constructed representation of – or mode of representing – truth.

The truth in genealogy

According to the juridical style, reason and truth are thought in the image of law as *ratio scripta*: the question of truth and legitimacy is posed as if it were a question of the succession and origin of (legal) texts. For the Roman jurist, the legitimacy of a text was determined by seeking its provenance: by asking: *Unde nomen iuris descendat?*, or quite simply *Unde?* This set in train a process of recapitulation, through which the authority of any given text was established by tracing its origin back through a chain of authority to an ultimate ground, or Absolute principle. So, Reason itself is represented as an order of lineage; or, to put it the other way around, the juridical order of kinship is essentially an expression – indeed, the paradigm – of Reason:

> [E]very lineage works *in the name of*. Normative communication refers back to the Political in its most abstract form, because, in accordance with a particular sort of logical formalism, the provenance of juridical products must be declared (in the same sense as one makes a customs declaration). The very fact of stating this

> provenance suffices in itself to establish the guarantee. Lineage functions as a legal – or a legally validated – answer to the question *Unde?*
>
> (Legendre 1985: 176)

All normative, institutional communication is – despite our functional, managerial, image of texts as nothing more than the information they bear on their surface – an enactment of this peculiar economy of power and truth. Indeed, normative communications can be taken at face value precisely because they refer back to a guarantee. In this sense, texts are accorded their credentials by their place in a sort of kinship of texts, each of which is validated by its relation to its immediate predecessor. This raises the question of the ultimate guarantee of this chain of causation, the principle which validates successive texts:

> The proof of lineage eventually runs up against an impossibility, just as did those proofs of title to property for which European lawyers coined a striking term: *probatio diabolica*. . . . In other words, the question reaches an impasse, but not just any impasse; it encounters this void, or vertiginous chasm, through those representations which, so to speak, inhabit the impasse. For westerners, the impasse is inhabited by God, or some functional equivalent, given that God is now dead as the founding signifier of secular western juridical systems . . .
>
> (Legendre 1985: 147)

So, ultimately, the accountancy of lineage reaches a space of myth, a necessary fiction which Legendre calls the Reference. The Reference is simply the Absolute, the Phallus, or the zero function in its pure form. As such, it is entirely a creature of faith, an assumption which is effective only in the fact of its repetition and reception. Because this justification of justifications cannot itself be justified, because, that is, it must simply be *supposed* (Legendre 1985: 240) to be true, it must be packaged and advertised in a quite irresistible style. Pure power – the Phallus – is intrinsically nothing, and can communicate nothing, so that the manner of representation is everything. The Reference is a myth like any other, and, like all myths, it stands or falls according to the unconscious appeal of the emblems through which it is communicated. These emblems are as insubstantial as they are vital:

> [T]he *non-juridical dimension of law* [is composed in] a body of discourses which, within any society, construct the founding image which is its subjects' marching banner. According to the industrial ethic, this body is composed as much of ideologies as of aesthetic, scientific, or other products. These are valorized institutionally; not according to their express content (which is a function of the declared intention of the author), but through the *fact* of being symbolically accorded a place within society as representations of the Reference. Structurally, they occupy the very place from which ancient theologies and myths exercised their [authority].
>
> (Legendre 1989: 70)

Truth is, therefore, produced by juridical reason as communicator of this non-juridical dimension of law, and manoeuvred through a function of paternity.

This affiliation of lineage and Reason accounts for the vital role of genealogical rules in the conquest of the uncivilized subject. The (partial) identity of the subject is essentially genealogical: it is from one's place in the order of kinship that the world, and the others who occupy it, are addressed. This prefabricated identity, or montage, is the bait used to lure unconscious desire into the genealogical order and to twist its megalomania into a belief in the power of the Reference. In the magic mirror held up by the montage, the subject encounters for the first time the image of the Absolute, and the intricate play of unconscious attachment to a symbolic identity begins to unfold.

Given Legendre's interpretation of the articulation of emblems of legitimacy in western culture, a genealogically constructed montage is almost uniquely persuasive. Lineage unfolds as the very paradigm of normative communication; each position in the family line is produced and represented according to the logic of the *Unde?* Indeed, just as the juridical problematic of descent constructs a succession of texts, so can one see the order of kinship as a succession of text analogues (Legendre 1985: 91). As a textual order, the order of lineage unfolds on the basis of an 'as if': things proceed as *though* there were indeed an ultimate justification for the order of causation. The subject must make this vital assumption if the montage is to be effective. In other words, something or somebody must be in a position to offer a definitive reply to the question *Unde?* The recapitulation of lineage must ultimately reach a respondent which the subject can take at its word. As articulations of power, genealogical lines must speak the truth: they must be guaranteed by the Reference.

The position of the father is vital here, because the father is for Legendre, as much as for Lacan, an *agent*. The *père de famille* enjoys a sort of juridical personality, a status conferred by the Reference: 'The father represents a representation: he represents that which on the juridical plane of society as a whole represents the very idea of a father, the principle of differentiation in the reproduction of the speaking species' (Legendre 1985: 314). Legendre makes an essential distinction here, between the father as progenitor and paternity as a function of the Absolute. According to a purely contingent arrangement of western culture, there is an overlap between the function of paternity and the office of the 'real' father. However, paternity is in essence a function which organizes the subject's introduction to two faces of the Absolute: first, as the pure Phallus, and, second, as guarantor of the order of kinship. And, ultimately, it serves as the principle of a structural reading of the symbolic order.

Fate and the institution

The model of structure is one of the most pervasive themes in Legendre's vision:

> To say that there is a structure (with the architectural connotations of the Latin) to history, and, accordingly, to the industrial system . . . is to say that things have congealed in a particular way and we have to reckon with this coagulation. It is of course possible to identify certain lines of force, or the lineaments of an evolutionary process (as in, for example, the identification of two Scholastic periods, one medieval and the other modern); or, one might locate certain points of amalgamation or rupture (as, for instance, in the emergence of the industrial era). However, there is something from which one cannot secede; namely, the logical relation which in the west melds the juridical mechanisms of industrial culture to the history of Roman law so as to form an institutional principle of Reason.
>
> (Legendre 1983: 36–7)

The role which this version of history has in organizing that vision, and in justifying some of its more polemical episodes, is vividly illustrated in *Le crime du caporal Lortie*. The crime in question – an attack on a government which, according to Lortie, bore the face of his father – is treated as an event programmed by the workings of the *structure* of society. Lortie was condemned to some sort of pathological response by the inexorable logic of the order of succession. His crime is presented as a consequence of an inherited burden of genealogical debt. Lortie's father had lived beyond his means, having indulged in various excesses of personality, notably incestuous relations with his daughters. Having refused to square things with the Absolute, this father was unable to represent the Reference to his son, who therefore inherited, at full tariff, the cost of defraying his father's debts to the Absolute. This sort of genealogical madness is, then, a genetically communicable disease; *culturally* speaking, of course.

In this idea of the extorting of accumulated genealogical dues, there is the notion of the logic of lineage as something that precedes and commands the subject: the madman is one who pays unpaid unconscious debts (Legendre 1983: 70). Like the Fates – the *Fata* – this logic is 'that which resists prayer, an immovable prohibition which, if it is transgressed, unfolds in a series of devastating and irrevocable effects' (Legendre 1988: 28). This is a particularly stern vision of the world as fate, because the parameters which we are given are immovable. The trials we suffer are attributable not simply to the content of our myth, but to the incongruity of contingent content and logical function. The order does not unfold only for the confirmed believer, it pre-exists its occupants. This characterization of the remorseless *Fata* prompts a polemical diagnosis of the degeneracy of western culture: '[I]n industrialized society, the younger generations are made to pay for the failure of adults to undo their genealogical attachments, so that thousands of children are driven towards psychosis and mental atrophy' (Legendre 1985: 336). Homosexual marriages and adoptions, the proliferation of reproductive technologies, womb leasing, and so on; these developments, and the way in which they are represented, constitute a purported derogation from the principle of paternity, and reveal our inability to go about things in the right way – that is, by engaging with our established (paternal) tradition. And, where many would blame our current dislocations on the decrepitude of the paternal metaphor, Legendre reinstates the Father with a vengeance. We bring our misfortunes on ourselves by denying the authority of this structurally constituted Father, and by attempting to cut free from the ties that bind us to him. The tale of the unfortunate Lortie simply offers a lurid allegory of our present condition.

A FATHER TO ALL MANKIND?

This father who is not one

With the father as with the veneration of a religious icon, 'it is not the wood itself that is honoured, but that which is represented on the wood' (Legendre 1985: 63). Formulae such as this refer of course to the place of ritual, but they also develop a more prosaic reading of things. In the distinction between father and Father, Legendre precipitates from the sober truths of Freud's science of 'real' families a differently 'scientific' analysis of a structure or logic to which desire is subjected. This abstraction from the domestic scene supports a reading of psychoanalysis according to which theory transcends the scene of patriarchal authority to reveal a logic of subjectification. More to the point, it serves as a justification for the claim that the process of subjectification implicates male and female equally: 'in psychoanalysis, the phallus is not a reference to the masculine organ, but a representation incorporating the dual reference to desire and the impossibility of desire' (Legendre 1985: 318). The account of this logic of paternity reveals Legendre at his least flamboyant. The texts are rather more prosaic than the vibrant stories of dance, ritual and heraldry through which the question of subjectification is pursued elsewhere. They are none the less essential because they develop the manoeuvre through which Legendre dissolves the appearance of culture into a logic which imprisons both sexes in a machinery of structure.

We begin again with the descent of texts. That the vital question – *Unde?* – should resonate so harmoniously through the lineages of family and power is due to the peculiar way in which these genealogical orders unravel. The descent of the order enacts what might be called a sort of arithmetic of sovereignty, a process in which the claim to be the ultimate respondent to the question is repeated so often, and in such enchanting terms, that its very implausibility is overlooked. The Reference as unmoved mover is constituted as such by the faith of its subjects. The institutional show is kept on the road on the basis of an essential, but obscured, assumption:

> Every juridical system is guaranteed by a founding supposition, the expressed content of which may vary according to social and political factors, but which derives its power from its function as a general presupposition, or, in other words, as the axiom from which all particular axioms are derived. This general axiom

> operates within institutional systems as a general normative affirmation having the status of a mythical justification for the system as a whole: for example, God, or the People, etc.
>
> (Legendre 1985: 240)

This function of myth is illustrated by analogy to the role of the 'number' zero in mathematics. Just as the sequence of numbers is founded in a concept which is paradoxical – the concept of zero being in practice counted as one whilst being named as emptiness – so the accountancy of lineage continually restates the fiction of a beginning which is paradoxically presence *and* absence. Hence, the primary quality of the Reference is its role as a pure function, the inaugural moment of the structural order. The fact of having a myth is more important than the content of the particular myth which we have, despite, it would seem, the fact that the myth is nothing without its mode of representation.

The principle of myth is also the principle of paternity. In the latter context, the zero function renders Freud in the language of Frege. Stripped to the bare bones of its 'structure', the symbolic order is revealed as an order of succession in which each of the succeeding units in the chain is constructed through the same repeated operation as that which sustains the progression of numbers. So, the montage which each subject-to-be is called upon to occupy is reducible to a quality resembling that of the whole number as an entity which, because it incorporates the zero as a moment of a radical lack, is not all that it claims to be. The task for the subject is to learn to count itself as such a 'one', to assume the lack that the whole number conceals within it; in short, to interiorize absence – namely, the *impossibility of the mother as origin*. The arithmetic of paternity is therefore a transcription of Freud's *fort-da*, the game in which the child learns to symbolize the presence–absence of the mother, and to symbolize *itself* in those terms. As in Freud's version, accession to the symbolic order is based on castration. For Legendre, the rather dry logic of presence–absence which characterizes the zero function is dramatically infused with the charisma of the divine, so that the zero stands in for the Phallus, the Absolute which commands the belief of the subject in the radical paradox which it stands for. For future reference, it should be noted just *how* empty the function of myth really is in this representation, and just how much is left to the particular mode or style of its communication; in short, just how far *structure* is subordinated to *content*.

The most significant implication of this is that it enables the Reference to be abstracted from what Freud might have been more inclined to see as the *facts* of the matter. Genealogy is crystallized as structure: 'Genealogical systems are not arbitrary, they respond not only to the exigencies of socio-historic conditions, but to the necessity of a logical function. I have attempted to grasp that logical function with the assistance of the concept of a zero function' (Legendre 1985: 244–5). So, paternity in this mode is reducible to a slender logical function: a father who is not one but zero. This account of these juridical and institutional techniques of subjectification de-centres the target that feminism (which is a problematic label for Irigaray's critique) has made of psychoanalysis. The discussion of law-as-lineage is manoeuvred in such a way as to illuminate a female genealogical line, and to suggest that there is such a thing as 'structural equality' between the sexes. This role for the feminine, or women – and it is never entirely clear who or what Legendre has in mind when he distinguishes women as mothers from women as subjects – constructs them as agents of the (paternal) Reference.

As a simple biological fact, the production of a child is not something that can be registered in its raw state; it is an event which is necessarily inscribed and symbolized in a narrative which 'institutes' the biological, giving it a human form. Motherhood is a state – or a status – which is constructed according to the order of the Reference. To be a mother is not simply to function as a sort of mechanical womb; it is to accede to the status of a distinct subject within the lineage of the Reference. To see things otherwise, says Legendre, is to settle into a rather hackneyed corruption of psychoanalysis, in which the mother is portrayed as nothing more than a womb, and therefore nothing more than the all-powerful Mother or the partial object. His account seeks to reinstate the mother as *subject*: to construct for her an identity that is as securely grounded – and grounded in the same way – as that of the father.

In Legendre's version of things, the Oedipal family is not a self-contained entity structured by relations of rivalry. The basic elements of Lacan's *Nom-du-Père* are transported to an arena composed within the descending order of genealogy. Each of the participants in the staging of the paternal metaphor therefore acts under an authority issued by the law of the Reference. The principal effect of this is apparently to dislodge the father from the position of dominance that is attributed to him in other commentaries on Lacan. For Legendre, of course, the father is only an intermediary – a sort of emissary or ambassador of the Reference. Both father and mother occupy montages constructed and warranted by the Reference, so the basic family unit cannot be portrayed as a composite in which the father is the dominant element. Instead, it must be grounded in a sort of dialectical relation between father and mother, and the play of this dialectic assigns the father and mother to positions which are separate but equal. Father and mother *jointly* communicate the principle of the Reference: 'The genealogical phenomenon, as a juridical ordering of reproduction within society, promotes two linked powers, two functions, each of which mobilizes the subject, and translates the relation of each human subject to the absolute Reference' (Legendre 1985: 317). The child, in its accession to the status of subject, must chart a course by reference to these *two* poles, so that it is inadequate simply to portray the process of subjectification as a course of (masculine) becoming in which the child rejects the mother in favour of the father as (natural) possessor of the Phallus.

Symbolic permutations: the modalities of identification

All lines lead to *Ego*: the genealogical order is *Ego*-centric in the sense that it is from that perspective that the horizon of lineage is seen to unfold. To map out his place in this world, *Ego* must first take his bearings according to two essential cadastral references: the distinct montages occupied by each parent. *Ego* can then begin the process of genealogical accounting, retracing the map that shows the place with which he must identify. It is essential that two distinct lines be represented – for two reasons. In the first instance, to communicate the 'general axiom' of differentiation, the *principle* of division; namely, the *Tiers*. A representation of the division of the sexes confronts the subject with the principle of division in general, with the idea of mortality or limitation, and through that with the power of the Reference which makes those representations effective. Second, the two distinct threads of the male and female lineage serve as clues to the *particular* axioms of genealogical accounting, to the practical techniques through which the general principle of division is instituted. In this way, a representation of division according to sex is the kernel from which the full panoply of the family tree unfurls into an intricate structure made up of lines, generations, and degrees of kinship.

For all these reasons, *Ego* can only accede to his appointed position as subject if each of his parents has established his or her credentials as an emissary of the Reference. Acquiring those credentials – in short, becoming a parent in the order of the Reference – is not a straightforward matter. One is not simply decanted from one genealogical position to the next in some natural order of progression. What is involved is a painful process in which each parent extricates himself or herself from an identification with a desirable montage so as to redraw the map of family relations. To be refamiliarized, each parent must undo the attachments that he or she has formed to his or her own parents, so as to renounce the ties that bind each as son or daughter in their own right. The birth of the child therefore occasions the birth of the parents *as parents*. It is an event which demands of each that they should realign themselves according to a new set of 'vertical' and 'horizontal' co-ordinates.

For the mother-to-be, this involves representing – to herself – the fact of the birth in terms of the narrative of the Reference. In other words, she must recognize her own image in the fiction of the Mother. The price of identification with that image is the deliverance of her child to the paternity of the Reference, and the inducement offered for participation in this transaction is the representation of paternity presented by the father of her child. Given the image of paternity which her partner represents – namely, paternity in a register other than that occupied by her own father – the mother-to-be has a reference point, or lever, which she can use to prise herself away from her attachments to her father. Through this transfer of allegiance from father to partner, the mother gains an identity as a woman other than her mother, as a woman distinct from men in general, and as '*femme d'un autre homme que son père*' (Legendre 1985: 330). The story is similar for the father, who must replay the drama of his Oedipal attachments on the screen presented by the mother of the child. This slippage down through the 'vertical' order is initiated and stabilized by a horizontal or dialectical relation between the new-born parents. The 'dialectic' that is supposedly in operation consists in the mutually supportive functions of maternity and paternity. Just as the mother's progress to motherhood cannot begin unless she is confronted with paternity in the register occupied by her partner, so the father's progress will be obstructed unless he is offered a similarly displaced image of maternity.

The progress of subjectification is characterized by a principle of equality, or, more precisely, equality before the Phallus. Men do not possess the phallus as of right. According to Legendre, both sexes have to go through the same process of differentiation, both have to *earn* their place in the order of the Reference. Men are not 'naturally' accorded credentials which women 'naturally' lack. The relation to the symbolic order – or to the phallus as Absolute – is not mediated by reference to (a desire for) something that men possess but women do not. The process of becoming a subject does not describe an exclusively masculine trajectory. Further, the place in the symbolic order to which the subject accedes can be occupied as much by women as by men. Each performs a different function, but, as Legendre puts it, 'neither side is master of the absolute Reference' (Legendre 1985: 321). Thus, the feminine can find a place in the symbolic order – or, rather, in the *structure* or *logic* of that order. So, for Legendre, the sexes are structurally equal:

> The west – in common with many other civilizations, will inevitably have great difficulty in desexualizing the problematic of power. Assuming that campaigns for equality can rise above the simplistic tone of our current confusion, desexualization would be a matter of establishing the process of recognizing one's identifications with the genealogical principle of pure power (the principle which the jargon of psychoanalysis constitutes as the Phallus), as a process which implicates both sexes, not only the masculine sex.
>
> (Legendre 1985: 150)

Here, one should be clear. 'Structural equality' does not mean equality according to the canons of some sort of 'ethics'; it refers to *equality before the Phallus*. The point is that, whereas some would make of this symbol the key to a *masculine* symbolic order, Legendre's is a reading of the Phallus as a pure signifier, detached not only from any representation of anatomical differences, but effective in structuring the becoming of individuals of either sex.

The question of the feminine

At first sight, the terms of this response do little to address the demands of the question. The question of the feminine, and of the place accorded to women or Woman within or without the economy of desire, is essentially a question of the discursive limits of the psychoanalytical enterprise. Lacan marks those limits with the figures of Woman and the *réel*. In the case of Woman the limit is posed because '[there] is no woman except she who is excluded by the nature of things which is the nature of words' (Lacan 1975: 68). The *réel* – this realm of what cannot be anticipated, and whose only presence is as the lack which motivates the temporality of desire – is the condition of all discourse, including the *discours analytique*. Irigaray poses those limits *as* limits in her attempt to twist the theory outside-in so as to reveal its dependence on a repressed specular substance.

This story of Woman as the Other of psychoanalytical discourse is well known (though for a restatement see Irigaray 1992: 101–16). The exercise attributes to the theory precisely the *imaginaire* – the web of phantasmic representations – through which the desiring subject apprehends, or rather constructs, a habitable world. And that *imaginaire* is gendered as masculine. The theory's desiring body is characterized as 'phallomorphic', as constructed or predisposed to a style of engagement with the world which privileges the gaze as an instrument of diacritical judgment, a tool for separating and distinguishing identities. The scopic drive – or the search for the gaze of the Other – is privileged in the masculine imaginary because, in becoming an eye for the Other, the subject is committed to a never-ending search for confirmation of identity or plenitude. This search expresses the radical lack experienced by the subject, the lack of a total envelope, or a proper place in which it might once again experience the identity imparted by the primal *lieu*. Like all the drives – or *pulsions* – it traces a circular movement of attempted closure or encirclement; in encompassing the object in question, the drive seeks to make of that object the negation of the desiring body. It seeks to make of its inner surface (that which touches and encloses the object) its *outer* surface. The desiring body attempts to twist itself inside out so that its total encirclement of the *objet pusionnel* might be experienced as a total encirclement *of it* by the object. It is, in other words, an attempt to fashion a new dwelling out of a movement of capture.

This movement is expressed by Irigaray as the model of specular relation to the world, in which substance is interrogated and experienced as a potential confirmation of plenitude and identity. The limit of psychoanalytical theory is posed by its need – as a phallomorphic discourse – for a similar confirmation or support of its existence. This is one way of playing the Other against the Same. Although for Irigaray the feminine is not styled the Other of the Same, as it is according to the role accorded Woman by Lacan, an analysis of the role of the repressed Other to the Same defines the limits of the psychoanalytical discourse and its implication in a culture founded on 'the murder of the mother' (Irigaray 1987: 31).

The model of structural equality addresses none of this. The assumption implicit within it seems to be that the Reference is somehow exempt from this play of Same and Other. The Reference is presented as a principle which *creates* the distinction between the two sexes according to its own internal logic: each sex is a different, but equal, relation to this singular presence. So the division of the sexes is not a replication of a distinction between Same and Other. This claim that desire is singular but undiscriminating in its application is problematic, not least because it ultimately confirms the blindness of the theory to its own cognitive or discursive limits. The point is that the model of desire is at once an expression of the *opus operatum* and the *modus operandi* of Legendre's theory (for the distinction, see Bourdieu 1980: preface and ch. 1). The theory's object is an objectification of a method, or, to use Irigaray's formula, of a given (masculine) *imaginaire*. So, to suggest that the prototypical universal subject (or principle of subjectification) – the Phallus – is not constituted by an opposition of Same and Other, and that it does not distinguish and value the sexes according to that valorized opposition, is not only to say something about the object of study, it is (more significantly) to say something about the method. More precisely, to suggest that the sexes are 'structurally equal' is to say first that the model of desire is neutral, and second to say that the theory itself is neutral in the gathering of its insights.

This is an occlusion or evasion of the problem rather than an answer because the notion of neutrality as between the sexes seems, even according to Legendre's own lights, soon to dissolve. Because the totem of the Reference – as with all totems – consists only in the form which ritual performance lends it, the principle of neutrality is impossible to maintain. There can be no pure logic when the logic itself is nothing other than a distillation of this cultural performance. This is plain even in the studies of the western family tree which support the account of subjective identifications. And, it is not met by the proposition that there is a meaningful distinction to be made here between a structure and content of cultural representation. That distinction is implausible here because, even if one can, as did our forebears, draw a family tree in which the maternal line mirrors the trajectory of the paternal line, this would not be a description of how the genealogical message is *received* by the desiring subject. As Legendre observes, the structure is nothing other than the representations which render it tangible; and, indeed, the answer to the question *qu'est-ce que?* must ultimately be 'nothing' if the account of desire is to be sustained. However, this leads Legendre to adopt a distinction between structure and content, according to which a patriarchal order, or style of representation, can be categorized as a question of content. Although the entire genealogical order functions as a representation of the Absolute, there is in our culture an essential *structure* to that representation, which is communicated in the logic of the zero function.

However, for the insider, the subject who has been brought to believe, one's place in the order is communicated through the representation of captivating emblems and images, a theatre which considerably exceeds the pure logical function. For example, the reading and representation of the genealogical map follows a particular scheme of distribution and valorization, so that the right (male) side is accorded priority over the left: it is drawn first and *seen* first, according to one of those schemes of perception that are most instructively presented in Pierre Bourdieu's studies. Of course, Bourdieu's *habitus* is not a depository of actions and representations in the same sense as are the *imaginaire* and the *symbolique*, but it would not be at all inappropriate to weave these elements into the screens through which our world is apprehended: in terms of those *'principes de vision qui sont aussi des principes de division'* (Bourdieu 1987: 98). In those terms, the cultural arrangements of our tradition, symbolized as they are in such things as conventional naming strategies, mean that the family tree is inevitably projected on to a culturally specific grid of perception. *Ego* necessarily situates himself according to culturally interpreted co-ordinates. And, to say that behind those co-ordinates there lies a structure is quite unhelpful.

In other words, structural equality is equality without difference. The twin orders of the Reference are the double reflection of the movement of a singular principle. If only for that reason, the idea of structural equality is implausible. Legendre's scheme would not resonate except as a representation of a social arrangement, except as a hypostatization of a singular experience (which it might or might not be helpful to label 'patriarchal'). Legendre writes his *modus operandi* into the human condition in western culture, so etching the normalizing perspective even more sharply into the framework of psychoanalytical theory. 'Normalization' here involves exclusion – namely, the exclusion of the possibility of any sort of symbolic order, and hence any sort of subjectivity, other than that described by the paternal order of succession. The paternal metaphor is so vital that if we are to have any sort of order at all, it must be on the terms dictated by structure:

> The idea which we have of the principle of division and its modalities of rationality by way of the law of human reproduction will have to change, and take shape through novel techniques, without, however, giving any ground. The West remains Christian and rationalist.
>
> (Legendre 1985: 310)

Women and men are not 'equal' before the phallus. The cultural schema valorize the male line according to criteria which suppress the feminine. The influence of the *modus operandi* of the theory in shaping the *opus operatum* is most evident in the distillation of a logic of paternity from cultural and institutional material. The function of paternity – of communicating a transcendent principle so as to manufacture the subject matter of the social order – is only thinkable against the horizon of our (or Freud's) experience of the bourgeois family. For all the assertions to the effect that the father in the order of the Reference is *not* simply a *principe séparateur* (see Legendre 1985: 242), it is plain that we remain with a family unit in which the father functions as the agent of a symbolic order which depends on the separation of mother and child. Despite the attempt to hide the phallus from view, it is plain that the model of the zero function is *no more* than Freud in the language of Frege. In Legendre's case the explanation of paternity becomes quasi-functional: *if* mother and child are to be separated, *if* desire is the will to confuse, and *if* the order of the Reference is to institute the subject, the father – or the paternity principle – must intervene. The vital *if* is shored up by the assumption of the necessity of a symbolic order which is nothing other than a narration of male lineage and male desire. Whatever the sequence and structure of the exposition, the starting point is always this paternal line.

In denying this, Legendre performs an implausible sort of extrusion, according to which the role of the father is presented as the function of a *principle* of paternity. It is not the father who, through the *fact* of being a father, or of being a man, lures the child away from its narcissistic embrace of the mother. It is the Absolute which the father represents, and whose recognition he has earned, that is desirable. The Phallus is not gratuitously conferred on fathers only, but is to be earned by both sexes. This is all very well, but we should recall that the very principle of the Absolute in the order of the Reference is simply the self-adoration, or *auto-affection* (see Irigaray 1977), of the masculine imaginary projected into the *au-delà* – the beyond – of the transcendental. This constitutive narcissism is the very principle of the symbolic order. What is exteriorized as the principle of paternity is simply the principle of the male imaginary and its need for a guarantor of its identity. Indeed, the maternal function is not genuinely different from that of the father. What is produced is maternity in the image of the father. Legendre proposes that the mother should be the homologue of the father, a figure modelled on his desire and his style of *auto-affection*. The discussions of *références croisées*, and *fonctions liées*, are simply a sort of trick of the light; a play of mirrors in which a singular paternal law is reflected off a sequence of spectacular surfaces, illuminated not according to natural or neutral light, but according to a luminosity of the masculine imaginary.

LOVE IN A SINGULAR MODE

For Legendre, words and things have not fallen apart (contra Jardine 1984: 103) because the Father waits in the wings, as the God guaranteeing the authority of the father. And this Father is not quite as insubstantial as he is made out to be; only a work of occlusion makes of Him a pure function; *nothing*, or at most *'très peu de chose'* (Legendre 1985: 243). This is as evident in the specification of this next-to-nothing as it is in the story of the *Fata* which it supports; even, that is, in the purest specification of the zero function. The subscription to paternity is therefore such that it cannot be a simple description. The function itself, in its very mode of articulation, describes a singular, masculine, experience of the world, remaining impervious to the possibility of difference. The possibility of difference is precisely the difference between Legendre and Irigaray.

There is, despite appearances, a sort of poetry to Legendre's paternal function. Even Lacan with his pseudo-geometric *mathemes* was simply constructing a myth. So too with Legendre: 'belief' is perhaps too dumb a formula for the Father's *potestas ligare*. The story of our intrications is a story of *love*: the Absolute is a figure that demands – or commands – love, and the identity it illuminates is a *structura caritatis*, or *montage d'amour* (Legendre 1983: 131). The webs spun by the dogmatic function to bind the subject to its *imago* are woven and embroidered with emblems of eroticism. The poetry of the founding myth – and Legendre's presentation of it – intoxicates because it manipulates the tensions and potentials of this bond of love. However, Irigaray's very different reports from the margins of language suggest that this may be a most impoverished style of eroticism. Irigaray's *nouvelle poïetique* suggests that Legendre's is an aesthetic born of nostalgia and abject hope. It betrays the sensibilities of an inverted soul, which, blind as it is to the material textures of beauty in the here and now, is anything but beautiful. It is the masculine subject for whom *l'amour de soi* is in some sense *'l'amour d'une partie de soi'* (Irigaray 1984: 64). This is a singular love which misses the point that *pour aimer, il faut être deux*, and which is closed to the faculty of *admiration* as the capacity to be continually surprised in 'the passion of the first encounter' of a relation of genuine sexual difference (Irigaray 1984: 78–84).

Irigaray's *nouvelle poïetique* captures the masculine body as the prisoner of a desire according to which total integrity and self-envelopment must be indefinitely postponed, so that any (self-) satisfaction is only partial and transient. Masculine desire is a perpetual movement towards an idealized home for the body, a movement which is alternately nostalgic and utopian, and which depends for its very vitality on the persistence of precisely that interval which it seeks to overcome. To sustain this dynamic, the masculine subject displaces the infinity of the movement to a *beyond*, to a transcendental principle of divinity. Irigaray describes this as a sort of intertwining of ascending and descending orders: 'Man is separated from that primary space which, for him, was plenitude. He lives, as though in exile, between the *never again* and the *not yet* there' (Irigaray 1984: 67).

So what Legendre presents as a universal and neutral process of becoming, Irigaray problematizes as the imposition of a singularly masculine model of subjectification:

> Because the subject deploys itself according to the model of the Moebius band, turning the inside out and the outside in without switching sides, it *closes* off the cycle of love between mother and daughter, between women. In enclosing a morphology and topology which would otherwise be open, the subject represses it, and treats it as a sort of substratum, as though it were no longer free and fertile in its becoming, and as though it were a domain of fearsome monsters.
>
> (Irigaray 1984: 103)

In other words, any potential basis for a maternal–feminine identity is metabolized and destroyed by the imposition of a symbolic order (see Irigaray 1977). Quite simply, the masculine transcendental principle cannot do what Legendre claims it should do – it cannot accommodate the feminine as genuine *difference*. And this inability to do other than repress the feminine leaves the masculine subject itself in a relation of futile subjection to a sterile transcendental principle:

> Man is locked in a master–slave dialectic. He is ultimately enslaved to a God to whom he attributes the qualities of an absolute master, and more secretly or obscurely enslaved to the power of the maternal–feminine which he diminishes or destroys.
>
> (Irigaray 1984: 17)

From this perspective, the logic of the zero function is simply the logic of psychoanalytical theory, or the logic of masculine desire. It serves as well as an illustration of Irigaray's critique of the theory, as it does as an illustration of the theory's *opus operatum*. In what Legendre presents as the limit of subjectivity, one can see the limits of the genealogical–analytical discourse. For Legendre, the Reference is the *lieu idéal supposé* (Legendre 1985: 263): appropriately, and whether or not it is intended to be taken as such, *lieu* here can be read as meaning both (primal) place and ultimate ground, or unmoved mover. As such, it accommodates this figure of a subject driven by the alternating current of nostalgia and hope. The arts of illusion do just enough to ensure that the *lieu premier* is perceived only through the mists of nostalgia; just enough, that is, to produce an experience of radical loss. At the same time, they do not do too much: the impetus generated out of nostalgia is preserved and redirected, engaging the subject in a pursuit of the transcendental principle. So, the concept of the zero function represents the Reference as a sort of displaced symbolic substitute for the Mother.

However, what is most striking about Legendre's model is that the calculative process it depicts – in which the impossible zero is carried over *ad infinitum* – seems perfectly to convey the balance in which Mother and God are held. In *Éthique de la différence sexuelle* (see esp. *'Le lieu, l'intervalle'*), Irigaray devotes a great deal of attention to the question of just how the two dynamics of masculine desire relate to and fuel each other. The problem is that of expressing a relation in which the Mother functions as a sort of origin, and God as a sort of ultimate destination, but which is neither a linear progression nor a sort of circular return. Neither of those representations will do, because origin and destiny are here constructed in separate, but intercommunicating, registers (according to the mode of the future anterior). The quest for God takes place in an order constructed as a sort of (false) confirmation of the masculine imaginary body: God is an Absolute which, even if it remains unapproachable – and indeed, it *must* do so if desire and subjectivity are to be sustainable – offers a different, and more sufferable, experience of lack. The symbolic order which God guarantees is more welcoming, more homely, because it holds out an anticipated state of solidity and *auto-affection* – *outside* or *beyond* the mother. And yet, the figure of the Mother remains present, as the lost origin for which *auto-affection* is the displaced substitute. The order of calculation seems to express this troublesome arrangement almost perfectly. The '1' with which the subject learns to identify incorporates both these registers. The zero that precedes the subject as '1' is the fulcrum of these two principles of desire. It is on the one hand the *assumption* – the 'as if' – which allows the symbolic order to unfold as a representation of possible desire, and, on the other, it is a reference to the Mother as that which is forever lost. The zero therefore keeps the moments of utopia and nostalgia elegantly balanced.

Irigaray's alternative account of our *paroles échappées* sees in the supposedly agnostic genealogical reading of culture a fidelity to the Father which obeys a 'diabolical' logic: 'In this approach, there is no announcement of the future. Everything is programmed and foreseeable. There remains nothing but the pursuit of this strange succession or series' (Irigaray 1987: 53). The rolling of the present into the past – the very exercise that makes of the present the revitalized thing that it is in Legendre's work – locks us into an endless repetition of the S/same. Doubtless Legendre would agree that 'humanity *is* in *narration*' (Jardine 1984: 69). What is either denied or ignored is the point that psychoanalytical theory is itself complicit in the construction and valorization of the narrative of the symbolic order. As with psychoanalysis, and culture generally, the presentation of institutional genealogies remains blind to 'a specifically feminine energy, linked more to communication and growth than it is to reproduction' (Irigaray 1992: 154). In contrast to Irigaray's elusive work of poetry – her *nouvelle poïetique* (Irigaray 1984: 13) – it seems remarkably uncritical. For Irigaray, words of poetry are enunciated in a rhythm of breath which denies 'obedience to a pre-scripted text or word expressing orders, laws and imperative truths' (Irigaray 1992: 190). Poetry is the art of critique in the name of nature, or, to be clearer, a nature that is composed of two irreducible energies. It is an ethical and aesthetic style of relation to the energy of the body, or, more radically, an attempt to think the unthought of western culture: the body (see Irigaray 1984: 99 ff.).

PSYCHOANALYSIS AS CRITIQUE

Of course, Irigaray's own myth-making is a denial of all psychoanalytical models of subjectivity as desire, or at least of the uses for which they are constructed and to which they are put (see Irigaray 1992). However, the critique is all the more problematic when applied to Legendre's genealogies because in tying desire to an order of kinship his institutional analytic accentuates and compounds the quality of closure which is instituted in the psychoanalytical reference to desire. Even for those who share Legendre's sense of pessimism, the paternity of law may construct a subject that is more obviously a creation of theory, and, in a curious sense, a less desperate figure than the subject of Lacan's *signifiant-maître*. In making Paternity a function of Law, and in portraying the unconscious as a jurist, Legendre leaves us with a very different sense of the subject. Where the *stade du miroir* constructs a subject of *anticipation*, Legendre's anthropology leaves us with the subject of a *supposition*. Law, for all its aesthetic flourishes, turns out to have a regularity such that desire must be portrayed as a tamer, less voracious, creature, simply because it has to be put to work in an order of causality. The point is that the order of lineage is constructed by Legendre as an essentially linear sequence driven by causality, and not as a deranged sort of railway network 'which goes everywhere' and on which 'those who travel have no choice but to use it, however little it can be relied upon to take them where they want to go' (Bowie 1991: 132).

Any (descending) order which is tuned to the question *Unde?* must accord each of its elements a causally situated position. Because the structure of the chain is ordered, so too are the elements from which it is composed. Granted, the sequence is – when seen from the *outsider's* point of view – a formally impossible one: each successor in a chain of succession is condemned to repeat the impossible claim to self-identity which is made in the number '1'. However, for the *insider*, he for whom the myth of the Reference has worked its charms, and for whom it speaks the truth, there *appears* a fixed order. Appearances may be deceptive, but having made the vital leap of faith, *Ego* – as he is then designated – has the precise co-ordinates needed to take his bearings and seize his place in the world. So, for the participant, the stations of lineage offer a secure, if uncomfortable, dwelling in the symbolic order, whatever torments the image of man as a *qu'est-ce-que?* might suggest.

This faith is conjured up by a poetry that *fascinates*, but which does not beguile and disrupt in the style of the linguistic Phallus. The leap of faith is made when desire is captivated; when the arts of illusion have done their work. Once ensnared, desire becomes rather listless, as though its vital impulse had been blunted. It is drawn in by the complexity of the genealogical map that spreads out before it, and fascinated by the Absolute principle by which the map is illuminated. In consequence, the play of desire acquires a certain stability or linearity. Indeed, if the genealogical order as it is described by Legendre is to be secured, things cannot be otherwise. So, the nature of the order prescribes the nature of desire. In more abstract terms, there is in play a determinate relation between universal and particular, or between whole and part, such that the nature of the elements is determined by the nature of a relation which is in turn determined by the *purpose* of the chain. The zero function – in its simplicity and apparent inexorability – fixes the sense of each element in such a way as to relegate the relations and promote the order.

With Lacan, on the other hand, the starting point is the relations *in themselves*. The symbolic order is what the relations between signifiers make (of) it. It is the activity of the signifier–subject in pursuit of its obscure object of desire which gives the linguistic chain its momentum and topography. The chain of signifiers, the order of language, is therefore composed of an infinite number of possible, virtual, routes, waiting to be created and articulated through this quite incoherent desire of the subject. Each of these instances of creation – each interruption–constitution – of the chain is the act of a subject-in-the-future-anterior; a subject who is, to borrow an expressive phrase, 'broken on the wheel of . . . the signifying chain' (Juranville 1984: 154). The formally universal chain is therefore an extrapolation of a singular moment of desire. The topography is nothing more than the evanescent trails of moments that have been – future anterior turned to past imperfect.

One difference between Lacan and Legendre may largely be a difference between Hegel's style of relational thought and the relational logic of Lévi-Strauss's indirect appropriation of Saussure. It is, as Bourdieu observes, a condition of Saussure's structuralism that the world addressed by the theorist be constructed from a position of *inaction*. A perspective, that is, from which the world unfolds as a network of closed logical relations, but which offers no view of the demands of practice: 'Unlike the orator, the grammarian has no interest in language other than that of studying it so as to codify it' (Bourdieu 1980: 53). This sets up a distinction or opposition between theory and practice – or thought and life – which obscures the dimension of *participation*. And, although Bourdieu's own model of the *champ* as a dimension of conflict and anticipation may make his neat phrase – *'le réel est relationnel'* (Bourdieu 1992: 72) – more than a reference to Hegel as aphorist, a great deal of Saussure (or perhaps one should say anthropology) remains. With Hegel's dialectic, something quite different is in play. For Hegel, thought *is* activity. Heidegger puts it most suggestively: the point is to 'make restlessness real' (Heidegger 1988: 69). It is, of course, the concept that is restless, and which demands the subsumption of particular existence to the rule of the universal. This accession to universality as a negation of particular identity is described in the *élan* of the dialectic of recognition.

Of course, in Lacan's writings, the exercise is given a peculiar twist; Catherine Clément refers to Lacan's *'hégélianisme malheureux'* (Clément 1981: 112). *'Malheureux'* in the sense that Lacan's is a reception of Hegel which assumes the death of the philosophical subject. The movement of reciprocal recognition is fatally disrupted by the introduction of the impossibly elusive *objet a*, and the perpetual deferral of any completed subjectivity. What remains, however, is the dynamic of the quest for recognition, which is in a sense rendered even more urgent and fluid by the absence of any final word from the Other, and hence the impossibility of any sort of reciprocity, or any transparent universality. The shift from present perfect to future anterior tunes the sense of anticipation to an impossibly high pitch, and it is the acuity of this anticipation which so dislocates the signifying chain. So, despite the prominence of Saussure in the *Écrits*, something quite different is going on here. The partial subject does not take its place in an established network: rather, each dislocated irruption into the order appears as a symptom of the desire of the partial subject. There is, quite simply, no sense of order at all.

What makes Lacan's thought so engaging is precisely this renunciation of totality. His brand of relational thought deals in the primary elements themselves – not things, or places even, but the senselessly repetitive movements of negation, desire, velocity, attraction and transformation. The dynamic of the subject caught in the void between origin and transcendental destiny dissolves any sort of institutional structure into an effect of the play of a desire which devours an enormous breadth of cultural experience. The image of desire as the unstoppable in pursuit of the unattainable brings far more of our tradition into view; and, in diffracting the elements of that experience through the prism of desire, an engaging vitality is brought to our reception of it. In Legendre's account, Law teaches us how and what to desire. Law is, of course, a capacious and diffuse body, but it may none the less be a constricting vehicle for desire. Lacan's oblique but suggestive weaving of cultural 'content' into his theory – through an ostentatiously erudite referencing of names from all points of the *champ lettré* – made a singular principle speak in a plurality of voices. His huge endeavour depended upon the style of presentation of a very slender principle.

With Legendre, this next-to-nothing that is desire, when it is fashioned into a structural principle of Law, loses the irony of that approach. Where Legendre was constantly in search of a more effective *medium* for the play of desire, Legendre imprisons desire itself in a structural model of social institutions. Desire as a version of the *ratio scripta* serves simply to make of law that which makes the world interesting. This often seems a rather reductive simplification, which accounts for few of the styles of *bricolage*, or of actualizing the cultural narrative so as to make ourselves at home in the world. To make law *everything*, as Freud makes sexuality everything (Irigaray 1989: 48), is either to adopt a reductive view of social institutions or to say very little about a great deal. In particular, it is – as the question of the feminine points out – to say nothing about the more subtle differentiations of the social order, or about the hierarchies of access to the totem, or (for instance) the exclusionary and marginalizing structures of Management and advertising as regards certain categories of individual. Even if Legendre's version of narrative coherence does constitute the basic structure of western belief, it may be that it is ordered by something more fragmentary than the juridically conceived Master supposed by Legendre.

REFERENCES

Bourdieu, P. (1980) *Le sens pratique*, Paris: Minuit.
—— (1987) *Choses dites*, Paris: Minuit.
—— (1992) *Réponses*, Paris: Seuil.
Bowie, M. (1991) *Lacan*, London: Fontana.
Braidotti, R. (1991) *Patterns of Dissonance*, Oxford: Polity Press.
Clément, C. (1981) *Vies et légendes de Jacques Lacan*, Paris: Grasset.
Goodrich, P. (1990) *The Languages of Law*, London: Weidenfeld and Nicolson.

Hegel, G. W. F. (1977) *The Phenomenology of Spirit* (trans. A. V. Miller), Oxford: Oxford University Press.
Heidegger, M. (1988) *Hegel's Phenomenology of Spirit* (trans. P. Emad and K. Maly), Bloomington and Indianapolis: Indiana University Press.
Irigaray, L. (1974) *Speculum, de l'autre femme*, Paris: Minuit.
—— (1977) *Ce sexe qui n'en est pas un*, Paris: Minuit.
—— (1984) *Éthique de la différence sexuelle*, Paris: Minuit.
—— (1987) *Sexes et parentés*, Paris: Minuit.
—— (1989) *Le temps de la différence*, Paris: Hachette.
—— (1992) *J'aime à toi*, Paris: Grasset.
Jardine, A. (1984) *Gynesis: Configurations of Woman and Modernity*, Ithaca and London: Cornell University Press.
Juranville, A. (1984) *Lacan et la philosophie*, Paris: PUF.
Lacan, J. (1966) *Écrits*, Paris: Seuil.
—— (1975) *Le séminaire, livre XX: Encore*, Paris: Seuil.
—— (1977) *Écrits: A Selection*, London: Tavistock.
—— (1991) *Le séminaire, livre XVI: L'envers de la psychanalyse*, Paris: Seuil.
Legendre, P. (1978) *La passion d'être un autre*, Paris: Seuil.
—— (1983) *Leçons II: L'empire de la vérité*, Paris: Fayard.
—— (1985) *Leçons IV: L'inestimable objet de la transmission*, Paris: Fayard.
—— (1988) 'Comment l'homme devient homme' (interview), *Le Monde*, 6 May.
—— (1989) *Leçons VIII: Le crime du caporal Lortie*, Paris: Fayard.
Papageorgiou-Legendre, A. (1990) *Leçons IV, Suite II, Filiation*, Paris: Fayard.
Weber, S. (1991) *Return to Freud*, Cambridge: Cambridge University Press.
Zizek, S. (1991) 'The truth arises from misrecognition', in E. Ragland-Sullivan and M. Bracher (eds), *Lacan and the Subject of Language*, London: Routledge.

Chapter 6

Antigone's law

A genealogy of jurisprudence

Costas Douzinas and Ronnie Warrington

Of all the masterpieces of the classical world – and I know them and you should and you can – the *Antigone* seems to me the most magnificent and satisfying work of art of its kind.

[T]he celestial Antigone, the most resplendent figure ever to have appeared on earth.

G. W. F. Hegel, *Aesthetics*

Like Hegel, we have been fascinated by Antigone, by this unbelievable relationship, this powerful liaison without desire, this immense impossible desire that could not live, capable only of overturning, paralysing, or exceeding any system and history, of interrupting the life of the concept, of cutting off its breath, or better, what comes down to the same thing, of supporting it from outside or underneath a crypt.

J. Derrida, *Glas*

Is there anyone who doesn't evoke *Antigone* whenever there is a question of a law that causes conflict in us even though it is acknowledged by the community to be a just law?

J. Lacan, *The Ethics of Psychoanalysis*

I was not born to hate but to love.

Antigone

I

We shall start where we should, at the start. What is the site of law's emergence? Where does it come from? Our enquiry will attempt to trace the 'question of law'; of law's origins and of its value, of law's validity and force. The question is haunted. It is persecuted by two ghosts both deriving from *Antigone*. The more ancient emerges from

Antigone's tomb and yet never leaves it. The more recent, but in another sense also the most ancient, answers to the name of Heidegger, the recorder of the closure of metaphysics and of the death of jurisprudence. We will follow the lead of these two spectres in our attempt to approach the ground of law, the law of law, and to answer the most ancient and most urgent question.

At the beginning of Sophocles' *Antigone*, the tragic heroine states her own law in the most categorical way. She will bury the corpse of her brother Polynices. There is no equivocation, no ambiguity, no hesitation in Antigone's voice in the face of the disreputable death of her brother or the command of her uncle King Creon who has prohibited the burial of a traitor. Only an immediate and unquestioning acceptance of the 'should', an unwavering assumption of responsibility.

> ISMENE: You cannot mean to bury him
> Against the order.
> ANTIGONE: Yes! He is my brother . . .
> I must bury him myself . . .
> ISMENE: Then go if you must . . .
> wild, irrational as you are.
>
> (44, 45, 98–9)[1]

We cannot remain indifferent in the face of the force of this wild, irrational law. Where does this 'must' come from? To answer this question, the question of law, we turn to the tragedy handed down through the thick matter of philological and philosophical commentary that has covered Antigone's face like a wedding veil and sepulchral curtain. But why turn to *Antigone*? What is the relevance of a text written in Athens in the fifth century BC for the understanding of the law of law?

For centuries, Greek drama has been the meeting point of philosophy, literature and ethics, of reason, form and law. Greek tragedy, Nietzsche's 'philosophical opus *par excellence*', was the testing ground of the Odyssey of Spirit for Hegel, of unconscious desire for Freud and of the primordial memory of Being for Heidegger. The tragedies have been translated, interpreted and incorporated into the concerns of modern philosophy as the imagination of modernity returns time and again to its grounding myths. For classical philologists, aestheticians and poets, on the other hand, lyrical poetry and tragedy are the highest achievements of Greek culture and are considered an unparalleled yardstick for western literature both in style and content.

And, according to Steiner, amongst the great works of world literature no one 'has elicited the strengths of philosophic and poetic interest focused on Sophocles' *Antigone*'.[2]

Interestingly, while philosophy has consistently turned to tragedy as the ground of the dialectic and to *Antigone* in particular in order to understand the nature of the law and of law's power, jurisprudence has virtually ignored it. Jurisprudence textbooks usually refer to *Antigone* in passing, in the chapter on natural law.[3] They present the tragedy as an early statement of the potential conflict between a superior source of duty and the law of the state. Antigone is the 'first great heroine of civil resistance, almost the leader or inspirator of a resistance movement against tyranny' (Weinreb 1987: 21). And as most jurisprudence improbably presents modern conceptions of natural law as the outcome and perfection of an unbroken, continuous history that started with the Greeks, *Antigone* gets a statutory mention alongside Aristotle and the Stoics, Aquinas and Locke. But this is merely to attribute to it a certain foundational status without attempting to listen to *Antigone*'s call. Despite the imprudent neglect of jurisprudence the praise of philosophy should alert us to the importance of *Antigone* for the moral unconscious of law. *Oedipus Rex* and the myth of Oedipus have been recognized as key texts for the understanding of psyche and identity. The daughter of Oedipus, Antigone, must be similarly acknowledged as a foundation of thought and action concerning *physis* and *nomos*, *nomos* and *dike*, law and justice.

The presence of these myths is so pervasive in our culture, that only a sense of misplaced arrogance and originality have stopped us from acknowledging the 'repetitive and epigonal character of our consciousness and expression' (Steiner 1986: 113). Heidegger fully agrees:

> all progressivist and evolutionary anthropology is false. The beginning is the strangest and the mightiest. What comes after that is not a development but flattening that results from mere spreading out. . . . Historical knowledge is an understanding of the mysterious character of this beginning. If anything it is knowledge of mythology.
>
> (Heidegger 1961: 155)

Our claim is that *Antigone* is as important for the exploration of the origins and force of law and ethics as Freud believed Oedipus was for the foundations of psychoanalysis. But 'origins' does not refer here to some idealized Greek 'childhood of man' that was perfected in his western maturity. Instead it refers to the leap, both original and final, in which man founded himself by finding himself before the 'other' who put to him the first, continuing, and last, ethical command which constitutes the philosophical foundation of law as laid down in *Antigone*.

To follow the ethical command that the other always makes we will conduct three readings of *Antigone*: a juridical, a dialectical-speculative and an ontological. But each will be 'deconstructed' by being directed to the question of law and justice. The juridical reading will show the impossibility of a *nomos* with(out) *dike*; the dialectical will reveal the universal and the (legal) system devoured by the singular; finally, the ontological will show that ethics comes before the destiny of Being and ontology and brings the law before the question of justice.

*

At the start of the play, the two daughters of Oedipus are in conversation. Antigone tells Ismene of the latest catastrophe to visit the house of Laius. Creon has issued a decree prohibiting the burial of their brother Polynices and threatens disobedience with death. Both Polynices and his brother, Eteocles, perished in the battle at Thebes. Eteocles was given the full funeral honours of a dead hero; but Creon's edict was that the traitor Polynices should be left unburied. As a result his soul will be unable to enter Hades. Antigone tells her sister that she will defy the King's proclamation and tries to involve her in the act. Ismene is not prepared to challenge the law and tries to reason with Antigone. Antigone, fearless and determined, despairs at her sister's indecisiveness and sets off to bury Polynices on her own.

Creon then proclaims his vision of politics based on utilitarian calculation and pragmatic compromise. He announces his harsh edict and informs the Thebans that he has posted sentinels to guard the corpse. He is interrupted by a terrified soldier who comes to announce a 'miracle'; Polynices corpse has been covered by a film of dust, but no one was seen carrying out the libation. The chorus suspects divine intervention, but Creon is convinced that it is the work of political conspirators and accuses the guard of complicity, threatening terrible punishments.

Antigone is brought before Creon by the guard who caught her in the act of burying Polynices. She freely admits her guilt and appeals to the eternal laws of the gods who ordain that the dead should be properly buried in order to travel from this world to Hades. Creon condemns her to be buried alive. The King's son and Antigone's fiancé, Haemon, tries to convince his father that Antigone's action was holy and her life should be spared. Creon sees in his pleadings the work of a feeble person, infatuated by love and unable to reason. Incensed by his son's disobedience, that threatens both paternal and political authority, he confirms Antigone's sentence.

Tiresias, the blind seer, tells the King he has received terrible omens. The gods will not accept his sacrifices and a plague is tormenting Thebes. The carrion of Polynices' corpse that the beasts bring into the city has polluted the temples. As the signs of divine anger multiply, Creon relents. He will save Antigone from her grave and bury the corpse. But fate has ordained differently. When Creon arrives at the burial site, Antigone has killed herself. Haemon, who has followed her, mad with anger and remorse, attacks his father and kills himself. Creon returns to Thebes to hear the final part of his family's destruction; his wife Euridice, on hearing the news, is overcome with grief and she too commits suicide on the family altar. The houses of Creon and of Oedipus have been destroyed.

II

Unusually for tragedy, *Antigone* has 'a double centre of gravity' (Goheen 1951: 97). The tragedy progresses through the clearly defined conflict of the two protagonists, Antigone and Creon. Their arguments, principles and actions in relation to the moral and political issues and dilemmas involved are sharply distinguished and are presented consistently from two diametrically opposed perspectives. As a result some of the most influential readings of *Antigone* have treated the tragedy as the manifestation of a series of underlying conflicts of value and standpoint that move the action inexorably towards its doom-laden conclusion. The trend started with Hegel's influential philosophical interpretation, and has been repeated in many critical readings.

In general terms, philosophy has treated oppositions of principle or concept either as the inevitable preparatory step towards their eventual dialectical synthesis, or as eternally circulating and irreconcilable antitheses that constitute the subterranean 'grammar' of action. To be sure, conceptual oppositions invite or inhabit axiological priorities in which one side is presented as superior to the other. If Creon and Antigone are the human embodiments of a double perspective, inescapably bound to each other, the attribution of guilt and responsibility for the monstrous catastrophe that befalls all the main characters by the end of the tragedy becomes the key question in the interpretation of *Antigone*. If the two protagonists are masks of a fatal conflict, the question of supremacy of one of the antagonistic principles, of 'who is right' has correctly dominated the commentaries.

Many principles have been proposed as the key organizing oppositions of the conflict.[4] But it is the attitude of the protagonists to the law that has received one of the clearest presentations and has dominated the critical literature. It is a question of law, justice and punishment.

CREON: Now, tell me – not in many words but briefly –
did you know that an edict (*kerychthenta*) had forbidden this?
ANTIGONE: Of course I knew it; it was public (*emphane*)
CREON: And did you dare to transgress these laws (*nomous*)?
ANTIGONE: It wasn't Zeus, not in the least,
who made this proclamation (*keryxas*) – not to me.
Nor did that Justice (*Dike*), dwelling with the gods
beneath the earth, ordain such laws (*nomous*) for men.
Nor did I think your edicts (*kerygmata*) had such force
that you a mere man, could override
the great unwritten and certain laws of the gods
(*agrapta kasphale theon nomima*).
They are alive, not just today or yesterday:
they live forever, and no one knows
when they were first legislated.

(446–57)

A strict dichotomy is established. The divine proclamations of Zeus and the laws of the chthonic gods of the underworld are juxtaposed to the *nomos* or *kerygmata* of the *polis*. Divine law is unwritten, certain and eternal. As unwritten it is felt and acted upon by those who receive its call. It lives in the actions of people rather than in public proclamations. Its certainty does not call for interpretation but for an immediate obedience that does not calculate the consequences. To die before her time carrying out her duty is for Antigone a 'gain', *kerdos* (464). Finally, *ta theon nomima* are everlasting; they exist before and beyond the time of political institutions and of human machinations and devices like writing. The worlds of heaven and of *Hades* intrude upon history as disturbances of temporality and rationality. The timelessness of their commands is a permanent challenge to the timeliness of the laws and institutions that establish the boundaries of the *polis*.

At the other end stand the *nomoi* of the *polis* legislated by the rightful King. Creon's law is man-made, secular and civic; it is the basis of all civilizing values of the *polis* and the cause of its salvation. There is no greater test for a man than 'rule and law-giving', *archais te kai nomoisin* (177), and Creon boasts that he has passed it: his *nomoi* guard the city's greatness (191). It is in his first speech to the chorus, which parallels Pericles' funeral oration to the Athenians, that Creon sets out the general principles and the law of the democratic state which is always threatened by enemies external and within. Polynices, a traitor who attacked his city and family, deserves the cruellest punishment; Creon's edict is a straightforward application of the general law of state necessity.

> CREON: I could never stand by silent,
> watching destruction march against our city, putting safety to rout,
> nor could I ever make that man a friend of mine
> who menaces our country. Remember this:
> our country is our safety.
> Only while she voyages true on course
> can we establish friendships, truer than blood itself. Such are my laws (*nomoisi*).
> They make our city great.
>
> (184–91)

Creon's words sound no different from any other leader's in the midst of strife and war. The chorus thoroughly agrees with him:

> It's true your word is law (*nomo de chresthai*)
> and you can legislate
> both for the living and the dead.
>
> (213–14)

The chorus has no kind words for Antigone until much later in the play when the displeasure of the gods at Creon's impiety becomes clear. To understand the impact of the developing conflict for the *phronimous andres* of the chorus we should compare the contrasting positions with the dominant political and ethical theories of classical Greece.

For the Athenians of the fifth century, the *polis* is both spatially and metaphorically the focus of man's civilizing influence. In his *Ethics*, Aristotle presented the city as the median place between the world of the gods above and of the animals (*zoa*) below. Civic virtue can only develop in the institutions of the *polis* which lie between divinity and bestiality. Man overcomes his state of animality (*zoon*) only when he belongs to the city (*politicon*). Thucydides reported that the Athenians prided themselves on being law-abiding (ii, 37, 3) and Euripides believed that it is the enactment of laws that distinguishes Greeks from barbarians. No wisdom or experience should set them aside (*Medea* 536–7; *Bacchae* 881–2), a sentiment that echoes Plato's life-long dislike of civil disobedience.

In the *Crito*, Socrates is visited by his old friend Crito in his prison where he is awaiting execution. Crito has prepared his master's escape. Socrates, in a dream-like encounter with the Laws of Athens, is reminded that a state cannot survive if individuals disobey the decisions of the laws. To the argument that unjust laws may be disobeyed, the Laws respond that their binding agreement with Socrates was that the Laws were to be followed at all times. Their authority should not be undermined as they protect the state which is holier than mother and father (50b, 51b).

To Athenian ears, therefore, Creon's opening speech, with its moving references to the paramount importance of the salvation of the ship of state, would not have sounded very different from Socrates' argument or from Pericles' *Epitaphios* (Funeral Oration). The great rhetor Demosthenes is reported to have used part of Creon's address in defending his own case against Aeschines whom he attacks for having forgotten these great principles in his political life (xix, 247). Despite some fanciful interpretations of the tragedy (Whitman 1951: 90), the Greek citizen, Aristotle's *zoon politicon*, knows that his and his family's salvation and well-being depend on the safety of the *polis* which cannot be easily gainsaid.

As the action unfolds, however, Creon's attitude gradually changes as does the positive, all-conquering image of the law. First, he identifies *nomos* with his own pronouncements (449, 481) which are declared equivalent to earth, the 'highest goddess', and the temples (284–7). In his confrontation with Haemon, Creon claims absolute obedience for his laws:

> But that man the city places in authority,
> his orders must be obeyed, in small things and
> large, in just and unjust, *dikaia kai t'enantia*.
> (667–9)

There is no greater evil than *anarcheia*, proclaims the King in his argument with Haemon (672). But as his arguments do not alter Haemon's position, the desperate Creon abandons his earlier high-minded claims and asserts that the city belongs to him (738). This change of attitude turns Creon from a legitimate King to a demagogue and a tyrant who will soon forfeit whatever sympathy the chorus still has for him.

But if the two protagonists seem to have totally antagonistic conceptions of law, the same appears to be true in relation to their attitudes to *dike*, justice. In Creon's vocabulary *dike* is an attribute of civic rule closely associated with positive law, and *dikaios* is the obedient and virtuous citizen (208, 400). On two occasions the expression *dounai diken* (to give or to do justice) is used, which identifies *dike*, like much contemporary jurisprudence, with procedure, the administration of justice and punishment (228, 303). Creon is not impervious to the claims of divine justice; in his opening address he appeals to Zeus as witness to the justice of his rule and as protector of Thebes. But as the confrontation with Antigone and her claim to follow divine law intensifies, he distances himself from godly appelations and claims supreme validity for his own edicts. Creon distinguishes between the law-abiding (*dikaios*) man and the claims of Zeus (658–61). He demands obedience for both his just and unjust laws (665–7); he identifies justice with his laws (744) and uses the word *dike* pejoratively to mean feud, conflict (742). Finally, he denounces the seer and messenger of the gods, Tiresias, as a lover of injustice, *t'adikein philon* (1059). In Creon's enlightened and secular humanism, civic order and the rule of law are the highest principles. They subsume reasonable religious claims and try to turn them to advantage, according to the principles of political utilitarianism that Creon follows. Claims that deny the civilizing influence of the law are denigrated. But in not recognizing the proper rights of the gods he seems to prepare his own downfall.

By contrast Antigone's *dike* is divine in provenance and private in operation. *Dike* is personified, she is an infernal goddess who dwells with the gods below (451) and ordains what is due to the dead (94) and to the gods (459–60). Her commands are specific and are addressed individually and privately to a chosen few rather than to the whole *polis*; she who receives the *nomous* of Hades (519) is immediately obliged to answer through deeds, irrespective of personal interest or the consequences of action (538–43). The responsibility of the recipient of the law is original and unique (908,

914) and forces her to action. It cannot be shared after the deed through words of sympathy or a merely verbal undertaking of responsibility. Ismene cannot join in Antigone's punishment as she did not answer the call of *dike* (542–7).

Antigone is not impervious to the interests of the state. She believes that her fellow-citizens support her action and would do so publicly but for the fear of reprisals from Creon (519), a claim repeated by Haemon. She would not have acted against the wishes of the *polis* if the dead was a husband or son (905–7). But the call of the dead brother and the law of the chthonic *dike* make her, exceptionally, disobey. She has received her own law and she is acting upon it of her own free will. As a consequence she will suffer a fate no other mortal has ever known: she will be buried alive. She is *autonomos*, says the awe-struck chorus (821).

On the few occasions legal literature turned to *Antigone*, it is this dichotomy that was mostly discussed. It is presented as the first clear statement of the conflict between natural and positive law. The law that comes from God, let us call it for the sake of analytical clarity and only provisionally justice (*dike*) against the law of the state (*nomos*). In this sense *Antigone* is acknowledged as the foundation stone of jurisprudence. It sets up, it starts an eternal confrontation at the heart of the 'ought'. Antigone splits the ethical substance between a divine and a secular component, the unwritten and the written, the eternal and the temporary. The two poles are placed in their unceasing circulation, they create an economy of conflict and of revolving hierarchies, which becomes the history of law and of law's consciousness–jurisprudence.

There is, however, a parallel narrative of the tragedy, which deeply affected Hegel. Antigone stands for the principle of family, for the realm of the private, of individuality and love. Time and again she reminds both her sister Ismene and Creon of her familial duty to her brother, which in some instances appears ordained by the 'unwritten laws' but more often is presented as the result of Antigone's *philia* love, loyalty, affection and kinship.

She and Ismene are the only survivors from the house of Oedipus. In her moving soliloquy, before she is led to the tomb, Antigone recounts how she carried out the funeral rites for her father, mother and her other brother Eteocles. Her duty now finally extends to Polynices.

ANTIGONE: And even if I die in the act, a good death
I will lie loved with the one I love (*phile philou*) . . .
If I had allowed
my own mother's son to rot, an unburied corpse
that would have been agony . . .
Not ashamed for a moment
to honor my brother, my own flesh and blood.

(67–73)

No death is nobler than that imposed for burying her *philtatos*, dearest brother (81, 503, 512, 517). She will bury Polynices both because he is a brother and out of the deepest affection for him. Throughout the play, Antigone uses the language of love and of family kinship as demanding with equal force that she defies the law of the *polis*.

Antigone stands for the rights of the *genos*, of blood lineage. As the sister, she is the kinswoman who has the duty to perform the burial rites necessary for her kin to enter the netherland, the dark region of Hades. The origin of her duty and her affection is the common womb from which she and Polynices have emerged. The references to the womb as the place that founds clear bonds of affection and duty are continuous. From the first striking line of the play Antigone establishes her strong link with kinship morality. She calls Ismene 'my sister my own dear sister' and uses an uncommon word for sister (*autadelphos*) which emphasizes their link through the *delphys* (womb). Her brothers and sisters are *adelphoi*, *homogastrioi* (co-uterine), *homosplanchnoi* (of the same belly).

In his first speech, on the other hand, Creon had defined *philia* in terms of civic obedience, political friendship and right (182–3):

CREON: Only while our city voyages true on course can we establish friendships,
truer than blood itself.

(190)

Blood friendship must be subordinated to the salvation of the city; moreover, Creon reminds Antigone, the two brothers found themselves the worst of enemies and killed each other in battle, impervious to their common descent.

Miserable wretches who, born from one father and mother,
leveled double-conquering spears against one another and so won, both of them,
a common share in death.

(143–6)

CREON: The foe (*echtros*) is never a friend (*philos*) – not even in death.

ANTIGONE: I was not born to hate but to love (*symphilein*)

(522–3)

Antigone's answer is perhaps the most famous line of the tragedy. Against Creon's distinctions of the primordial commonality of matrilinear belonging, Antigone allies nature with her own idea of love. She undertakes to purify the *miasma* (170–2) and heal the infectious division of the house of Oedipus by re-uniting the two brothers in Hades and following them there.

Antigone stands *anti* the *genos* or *gonos*. She compensates for the curse of her house that turned mother and son into husband and wife, father and offspring into brothers and sisters – in other words she stands for the basic laws and taboos of womb integrity. But she also consciously runs the risk of destroying the family of Oedipus. Her maiden betrothal with death virtually ensures the destruction of her father's line.

Antigone therefore stands both for and against the family. Her name alone should alert us to the excessive formalism of the 'structuralist' or 'jurisprudential' readings of *Antigone*. Their confrontations and reversals, oppositions and syntheses, provide too neat and formal readings of the text. Characters and principles, actions and words do not stand ready formed, closed and totally opposed to each other. Ambiguity, conflict and tension exists both within all main characters and concepts of the tragedy as well as between them. This tension is all too apparent at the level of the legal terms and institutions that form the background against which the action takes place.

Language generally, and legal discourse in particular, is a battleground for the protagonists, who use the same legal concepts with profoundly different meanings. Take for example the key term *nomos*, the law. Its semantic field is beset with extreme ambiguity. The same word is being used by different characters and occasionally by the same character with totally different meanings. For Antigone *nomos* is religious law and the ancient and unwritten customs of family, kinship and Hades. For Creon *nomos* is the edict of the King, his *kerygma*, promulgated in his sovereign speech (*keryttein*: to announce, pronounce). *Nomos*, of course, derives from *nemein*, regular attribution fixed by custom but also territorial attribution fixed by pastorage. The fecundity of the term allows both uses to exist even though they totally contradict each other.

The sharp contrasts between the totally antagonistic laws and principles all too easily identified by jurisprudence, are soon upset. Creon, for whom *nomos* is the edict of the state enunciated in his authoritative commands, comes soon to meet the laws of those forces that do not follow his rationalism. Such laws are not promulgated in speech (*logos*) nor are they the products of reason (*logos*). He is reminded of the law of fate and of the gods connected with the unleashing and punishment of wanton boastfulness (*ate*). 'Nothing that is vast enters into the life of mortals without a curse' (614). The wonderful power that lies at the centre of all human greatness and achievement (352 ff.) carries with it the violence of destruction thus linking unbreakably the greatest and basest in man. The law of *eros* next, of love and sexual passion, is inescapable by mortal men and immortal gods alike (786–90) and is enthroned on the side of the eternal laws (799); love makes people forget and disobey the orders of state law, as it did with Haemon, whose infatuation with Antigone wreaked havoc on the royal court. Finally, as the scale of destruction of his home becomes clear, Creon has to acknowledge the existence of the *kathestotas nomous* – the laws established by powers beyond his sovereignty (1113–14) – which however are fully valid and necessary for the well-ruled city, *eunomousa polin*. Too late, responds the chorus. Creon 'saw *diken*' at last but not in time to save himself and his *oikos* (1270).

But Antigone too comes to experience a *dike* different from that of the underground gods she cherishes. In her last exchanges with her fellow citizens, as she tries to understand her fate and solicit sympathy for herself, the chorus explains:

> CHORUS: You went too far, the last limits of daring –
> smashing against the high throne of *Dike*.
>
> (853–5)

Dike forbids the suppliants to come too close; there is a point after which no further advance to the throne of *dike* is allowed. Antigone rushes forward nevertheless; but she stumbles, smashes herself against the throne and falls. We can never know *dike* fully. Justice forbids and she forbids herself. And Antigone teaches that to come close to *dike*, we must launch ourselves, attempt to transcend self and the law and experience the inevitable fall.

But the possibility that Antigone too may have miscalculated in attributing exclusive significance to one set of laws does enter her mind. This comes eventually to engulf her in mortal amphiboly as she is led away to her grave. The gods, for whose law she is about to suffer the ignominious fate of the living corpse, do not seem to acknowledge her resolution or to support her in her martyrdom.

> ANTIGONE: What law of the mighty gods (*daimonon diken*) have I transgressed?
> Why look to the heavens any more, tormented as I am?
> Whom to call, what comrades now? Just think
> my reverence only brands me for irreverence!
> Very well: if this is the pleasure of the gods,
> once I suffer my doom I shall come to know my sin.
> But if these men are wrong, let them suffer
> nothing worse than they mete out to me –
> these masters of injustice!
>
> (921–8)

This is an awesome combination of defiance of the injustice of the law, of abandonment in the face of the unknown wishes of the gods and of extreme agony that prefigures Christ at Gethsemane. The *dike* she has appealed to throughout remains uncommunicative and the law she gives to herself as *autonomos* may still turn out to be unjust. Antigone accepts that the law – her own and Creon's – will take its course and will not allow her to know whether she is pious or sinful before her terrible death. The law metes out its punishment before we know its command fully, like the infernal machine in Kafka's *Penal Colony* that physically inscribes the law and their crimes on the bodies of the convicts who will come to know their transgression in their punishment.

Antigone goes to her death 'pious out of impiety' (924), a criminal whose crime has been the most holy (74). She is a tragic and heroic persona on whose corporeal body, law and *dike*, the highest and the lowest will play out to the end both their catastrophic antithesis and eternal symbiosis (Whitman 1951). And if this is the law, it is given to the solitary person in unpredictable fashion and is never beyond doubt. But the wavering of ethical solitude is only temporary. The terrible law can only be fully known after it has taken its course. And it is the fate of Antigone, the *isothea* of Hölderlin, to take this course and defy both earthly and godly powers. This simultaneous acceptance and defiance of both laws fascinated Hegel. Antigone's sacrifice could lead the antagonistic principles to their necessary sublation and transcendence.

III

Hegel's interest in Greek tragedy is linked with his understanding of the modern social and philosophical condition as exemplified in Kantianism. Kant had inaugurated the modern obsession with the split between subject and object, and the fragmentation of self and the world. The main philosophical task of German romanticism was to heal the rift and assert again the oneness of existence. Hegel's answer was to internalize and historicize the split; the fragmentation of modernity was a necessary and evolving part of the movement of the spirit towards its self-consciousness. The key oppositions of modernity are the expression of an ongoing conflict, an *agon* internal to our existence, and the inescapable condition of our consciousness. Thought, consciousness and the spirit are action, a continuous struggle. The spirit must fight a civil war against its own alienation, and must recognize itself in, and return itself through, its other. It is only through this *emphilios polemos* (war of friends) that the spirit gathers and sublates the fragments in the totality of history. Against what he saw as Kant's moral formalism, Hegel claims that freedom and the possibility of ethical life are intrinsically linked – indeed they are the outcome of the split existence within the organic community. But the condition of ethical life, *Sittlichkeit*, the ethical substance as realized in the state, is necessarily tragic.

In the *Philosophy of Right* (Hegel 1967) the movement to the absolute Spirit, to Reason's self-consciousness is presented in the usual triurnal progression but in explicitly legal terms; from abstract, formal right to *Moralität*, the morality of the Kantian type, finally to *Sittlichkeit* (ethical life or substance). Abstract right, both as law and morality, is the immediate, undifferentiated unity of the universal. As such it has no determinate content, only a formal existence; its concept, that of the personality, exists only in the abstract. Human will is absolutely free but has no content other than to relate self to itself thus turning self into a person. This abstract personality can only be legal; it is the abstract capacity of the persona to have rights and it forms the basis of all systems of property, contract and criminal law.

The passage from right to morality involves differentiation and concretization; the bare, abstract universality of will, of personality and of formal right are turned into individual subjectivity. The subject becomes aware of his freedom as he stands out against the world presented to his will. In this inner sphere, it is my intention and purpose that counts, as it stands at the bar of the good, of universal morality. But the good should not remain internal to my conscience; it must be realized in the external world as it is the universal end.

In morality, however, the two domains remain formal and unmediated; moral conscience on the one side, in its Kantian abstract form, faces the Good, the universal essence of freedom, as two sides external to each other. The Good has no content nor has it become yet a concrete part of subjectivity. The subjects are now differentiated but their morality is still abstract.

It is in the third moment of *Sittlichkeit*, ethical life, that formal right and morality are finally absorbed and cancelled. The differentiated universal with its objective and subjective moments is now superseded by the concrete synthesis of the universal and particular. The good and conscience that were kept abstract and apart in morality come together and become present in the actions of concrete individuals. The ethical life is freedom become concrete, the unity of subject and object and of content and form; it constrains 'subjective opinion and caprice' (Hegel 1967: 144), not as an externally posited law but as the living good which is particularized in each individual. The individual can realize his freedom and his satisfaction only in and through the ethical order; virtue is 'the ethical order reflected in the individual character' (Hegel 1967: 153, 154, 150). The concrete embodiment of this ethical substance is posited without hesitation: it is the 'valid laws and institutions' (Hegel 1967: 144); and again in the *Phenomenology of Spirit*, 'this Spirit can be called the human law, because it is essentially in the form of a reality that is conscious of itself. In the form of universality it is the *known* law, and the prevailing custom' (Hegel 1977: 448).

This is then the movement of the Spirit: from right to morality to the ethical life which realizes itself in the passage from family to civil society to the state. The movement is full of confirmations and contradictions that are absorbed in the inexorable sublation and transcendence of the opposites. Political philosophy and economy have emphasized the conflict between civil society and the state. Yet the key opposition in the Hegelian edifice is that between family and state.

Both principles are immanent in human history; the state is the embodiment of positive law as generality, equality and legality. Family on the other hand is law's other, it stands for love and death, for specificity and individuality. *Sittlichkeit* and the dialectical path to it are split between the demands of the political realm and those of private right, the main aim of which is the preservation of family.

This split becomes concrete in the actions of individuals. In extreme cases, the conflict between the abstract formalism of the state and the substantive autonomy of an individual who is not prepared to give way becomes catastrophic. Antigone is one such authentic person; she answers the inner voice, acquires self-consciousness and thus realizes the ethical substance. In her action absolute ethicity becomes actual and historical, as the conflict between its two principles is fought around the burial of the dead.

The family has as its object the absolutely singular. Its field of intervention is man in the abstract, manhood without its everyday empirical characteristics. In the consciousness of the family, its member is the most concrete and unique person, an *individualized particularity*, and it is this singularity that makes him worthy of the family's ontological valuation. The state, on the other hand, is concerned with the citizen's actions, and assesses him for what he does. In particular, the pagan state demands that its citizens risk their lives and die for the universal cause of personal and state recognition. And as these actions can be performed by many people, the citizen is a *generalized individuality*.

For Hegel, of course, the ethical purpose of the family is not acquired in its pure natural existence. When 'the brother leaves the family . . . and the sister becomes, or the wife remains, the head of the household and the guardian of divine law . . . the two sexes overcome their merely natural being and appear in their ethical significance' (Hegel 1977: 275). And while each of the laws is assigned to each sex by nature, the importance of the family is to prepare man, *vir*, for a life of virtue and virility in the community, transform him from *homme* into *citoyen* and install him in the service of universality and citizenship. Family, the place of the individual and the private, fulfils itself by educating men to renounce the family's principle of privacy and love and teaching them to adopt the public life of state and the spirit. The family's *telos* is to sacrifice itself for the *polis*. State and family are as opposed as earth and the underworld, their respective principles as those of Zeus and Hades.

Hegel is quite explicit: the ultimate and most complete family deed no longer concerns the living but the dead,

> the individual [man] who, after a long succession of separate disconnected experiences, concentrates himself into a single completed shape, and thus raises himself out of the unrest of the accidents of life into the calm of simple universality. But because it

> is only as a citizen that he is actual and substantial, the individual, so far as he is not a citizen but belongs to the family, is only an unreal impotent shadow.
>
> (Hegel 1977: 270)

But although the duty of the family, especially of the female members, encompasses the requirement to bury the dead, the state does not always recognize women's funeral function and rights. When Creon condemns Polynices' corpse to the birds and dogs, he punishes him for the only thing that concerns the state, his acts. And again when Antigone buries him, she knowingly commits a crime. Creon must threaten death to sustain his rule and he must carry out his threat. The law of the state establishes government and abstract rule and assembles the dispersed and conflicting members of community around the King's head. But the community's real life, property, labour and personal rights still belong to and are exercised in the family. The state and its law recognizes and protects the family as it knows that it owes its existence and aggrandizement to family's law and function. But individuality can degenerate into anarchy and ownership into untrammelled self-interest, and endanger the city. To prevent the degeneration of the spirit of individuality the government must 'from time to time shake [people] to their core by war. . . . By this means . . . individuals are made to feel by government in the labour laid on them, their lord and master, death' (Hegel 1977: 272–3). Death, the province of the law of gods, is mobilized by the law of state as a guarantee of its validity. Each of the two laws carries death as its work or as its limit; death as the proper business of woman that takes her outwards to community or death as the threat and the weapon of man that takes him inwards to family. As an inner limit attached to one of the antagonistic principles, which at the same time acts as the principle of transcendence of the antagonism itself, death becomes the symbol of the dialectic and the (burial) ground upon which the family/state conflict rises and falls.

We can conclude that for Hegel the state must try to absorb the activity of family and direct it towards its aims and policies; but it cannot extend itself beyond a certain limit because the very existence of the family upon which the state bases itself will be threatened. This division between the domain of private and public exemplifies, and is one layer or moment of, the wider speculative conflict between the Absolute and the contingent or the Universal and the singular.

Antigone knows the law, unlike Oedipus, and she publicly violates it without remorse or regret. 'The ethical consciousness is more complete, its guilt more inexcusable, if it knows beforehand the law and the power it opposes, if it takes them to be violence and wrong, to be ethical merely by accident, and, like Antigone knowingly commits the crime' (Hegel 1977: 284). Antigone thus becomes the symbol and embodiment of pure criminality who must be punished by the law, 'the manhood of community' that establishes itself by 'consuming' the family. But at the same time in defying the law to defend the divine and family principle, Antigone abandons the realm of the private. She rejects Creon's angry suggestion that the two brothers should be differentiated according to their actions and makes a public principle out of her own personal devotion to the singular being of the traitor brother's corpse. Antigone is a rebel in the cause of family love who reverses the order of priority and dependence between state and family and inscribes the ontological principle of law in the heart of the community. In dying for love, Antigone becomes the law; her irony and passion inscribe themselves in the midst of the disembodied sobriety of the universal.

> Since the community only gets an existence through its interference with the happiness of the Family, and by dissolving (individual) self-consciousness into the universal, it creates for itself in what it suppresses and what is at the same time essential to it an internal enemy – womankind in general. Womankind – the everlasting irony (in the life) of the community – changes by intrigue the universal end of the government into a private end, transforms its universal property of the state into a possession and ornament for the family. Woman in this way turns to ridicule the earnest wisdom of the mature age which, indifferent to purely private pleasures and enjoyments, as well as to playing an active part, only thinks of and cares for the universal.
>
> (Hegel 1977: 288)

IV

What is it that makes Antigone stand against the force of Creon's state? It is the call not just of the dead but of one particular dead.

> ANTIGONE: Never I tell you,
> if I had been the mother of children
> or if my husband died, exposed and rotting –
> I'd never have taken this ordeal upon myself,

never defied our people's will. What law (*nomou*)
you ask, is my warrant for what I say?
A husband dead, there might have been another.
A child by another too, if I had lost the first.
But mother and father both lost in the halls of death,
no brother could ever bloom for me.
For this law alone I held you first in honour.

(905–15)

Antigone defied the state because Polynices was her brother; she would not have buried a husband or son in flagrant defiance of law and blood. She goes on to confound her 'bizarre', 'disturbing' argument[5] with an even greater assault on the presumed principles of logic, consistency and publicity. Husband and sons can be replaced if they perish; but the brother is irreplaceable and this fact makes her duty to him paramount.

The irreplaceability of the brother lends force to the demand to bury Polynices and moves Antigone to her mad sacrifice. Her act is not a violation of the law but the ground upon which the law rises and becomes a potent source of duty alongside the law of the state and divine/family law. This archaic source of duty responds to the concrete call and demand of the most unique and singular person. 'Antigone's position represents the radical limit that affirms the unique value of his being without reference to any content, to whatever good or evil Polynices may have done, or to whatever he may have been subjected' (Lacan 1992: 279). The call exerted upon Antigone by her dead brother stands before the Platonic divisions into good and evil, right and wrong. It is the uniqueness of the relationship and the liminality of the demand that gather and apply the irresistible force that Antigone feels. Whatever is repeated or repeatable loses its urgent character and lowers the expectation of absolute obedience. Could we not argue, then, that repetition and the law arise only on the ground of unrepeatability, that the singular comes always before the law, in both senses of before?

The uniqueness of the demand is determined by the singular corporeality, the incarnate presence of the individual who arises in the field of vision and puts the demand. Antigone when speaking to Polynices addresses him as *kasigneton kara*, beloved head, face of my brother. Three times in the tragedy Antigone speaks to her siblings, face to face; to Ismene in the first line and to Eteocles and Polynices in the disputed passage. In all three they are called *kara* (head or face). It is Polynices' head, in its beloved physicality, suspended between the earth from which he has departed and Hades where he cannot arrive without the love of Antigone, that gave her the 'law whereby I held you first in honour' (914–15). The reference to the beloved head reminds us of Antigone's physical longing to lie with her brother, 'her own' as she calls him to Ismene (48). The ethical demand arises not out of a form or an idea but out of desire, in a somatic encounter and through the *epiphany* of a head in need.

And if the ethical demand arises concretely in the meetings of heads and bodies, its structure is not dissimilar to that of the unconscious and its action bestows singularity upon its addressee who answers its request. Antigone is Hegel's eternal sister who following the law of singularity, femininity and the unconscious has a presentiment of the ethical. But her ethicity rises on the ground of a necessary contingency: it is the death of the parents that makes the brother unique and turns the unconscious desire into the law of desire, this internally fissured law which demands that Antigone protects Polynices both from her own law and from that of the state. Similarly, if the ethical substance is the union of opposites, of man and woman, of consciousness and the unconscious, of universal and singular, of state and divine law, Antigone shows that the pleasure of the copulation and of the concept(ion) never fully arrives and that, *contra* Hegel, the law of reason and man will be judged in the (nocturnal) light of desire and woman. Indeed, although Hegel adored the play, in making *Antigone* fit his overall scheme he failed to come to grips with the strength of Antigone's desire for death. In the Hegelian universe the conflicting principles between family and state, individual and community had to be reconciled. But as Lacan somewhat cuttingly asks: 'I just wonder what the reconciliation of the end of *Antigone* might be' (Lacan 1992: 249).

Antigone obeys the law, but the law she obeys is not just some universally valid rule; its command arises in her overwhelming desire and in the unrepeatable encounter with the suffering (br)other and as such it is irreducibly unique. Antigone's 'transcendental surfeit' is not to be found in her *pleromatic* existence but in her standing for and before (*anti*) the other. In some traditions this incarnate Other, the absolute alien and the most proximate, is the earthly face of God. It could be that Antigone is an *antitheos* after all, whose ethical action is constitutively and necessarily a casuistry.

V

While repeated indications of desire and sexual love form the background of Antigone's obedience to *dike*, her *eros* is monstrous; she is besotted with *thanatos*, and will be betrothed with Hades and death. For Hegel, as for Nietzsche and Heidegger, death is an existential yardstick; its recognition and acceptance as the inescapable horizon of being is the *differentia specifica* of the human species. *Antigone* is full of references to the momentous linking of the primordial forces of love and death. Antigone, we are told, is in love with the impossible and with death (90, 220). The chorus's 'Ode on Eros' is immediately preceded by Creon's accusation that she is devoted to Hades (776–80). The Ode's praises to maddening *Eros* are followed by the announcement that the maiden is making her way 'to the bridal vault where all are laid to rest' (821–2) and her own moving, 'I go to wed the lord of the dark lake (*Acheronti nympheuso*)' (816).

Antigone consummates her passionate and destructive love with her *philtatoi* in death; her affection for Polynices but also for the unlucky Haemon, caught in the *maelstrom* of forces larger than life and death, will be fulfilled in the wedding chamber of Hades:

> MESSENGER: And there he lies, body enfolding body . . .
> he has won his bride at last, poor boy,
> not here but in the houses of the dead.
>
> (1240–1)

This is not the *eros* of Platonic harmony nor the Hegelian familial love that unites the spouses and sublates them in the coming son. There is no gain to be made from it against Creon's enlightened utilitarianism according to which there must be return for all investment (93). Antigone's *eros* is pure expenditure, a gift with no return, Sappho's 'elemental force of nature, a whirlwind running down the mountains' (frag. 47LP, quoted in Segal 1981: 198). It belongs to an *oiko-nome* of monstrosity.

But what is Antigone's desire? We must ask both questions implied in the double genitive. What does Antigone want and what do we want of Antigone? Does she follow the law of family and of gods, the Big O of the symbolic order, or does she act out her desire for Polynices? I hear what she says and what she asks of me but what does she really want? This is the question that Creon asks of her and Freud was to repeat. Creon is convinced that there is a dislocation between Antigone's demand and act and her desire. Within the framework of his political rationalism, Antigone can only act for gain or as part of a conspiracy: she wants to overthrow him. The only alternative is that she is 'mad', that a permanent and unbridgeable gap has opened between her locution (what she says) and her illocution (what she aims at), a state that psychoanalysis examines under the name of hysteria. A dangerous political rebel or an unhinged hysteric?

Antigone's answer is: 'I was not born to hate but to love'. In Lacanian theory love has the character of fundamental deception:

> We try to fill out the unbearable gap of 'Che vuoi?', the opening of the Other's desire, by offering ourselves to the Other as object of its desire. . . . The operation of love is therefore double: the subject fills in his own lack by offering himself to the other as the object filling out the lack in the Other – love's deception is that this overlapping of two lacks annuls lack as such in a mutual completion. (Zizek 1989: 116)

Antigone's sacrifice is the sign of absolute love. She offers herself to Polynices in order to complete his passage and fill in his lack, and at the same time she removes herself from the commotion of activity and passion onto the plane of pure desire and existence.

It has been repeatedly observed that Antigone's character does not develop during the tragedy. From the first scene to the end she remains committed to her act, although she occasionally wavers about its justifications. Neither Creon nor we can know for certain Antigone's object of desire. The only thing we know is that Antigone desires and that she will always act on her desire. But the acting appears secondary. Her calm serenity intimates a saintly passivity, an ontological aloofness: she is already elsewhere, her inscrutable desire is a state of being rather than an act. Her desire is a death drive, in desiring she becomes a deathbound being but 'she will not give way on her desire'. Creon's utilitarianism makes him unable to understand this 'bizarre' calculation and he finally adopts the 'female madness' alternative. But that makes her even more dangerous in his eyes. Her stubborn persistence to death, her frightening ontological ruthlessness which exempts her from the 'circle of everyday feelings and considerations, passions and fears' (Zizek 1989: 117) turns her into a symbol of sedition. In desiring unto death, Antigone challenges the symbolic order of state law and male authority and becomes a rebel in the name of desire.

Creon's repeated refusals of god, family ties, love and the dead, on the other hand, are necessary parts of all rationalist politics. They are part of a considered 'politics of forgetting' that every *polis* must use in order to ban what questions the legitimacy of the institution. This politics turns the imponderable powers that threaten the city into past, memory and recitation and the discourse of rational legitimation into a Periclean funeral oration. It transcribes the forces beyond into a well-organized narrative that re-presents and thus transcends the fearful past presence by putting them into *logos* and enclosing them into a singular and familiar order of argument and persuasion. Our repeated and memorized myths help us elevate and remove the terrible predicaments of life, and forget the pain of the event.

Creon is a master of the strategy of forgetting and concealing through denial and memorization. The temporal order he refers to is finite; the repeated past comes to the service of the future through a temporality that is linear and quantitative, rationally organized and mastered. His time and the time of state and legality cannot answer to eternity or the time of the event. The function of the time of repetition and of memory is therapeutic. Their representations aim to make, forget and sublate, what is alien to self and the alien itself and thus heal the wound that the abyss opens in the psyche and the social bond. But what was never a presence in the homogeneous time of *logos*, cannot be fully represented and cannot be finally banned and forgotten. The abysmal always returns, as Creon learns at the end.

Antigone belongs to a different temporality. Her measure is not a natural lifetime. It is a gain to die before her time she says to Creon, and she adds to Ismene that her soul has died a long time ago (461, 559). Always, forever, eternity: these are the temporal markers of her existence. The sequential time of law and institutions that bind generations through calculations of gain and the totalizing time of history have intruded upon Antigone's timelessness and have upset the cyclical rhythm of earth and blood that pre-exists and survives the writing of the law. But Antigone's infinite temporality does not appeal just to the time of nature (*physis*) but to a timelessness of *dike*. It is the laws presided over by *dike*, unwritten and everlasting, the laws of Hades that Antigone gladly follows (456, 76).

This time of *dike*, which is opposed to the finite time of the institution but is not simply the time of nature, could be compared with the unsettling of temporal sequence that psychoanalysis diagnoses in the work of the unconscious. Antigone has suffered an original excitation, Freud's unconscious affect that has disturbed the psychic apparatus but has not been 'experienced'. It will only surface and be acted upon later in an action that will 'remember' the original blow which however was never recorded as a memory and was thus always a forgotten. Freud speaks of this parasite of the psyche which has been there uninvited and unacknowledged as 'the prehistoric, unforgettable other person who is never equalled by anyone later' (Freud, quoted in Lyotard 1990: 45). Freud has Oedipus in mind; but Antigone too is a timeless recorder of this forgetful memory as she acts out her desire. Antigone's devotion to Polynices is the outcome of a mad, immemorial desire that has been inscribed into her before and outside of the time of institutions and laws. Her action is the unconscious affect of a stranger in the house of being that has never entered it. An originary seduction has taken place, the self has been taken hostage by the primordial other whose desire is an excessive overflowing and an inexorable command. In this approach the conflict is between her passion for the brother that emanates from recesses of the psyche not open to the operations of reminiscence and *logos* and the unspeakable wrong against the love object that the institution commits. Can there be a law that emanates from this dark region of desire and challenges the legality of the city and the work of repression of the family? Psychoanalytic theory has been associated with such an ethic that incorporates the tragic necessity of our desire and the fatal love and excessive passion of femininity. For this law, which is unwritten and eternal but also the most unique and singular, the social bond is not just about good and evil or about right and wrong. Its time is neither that of natural eternity nor of historical totality, but the infinite time of the event; in this diachronous time, that 'there is' comes before what 'there is'.

Finally, if this is Antigone's desire what is the reason for our own fascination with Antigone? Could it be that Antigone's attraction must be sought in the stubborn way she has been pursuing her desire to die, coupled with her utter inscrutability? Our own desire for Antigone is based on this impossibility to know what the other wants from us, to turn it into a law, a demand upon which we can act. We cannot identify with Antigone, with her calm persistence to death that challenges the law, and we are left with an inescapable 'Che vuoi?' But if this is the case we could argue that *dike*, the justice of the law, arises on the ground of this question without answer, on the ground of the sphinx-like enigma of the inscrutable desire of Antigone. To use psychoanalytic terminology, justice is a 'fantacy', a frame we construct to explain away the unknown desire of the Other but which at the same time constitutes and organizes our own lack and desire for the Other. As Zizek puts it, '*desire itself is a defence against desire*: the desire structured through fantasy is a defence against the desire of the Other, against this "pure" trans-phantasmic desire (i.e. the "death drive" in its pure form)' (Zizek 1989: 118).

In this interpretation *dike* is not a goddess Antigone appeals to and even less the promised equity of the institution. On the contrary, it is not Antigone who follows justice but justice is the creation of Antigone. Justice is the fantasiacal screen that philosophers, poets and lawyers have erected to shield themselves from the question of the desire of the Other. The question of justice can only arise for us on the burial ground of Antigone. It is her death that first alerts us to the desire for the Other in the midst of the law, to the unique and contingent character of the demand of the Other – in other words to the reasons that make justice both necessary and impossible: we can only negotiate our own desire for the Other through our fantasies of justice, but the radical dissymmetry, the abyss of the Other's desire and of the 'Che vuoi?' will always leave behind a remainder that neither the law nor 'fantasy' can fully account for. In her own excessive love of her brother and death, Antigone may be the eternal reminder of an abyss that enfolds and enforces all law.

VI

We should remind ourselves here, as we approach an originary clearing and ground on which the law emerges, that the question of an 'originary ethics' and of the law of law is haunted by Heidegger's spectre in the same way that (Heidegger's) law is fascinated by Antigone's tomb. Heidegger claims that *Antigone*'s first *stasimon*, the 'Ode on Man', alongside Hölderlin's translation, could provide the basis of western metaphysics. In his *An Introduction to Metaphysics* (1961), Heidegger uses the Ode as a foundational text of ontology. His detailed interpretation is an attempt to cut through the impoverished post-Platonic philosophical language of false oppositions between Being and thought and Being and Ought and go back to the beginning, the originary opening in which Being presented and opened itself into the multiplicity of beings.

Heidegger believed that the Greek spirit and the language of the pre-Socratics was in close proximity to the truth (*aletheia*, unconcealment) of Being. The poetic thinkers, Anaximander, Heraclitus, Parmenides, and the thinking poets, Homer, Aeschylus and Sophocles were still able to understand and express in language the way in which the historical Being there, the *Dasein* of the Greeks, was created. They still possessed a *logos*, language, with the original capacity of truthful nomination and unconcealment of the being of Being and the essence of man. Language, could both 'say' this essence and show it; its inner structure and grammar, its syntactic and semantic clarity and archaic etymology could unconceal the structure of Being. Indeed, in its various uses, grammatical modes and interpretations of the copula 'to be', Greek poetry and philosophy opened the main avenues of western existence and knowledge. Like the radiant sun of Apollo and Attica, archaic *logos* both lights and reveals the Being of beings and blinds and conceals *Dasein* when it eventually degenerated into solidified and referential discourse.

This primordial power to perceive, name and bring forward *aletheia*, the truth in unconcealment of Being, was soon lost in the various Platonisms which distinguished between the sensory and the suprasensible and attributed priority to the latter in its various permutations from the Platonic world of forms to its Christian afterworld, Nietzsche's Platonism for the masses. The pre-Socratics still 'speak Being' and Heidegger turns to their obscure fragments with unprecedented interpretative violence to glimpse the original clearing of Being, the ground on which our consciousness of existence emerged and was articulated in language and myth. It is a glimpse of the unity of existence before Plato and metaphysics, and a genealogy of the great divides that fissured the wholeness of Being.

For Heraclitus and Parmenides, Being is *physis*, the power that emerges in its permanent presence against becoming. The original meaning of *logos* again, before it became discourse and language and even later reason and logic, is to gather, collecting and collectedness, both putting things together and marking them apart in their specificity. *Physis* and *logos* are aspects of Being, they are united in Being's common totality. For modernity and Kantianism, on the other hand, *physis* is objective while *logos qua* thought belongs to the subject. Heidegger could not disagree more; the separation between Being and beings is not a transcendental but a thoroughly historical question, indeed the essence of history which is also the essence of man.

The gathering together of *logos* maintains the common bond of all beings in a belonging together of antagonisms. For Heraclitus the essence of man is first manifested in *polemos*, war, in which men were separated from gods and the two were put forward in their being. We see man when we see him struggle with the various beings in the world 'striving to bring them into their being, i.e. into limit and form, that is to say when he projects something new (not yet present), when he creates original poetry, when he builds poetically' (Heidegger 1961: 144). And to exemplify this poetical creation of beings in their being through human action, and to appreciate the closest that man came to understanding Being and his essence, Heidegger turns to the 'Ode on Man'.

> Numberless wonders, terrible wonders walk the world
> but none the match of man
> *(polla ta deina kouden anthropou deinoteron pelei)*
>
> (332)

Man is the strangest, *deinotaton*, a word which in its ambiguity expresses both the extreme reaches and the abysmal depths of Being. Man is the most *deinon* in the sense of the terrible, the 'overpowering power' terrifying and awe-inspiring; but he is also the violent one, violence is of his Being. In his fundamental violence he uses power against overpowering. Man's strangeness, the basic trait of his uncanny essence, is that he always abandons violently the familiar and the secure for the strange and overpowering. But in this endless and violent fleeing to the unknown he becomes *pantoporos aporos* and *hypsipolis apolis*. He opens and follows a myriad of paths on his flight from home, *poros*, but he is cast out of all of them. He achieves his essence in and out and for the *polis*, historically. *Polis* is the time and place where the paths meet, the site of *Dasein*. But his *pol*itical action that makes him the highest in the city leaves him also without site, city and place, alien and lonely as he must first create the ground and order of his creation.

Having outlined the basic design of man, the strangest, most wonderful and terrifying of beings, Heidegger now looks closer at the poem to hear man's being unfold through the verses. The conquest of the sea, the earth, of animals and birds that opens the Chorus's 'Ode on Man' are not just descriptions of man's activities; they are an outline of his overpowering being that brings both his and all other beings into their own being. We have to turn to the pre-Socratics and *Antigone* because, against the evolutionism of modernity, man's beginning reflected there is the strangest and the mightiest of events. It is this original leap into overpowering wandering and alienation that makes man *deinotatos*; 'what comes afterward is not development but the flattening that results from mere spreading out' (Heidegger 1961: 155). We must return to *Antigone*, and our poets and philosophers, these 'shepherds of Being', have been returning to her because modernity, like Odysseus, suffers from the unquenchable nostalgia of the exile and the wanderer: the pain, *algos*, for the day of homecoming, *nostos*, of coming back to the original clearing of Being, before the great scissions of our age.

The second strophe of the Ode names the elements of the overpowering powers; language, thought, passion, laws and buildings rule man and must be taken up by him as he launches his ever-new ventures.

> And speech and thought, quick as the wind
> and the mood and mind for law that rules the city
> all these he has taught himself
> and shelter from the arrows of the frost
> when there is rough lodging under the cold clear sky
> and the shafts of lashing rain –
> ready resourceful man! Never without resources
> never an impasse as he marches on the future –
> only Death, from Death alone he will find no rescue.
>
> (354–61)

Heidegger's key interpretative shift is to read *edidaxato* to mean not that man has invented and taught himself language, thought and laws as a literal translation might suggest, but that he has found his way towards their overpowering order and there found himself. As soon as man departs into being he finds himself in language. Language and thought speak man; their power helps him speak and create the violent words and acts through which he breaks out into his myriad paths and breaks and subjects his world into its manifold beings.

The beginning of language is a mystery; it arose in the violent overpowering of power of originary, archaic poetry and philosophy in which the Greeks spoke Being. The original work of language is not a *semiurgy* but a *demiurgy*. Words are not wrappings in which things come ready-packed. On the contrary, it is in language and words that things first come into being and existence. In naming, language violently opens beings out of Being and only later words become signs of beings. Mastering the violence of language makes man; through his speech, understanding and building he tames and orders the powers of the world and moves into them as the violent creator of beings and history. But his existence is always at risk; the paths he violently opens are mischievous, they abort and throw him back to powerlessness. Finally, once words degenerate into mere signs or representations of something beyond them, language falls from its state of unconcealment and presentation into concealment and idleness and prepares for the functional semiology of Aristotle and the moderns. At this early stage of ontological nomination however, as the Ode insists, one limit surrounds and delimits man's creative violence – death. Man is defenceless against death; but in naming and thinking this inescapable barrier of human existence man once more carves out his violent specificity.

The third strophe brings together the two meanings of *deinon* and their interrelation in the *deinotaton*. *Deinon* as man's violent power is evident in knowledge and art (*techne*); these look beyond the familiar and cause beings to present themselves and stabilize in their being. *Techne* is the fundamental characteristic of man, and the work of art allows everything to come forward and shine in its being. On the other hand, *deinon* as the overpowering power is evident in the fundamental *dike*, the proper order and governing structure of Being against which the violence of speech and act will break out and break up. *Techne* confronts *dike* as man sails into the order of Being, violently tears it asunder using his power against its overpowering dispensation and brings forth the existence of beings. But the overpowering order can never be overcome fully and tosses man *pantoporos*, all resourceful and everywhere-going, back from pathbreaking to *aporia*, lack of passage and resource, from the greatest glory to the basest infamy and catastrophe.

> The *violent one*, the creative man, who sets forth into the un-said, who breaks into the un-thought, compels the un-happened to happen and makes the unseen appear – this violent one stands at all times in venture. . . . In venturing to master being, he must risk the assault of the non-essent, *me kalon*, he must risk instability, disorder, mischief. The higher the summit of historical being-there, the deeper will be the abyss, the more abrupt the fall into the unhistorical, which merely thrashes around in issueless and placeless confusion.
>
> (Heidegger 1961: 161)

Now, Heidegger proceeds to the final reading of the poem, a paradigmatic presentation of his combined ontology and hermeneutics and his own act as *deinotatos*. To move to the essence of *Antigone*'s text, the reader must abandon the arrogant 'scientific interpretation' and must use interpretative violence to show 'what does not stand in the words and is nevertheless said' (Heidegger 1961: 162). What lies between the lines is the writing of disaster. The possibility of catastrophe has an ontological permanence. The fall into disaster is a fundamental tenet that exists in waiting before every act or word, an inescapable condition of human existence, caught up and created as it is in the conflict and oscillation between power and overpowering, the violence of knowledge, art and deed and the order of the world. Man cultivates and guards the familiar, home, *polis* and hearth only 'to break out of it and let what overpowers break in'. The violent one desires the new and unprecedented and abandons all help and sympathy to fulfil the call of Being; but to achieve his humanness he knows of no peace and reconciliation, no permanent success and status. 'To him disaster is the deepest and broadest affirmation of the overpowering.' The greatness of the Greeks was to understand the suddenness and uniqueness of Being that forcefully revealed itself as *physis*, *logos* and *dike* and to respond to its awesome overpowering in the only way that could bring forward beings out of Being – that is, violently. They thus opened history.

In this superb example of Heideggerian hermeneutical ontology we are offered a good first insight into the place of ethics and law. Indeed, despite the strong emphasis in *Antigone* on *nomos* and *dike*, Heidegger gives only a general outline of the mythological position of *dike* and does not mention the repeated references to *nomos* in the 'Ode on Man' and throughout the tragedy almost at all. We will return to them shortly, but let us first situate their role in Heideggerian ontology in order to understand what is at stake in this 'lawless' reading of *Antigone*.

In the 'Letter on Humanism' Heidegger explicitly addresses the relationship between ontology and ethics (Heidegger 1977). In Homer, *ethea* are the dwelling places of animals; if the animal cannot return to its habitus its order has been violated. Heidegger defines ethics, according to this original meaning of *ethos*: 'ethics ponders the abode of man'. Original ethics is a 'thinking which thinks the truth of Being as the primordial element of man, as the one who *exists*' (Heidegger 1977: 235). The task of 'fundamental ontology', as defined in *Being and Time* (Heidegger 1962), is to ponder the truth and presence of Being. It follows that ontology does not need the supplement of an originary ethics as they both share the same field and their aim is to approach the joint clearing on which they emerge.

Human laws, ethical codes and rules are assigned by Being's dispensation which conditions and determines the substance of law. Law itself, *nómos*, like ethics, has a homonym, *nomós*, the original meaning of which is very similar to *ethos*. *Nomós* refers to the pastures of horses and to the wandering of animals randomly searching for grazing fields. The word later becomes associated with possession and regular usage of pasturage but also with division and distribution, with both habit and accepted practice and nomadic and disordered spreading out. Heidegger exploits these connections in what has been seen as an argument for the primacy of ontology over ethics.[6]

> In Greek to assign is *nemein*. *Nomos* is not only law but more originally the assignment contained in the dispensation of Being. Only the assignment is capable of dispatching man into Being. Only such dispatching is capable of supporting and obligating. Otherwise all law remains merely something fabricated by human reason.
>
> (Heidegger 1977: 238–9)

In the Heideggerian idiom then, *nomos* is what is assigned or allotted to us by the 'sending', the letter dispatched by Being, before it comes to mean law and rule. It is not the work of philosophy to 'legislate' an ethics nor to busy itself with specific laws, principles and ethical commands, the ethics of law and justice of the moral philosophers. Its task is rather to concentrate on the destiny and truth of Being and to trace the demand for an ethics and its various answers back to its primordial linkage with the dispatch of Being. The 'truth of Being' is the way a people 'dwells', the combination of knowledge, art and political arrangements and of their historical understanding of the world, Gods and themselves. In this sense ontological thinking abandons the futile and conflicting debates of the moralists in order to understand the fundamental constellation within which human life is organized in each epoch, and which is the historical realization of the primordial Being and ethos.

The demand for an ethics betrays the naïve position that ethics can be made to measure. The dispatch and allotment of Being, our lot and destiny, is the shape of our historical existence, our bond to our form of life. This bond cannot be of our making alone; it is not that impoverished to have been 'fabricated by human reason'. We found ourselves thrown in it, in *medias res*, answering its call. Its force lies in the 'demand placed on the individual to assume his place within his society (McIntyre), to answer the call of Being in his time' (Caputo 1987: 247). The thinker must not heed demands that come from elsewhere; he must concentrate on answering the call of destiny, to abide by the dispensation of Being.

It is this and similar arguments that have been used to suggest that fundamental ontology is a denigration of ethics. We should immediately add, however, that the Heideggerian injunction is itself a strong law. Indeed Heidegger repeatedly gives an ethical tone to the demand that we abide by the destiny of Being, the only way of a fitting life. But 'if this commandment has an ethical meaning, it is not that it belongs to the *domain* of the ethical, but in that it ultimately authorises every ethical law in general' (Derrida 1978, 1980). In other words, the Heideggerian injunction is not the law of rules, principles and codes, or the ethics of Derrida's 'ethical domain'. It is rather the law of law, before and outside ethics as discipline, the force that puts into circulation and authorizes all extant laws. The law of laws is the 'equivalent to what Heidegger calls law as the assignment of the dispensation of Being' (Bernasconi 1987: 125). In this reading destiny imposes an ethical demand that could even be called the originary ethic; but the answer to it cannot take the form of a code or a collection of principles and rules. It is the very refusal to issue an ethical code that abides by the ethical demand. 'To follow rules is to uproot oneself from dwelling. To provide ethical directives is to condemn to the everyday the person who adopts them' (Bernasconi 1987: 134). We can now fully appreciate the importance of Heidegger's reading of *Antigone* and of reading *Antigone* contra Heidegger; it can be used as the testing ground for the relationship between Being and ethics, the site of the originary ethics and of the law of law.

The key trope and strategy through which Heidegger claims the primacy of ontology over ethics is the presentation of *dike* as the primordial orderliness of the world and of *nomos* as our share in it. *Dike* is not justice but the overpowering structure of Being that emerges and shines in its permanent presence as *physis* and is gathered together in its collectedness as *logos*, which unites oppositions while keeping their tension. *Physis*, *logos* and *dike*, object and subject, law and justice are aspects of the essential unity of Being. Man's *techne*, violent knowledge, attacks *dike*, and in this original event and reciprocal relation man ceases to be at home and both home and the alien are disclosed. In his violent naming and acting the manifold of beings and his own being-there as history is made manifest and shatters itself in the catastrophe that lurks before every achievement as its existential precondition.

At first glance it looks as if Heidegger's ontological ethics is identical to Antigone's call and follows closely from *dike*'s unconscious. And yet something troubling remains. The *hypsipolis*,

Heidegger's violent one, according to the 'Ode on Man', honours both the laws of the land (*nomous chthonos*), and the justice of gods (*theon t'enorkon dikan*). If man comes into his historical being in the conflict between the violence of knowledge and deed (*techne*) and the overpowering order of the world (*dike*), *dike* is split right from the start. But what is the nature of this split?

This primordial division cannot be between the mere jurisprudential 'is' and 'ought'. Their separation will come about only at a later 'fallen' stage, heavily influenced by Plato. In Platonism Being and thought are sharply distinguished; thought becomes dominant while Being is defined as an essence and an idea. But as the Good is the idea of ideas, and Being consists in ideas, Being comes into opposition to the Good that stands beyond Being and acts as its model. Thus it is after the forgetfulness of Being has set in and Being has been defined as an idea that the 'ought' of moral systems arises and opposes itself to Being. The road to the strict modern split between is and ought and object and subject has been opened; it will come to its full and dogmatic fruition in Kant. But *Antigone* still speaks the unity in antagonisms of Being and it is here, according to Heidegger, that we should seek the ground of law.

If *dike* is the way of the world, the stuff on and out of which the basic distinctions of morality, religion and law emerge, it is the *nomos* of *nemein* the earth that works on *dike* and brings into the open the human being-there. *Nemein* means dividing, breaking up, sending away in many directions, without pattern, structure or aim. The *nomos* of Being is a nomadic assignation. In this version destiny is not belonging but exile, the Oedipal destiny of the blind wanderer, of the stranger in the house of Being. The truth of Being and of *nomos/ethos* is from the very start many conflictual, warring truths. The letter that Being sends is unwritten but follows the law of writing. It is never fully present in the historical presence; it finds itself always and already caught in the process of dissemination and difference, nomadic and polyvalent.

But even more fundamentally, as *Antigone* reminds us, there are two invincible and inescapable powers, unbreakably and fatefully linked, love and death. Heidegger famously showed how the knowledge of death opens the field of human possibilities in mortal living. The individual discovers her existential specificity by recognizing the singularity of her being to death. Nothing and no one underwrites and guarantees existence; no truth, history or ego can recentre a subject that opened herself to the mortal possibility of living. The flight of existence to death forces the individual to get hold of the only properly human being in possibility, the violent forcing of the over-powering. This is the specifically human being there, *Dasein*, of which the Ode gave Heidegger the best unconcealment: a continuous flight forward in pure, uncharted possibility that is being both opened and shattered against the totally Other of death.

If death, however, is the limit that gives *Dasein* its human specificity, *Antigone* shows that it is the loving turn to the suffering and unique other that bestows on the individual her own singularity. If death is the external limit that must be brought inside life to put human life into being, the other is the internal limit that in asking and receiving help creates individualities out of *Dasein*. And it is in this sense that the original *nomos* divides and breaks; the paths and byways that destiny opens take their unpredictable directions and map out mortal possibilities because they are signposted by the unique encounters with unrepeatable others who always come before us and impose on us the mystery of an originating 'must'. The law of law, destiny, is always open to an outside, an otherwise than Being, death and the Other.

Destiny, the universal force of law, lives and is enforced in singular, unpredictable and forceful manifestations. We can now understand why *moira* and *tyche*, fate and luck, are both necessary and contingent. The other who arises before me and the demand she puts to me are contingent, they happen unpredictably and without warning and could have happened otherwise. But there is an inexorable necessity, a strict legality to this contingency; some other will arise before me and I will have to answer her demand. Indeed my own individual *Dasein* is the necessary opening to the contingent demands of fate that appears to me in the face of the Other.

This reading retains the basic insights of Heidegger's ontology. It accepts that the demand for a moral code, while indicating the ethical character of the destiny of being, cannot be satisfied without violating the essence of the ethical relation. It affirms the contingent character of human *Dasein*, but insists on the necessarily relational nature of contingency. The reason why an ethics of norms is not strictly possible is that the human *Dasein* is primordially ethical and that openness to the other is part of the basic design of Being. Acts of destiny are not signs of an essence; they do not re-present an absent cause, fate, nor are they means used to achieve some unknown ends. On the contrary such acts are the manifestations, the epiphany of destiny.[7] And if destiny is the 'unwritten law' before human and divine, in a more modern and linguistically obsessed terminology, the writing of fate performs. It acts (forces) in speaking and it speaks by killing. In other words, destiny is life open to the call of something beyond self. This beyond is quite specific for Antigone. If she answers its call, she says, she could face her brother as the most beloved of friends and she will lie with him in eternal bliss.

Death, *eros*, and the force of the (br)other are the registers of destiny, they put into operation its unwritten and universal law. Its epiphany is always in the singular. Law is force. Both the ethical force of the living, embodied other, entombed in the 'you must' and the destructive force of the other as shrouded corpse and death. Both a force internal to law, that befalls and obligates, binds the I to the law and saves it; and an externally applied force, the sanction and limit of the law, that kills the I to save the law. Law's force: a force that binds and preserves or a force that severs and preserves.

We can conclude that at the mythical moment of its foundation the law is split into divine and human. On the one hand the madness of a 'must' gets hold of the I with an indescribable force and obliges the ego without any knowledge or calculation, without criteria or evaluation. On the other, the law of the state, the law of universality, of calculation and of uniform application applies its own force and persuasion. Antigone teaches that the *nomos* rises on the ground of the polemical symbiosis of female and male, singular and universal, justice and law. Force and form, value and validity, are both implicated in the ethical substance of the law, are both parts of law's original 'must'. And launched at the heart of both, encrypted in law's essence lurks the ghost of violence and death.

But the law of the law – destiny – is unknown. We can never know destiny but we must follow it, like Antigone. Fate comes as the Other, the dying/dead Other who asks me to save or bury him. The force of the 'must', is the force that the most remote and different from self imposes on self. Death as the Other of life; the stranger who is left outside the wall of Thebes to be devoured by the dogs; the force of *eros* as the total transcendence of the world projected by and revolving around self. Fate is the Other. We must follow the traces of its apparent extinction and ghostly life on the body of jurisprudence.

Could we not argue then that (unknown) fate is the Good (or God)? It stands before the law and it infuses it both with its opposition to Justice and with the superiority of Justice over Law. It is also destiny as the force of the multiplicity of Being (gods as Others) that propels the law into being. These are the horizons that shape the genealogy of jurisprudence. Greek philosophy founded ontology and sent out the letter that Heidegger gratefully received. But Greek tragedy, in its sense of tragic destiny, alludes to singularity and otherness, a destructive force and an unmediated duty, that has been always associated with the Greek's other, the Jew. This force could be the writing of the dead body or the Other. *Antigone* alludes to both, but as with everything else Antigone herself does not give a final answer. 'Who knows what the rules are among the dead?' She leaves it to (s)he who answers the call of the 'must'.

NOTES

1 The translations of *Antigone* are based on the Penguin edition of Sophocles, *The Three Theban Plays*, Robert Fagles translator, with an introduction and notes by Bernard Knox (London: Penguin, 1984). The line numbers in the text refer to the classical edition by the scholiast Richard Jebb (1966). Some translations have been amended by the authors to bring the text closer to the original Greek and to emphasize the legal concerns of the tragedy.

2 G. Steiner (1986) at 103. At key historical moments of state or foreign oppression playwrights throughout the world have turned to Sophocles and have interpreted the story of the self-sacrificed maiden as a symbol for their times. Anouilh's *Antigone* captured the spirit of the French resistance; Brecht's symbolized the desperate hope of redemption of German dissidents under the Nazis. And when the cultural embargo was lifted in early 1992, the first play to be performed in the homelands of South Africa by a European company was a contemporary version of *Antigone*. Towering over all modern translations stands Hölderlin's *Antigona*, the *isothea antithea*, the equal of Gods and their adversary. Antigone appears to have a magnetic pull, she is the object of a desire unabating through the centuries which incessantly attracts the modern back to her ancient bridal sepulchre. 'New Antigones are being imagined, thought and lived now; and will be tomorrow' (Steiner 1986: 304).

3 Amongst many references in passing to the play, see A. D'Entreves (1970) at 14; Lord Lloyd of Hampstead (1985) at 100, n.57; R. Posner (1988).

4 A strong tradition of reading *Antigone* in terms of juridical contrasts and binary oppositions finds its best representative in the works of the American classicist Charles Segal, who is strongly influenced by Lévi-Strauss. Segal's early, 'Sophocles's praise of men and conflicts of the Antigone' (1964) is followed by his magisterial *Tragedy and Civilization. An Interpretation of Sophocles* (1981) and *Interpreting Greek Tragedy. Myth, Poetry, Text* (1986). The themes of justice and law and their conflict exemplified by Antigone and Creon are treated as key interpretative principles in classical philology. See, amongst others, C. M. Bowra (1944), ch. 3; H. Lloyd-Jones, *Justice of Zeus* (1971), ch. V; C. Whitman (1951), ch. V; R. P. Winnington-Ingram, *Sophocles: An Interpretation* (1980), ch. 5.

5 The passage is one of the most controversial in the classical canon. Goethe, amongst others, is reported to have said that he would give a great deal 'if some talented young scholar could prove that those lines were interpolated, not genuine'. Jebb (1966) calls the argument 'unworthy' of Antigone, an abandonment of 'the immovable basis of her action – the universal and unqualified validity of divine law' (p. 259). Others have called it 'primitive sophism' and 'bad comedy' (Steiner 1986: 280). However the attempts to dispute the authenticity of the passage must fail because of an incontrovertible piece of evidence. Aristotle quotes part of the disputed passage in his *Rhetoric* (3.16, para. 9) and comments on it without mentioning any doubts as to its authenticity. For the 'jurisprudential' character of this impossible but persisting denial of the text see C. Douzinas and R. Warrington, *Justice Miscarried. Ethics and Aesthetics in Law* (London: Harvester, 1994), ch. 2.

6 The French philosopher Emanuel Levinas has criticized Heidegger's prioritization of ontology over ethics, which he links to the obsession of the Greek and Christian traditions with the *logos* and the self-same. Derrida, in his important early essay 'Violence and metaphysics' (1978), agreed with certain of Levinas's criticisms but concluded that his attack on Heidegger was unjustified as we can never fully abandon the predominantly 'Greek' ground of reason for an absolute Other. Levinas's response, 'Wholly otherwise', and the further and much more sympathetic rejoinder by Derrida, 'At this very moment in this work here I am', are found in R. Bernasconi and S. Critchley (1991). The recent interest of Derrida in legal philosophy and ethics, and his 'political turn', seem to draw much inspiration from Levinas. See J. Derrida, 'The force of law: the mystical foundation of authority', in D. Cornell, M. Rosenfeld and D. Carlson (1992), and J. Derrida (1992). A good review of the complex relations between Heidegger, Levinas and Derrida is found in Bernasconi (1987).

7 This analysis resembles Walter Benjamin's mythical semiology and his analysis of fate in 'Fate and character' and 'On language as such and on the language of man' in his *Reflections* (New York: Schocken Books, 1978).

BIBLIOGRAPHY

Benjamin, W. (1978) *Reflections*, New York: Schocken Books.

Bernasconi, R. (1987) 'Deconstruction and the possibility of ethics', in J. Sallis (ed.), *Deconstruction and Philosophy*, Chicago: University of Chicago Press.

—— and Critchley, S. (eds) (1991) *Re-reading Levinas*, London: Athlone.

Bowra, M. (1944) *Sophoclean Tragedy*, Oxford: Clarendon.

Caputo, J. (1987) *Radical Hermeneutics*, Bloomington: Indiana University Press.

Cornell, D., Rosenfeld, M. and Carlson, D. (eds) (1992) *Deconstruction and the Possibility of Justice*, London: Routledge.

D'Entreves, A. (1970) *Natural Law*, London: Hutchinson.

Derrida, J. (1978) 'Violence and metaphysics', in *Writing and Difference*, London: Routledge.

—— (1990) *Glas*, Lincoln and London: University of Nebraska Press.
—— (1992) *The Other Heading*, Bloomington: Indiana University Press.
Douzinas, C. and Warrington, R. (1991) ' "A well-founded fear of justice": law and ethics in postmodernity', *Law & Critique* II(2), 115.
—— —— (1994) *Justice Miscarried. Ethics and Aesthetics in Law*, London: Harvester.
—— —— (with S. McVeigh) (1991) *Postmodern Jurisprudence. The Law of Text in the Texts of Law*, London: Routledge.
Goheen, R. F. (1951) *The Imagery of Sophocles' Antigone*, Princeton: Princeton University Press.
Hegel, G. W. F. (1967) *The Philosophy of Right* (trans. by T. M. Knox), Oxford: Oxford University Press.
—— (1977) *Phenomenology of Spirit* (trans. by A. V. Miller), Oxford: Oxford University Press.
Heidegger, M. (1961) *An Introduction to Metaphysics* (trans. by R. Manheim), New York: Doubleday Anchor Books.
—— (1962) *Being and Time*, New York: Harper & Row.
—— (1977) *Basic Writings*, New York: HarperCollins.
Jebb, R. (1966) *The Antigone of Sophocles*, Cambridge: Cambridge University Press.
Lacan, J. (1992) *The Ethics of Psychoanalysis*, London: Routledge.
Lloyd-Jones, H. (1971) *Justice of Zeus*, Berkeley: University of California Press.
Lord Lloyd of Hampstead (1985) *Introduction to Jurisprudence* (5th edition, with M. D. A. Freeman), London: Stevens.
Lyotard, J.-F. (1990) *Heidegger and 'The Jews'*, Minneapolis: University of Minnesota Press.
Posner, R. (1988) *Law and Literature*, Cambridge, Mass.: Harvard University Press.
Segal, C. (1964) 'Sophocles's praise of men and the conflicts of the Antigone', *ARION* 3(2), 46.
—— (1981) *Tragedy and Civilization. An Interpretation of Sophocles*, Cambridge, Mass.: Harvard University Press.
—— (1986) *Interpreting Greek Tragedy. Myth, Poetry, Text*, Ithaca: Cornell University Press.
Steiner, G. (1986) *Antigones. The Antigone Myth in Western Literature, Art and Thought*, Oxford: Oxford University Press.
Weinreb, L. (1987) *Natural Law and Justice*, Cambridge, Mass.: Harvard University Press.
Whitman (1951) *Sophocles: A Study in Heroic Humanism*, Cambridge, Mass.: Harvard University Press.
Winnington-Ingram (1980) *Sophocles: An Interpretation*, Cambridge: Cambridge University Press.
Zizek, S. (1989) *The Sublime Object of Ideology*, London: Verso.

Index